"A timely resource for these turbulent times – this book provides terrific insight into both sophisticated methodology and the "soft" factors that must be contemplated in developing effective forecasts. The authors also include a valuable section providing practical guidance on implementation and development of forecasts."

Jack Alexander,
Former CFO, Consultant and Author of *Performance Dashboards and Analysis for Value Creation*

"As this book vividly demonstrates through its many case studies, forecasting quality is a life or death issue for organisations of all types, and the current economic turmoil makes strong "navigational" capabilities all the more critical. *Future Ready* is therefore a very timely call to action, challenging readers to rethink the many myths and practical flaws which bedevil their current approaches to forecasting and presenting a clear and radical blueprint for future success. This book is immensely readable, deeply practical and unquestionably authoritative – drawing on the authors' extensive practical experience of leading and reinventing forecasting processes in major corporations and the unique insights derived from their deep academic research. Its rich offering of theory, human and organisational observation, case studies and practical solutions will appeal to all actors in the drama of forecasting, and I would urge business leaders and forecasting practitioners alike to undertake the journey of transformation it advocates so powerfully."

Paul Baumann
Director of Finance and Investment. NHS London

"The business world needs more books like this one! Based on brilliant observations from their deep experience and knowledge of both the business front-line and the business library, Morlidge and Player not only reveals serious problems with current forecasting practices and offer valuable advice and alternatives, they also do so in a uniquely simple and entertaining way. Great analogies and stories are combined with rock solid theory in a language that even the most reading-averse manager will love from page one."

Bjarte Bogsnes.
Vice President Performance Management Development at StatoilHydro
and author of *Implementing Beyond Budgeting*

"In my opinion Player and Morlidge help Business Executives develop a robust and very sound process for decision making in today's hectically fast paced world. This book provides a cornerstone to business success."

A. J. Braniff,
Senior Vice President, Business Development, Whoop Inc

"Steve Player and Steve Morlidge have produced a 'must read' for CFOs. In these turbulent financial times, effective forecasting is vital to future business success. They have provided the blueprint to guide us to this success."

Patricia Cochran
Chief Financial Officer, VSP Vision Care

"This book on forecasting addresses an important topic as executive teams shift their managerial style from after-the-fact reaction to a forward-looking anticipatory planning so that executives, managers, and employee teams can be proactive in making adjustments and resolve small problems before they become big ones."

Gary Cokins,
SAS, Performance Management Solutions
Author of *Performance Management – Integrating Strategy Execution, Methodologies, Risk and Analytics*

"The ability to forecast has always been a precondition for any kind of successful navigation. In today's globally connected, constantly changing and fast evolving world of business, effective forecasting becomes a survival factor for any kind of enterprise. Yet, the discipline of effective business forecasting is still in its infancy – particularly the understanding of how to design and implement effective forecasting in an organization, especially in a larger organization. With "Future Ready" Steve Morlidge and Steve Player do an excellent job in putting together the pieces required for effective forecasting by integrating the thinking from various disciplines and different communities of thinking and in showing us how a more holistic, integrated approach to forecasting may lead to better enterprise management that is future ready."

Juergen Daum,
Management Advisor and Chief Solution Architect, SAP, and President and Founder,
International Institute of Enterprise – Heidelberg

"A detailed and thought provoking look at a fundamental area of corporate financial planning.
Provides a clear eyed analysis of an essential business process that many of us don't understand either as well or as in as much detail as we should.
Moves beyond theory to the mechanics of designing and implementing a genuinely useful forecasting system."

Liz Doherty,
CFO, Brambles Ltd

"Business Forecasting is a process all organizations do, but rarely do they do it well. Other books on the topic typically include complex analytical models that even most PhDs could not understand, or are so simplistic that they are not useful. This book provides a practical and understadable approach that can be put to use immediately. Steve and Steve have an ability to communicate complex concepts in simply lanaguage and provide an approach based real experience working with major corporations and non profits that will allow your organization to better predict future performance. Should be required reading for all executives and Business school students."

Mark Graham Brown,
Author of *Beyond the Balanced Scorecard*

"The roller-coaster of the last twelve months shows that this is a timely addition to management thinking. Those of us involved in the dark arts of forecasting know how difficult it can be in practice and that it can make or break the best laid of intentions. More importantly, we know that when done well, great forecasting as a core competency can be a source of competitive advantage in the way companies deploy and optimise the allocation of resources.

But, here we have a text that helps shine a bright light on this whole area and it does so in a practical, engaging, and thought provoking way. The deep practical experience of the authors shines through. I can recommend that reading this book will be a good investment of your time and will make a difference to the way you think about forecasting going forward."

Howard Green,
Group Controller and SVP Finance Categories, Unilever PLC

"Knowing the authors well, I wasn't surprised when I read this thoughtful, well grounded book. But, working in a company that prides itself on its intensely pragmatic approach to business, I was delighted by the simple and straightforward way in which sophisticated ideas have been expressed and the focus on practical application. This combination makes this a book for the executive suite – as well as the back office."

Andrew Higginson.
Chief Executive of Retailing Services, and former CFO, Tesco PLC.

"*Future Ready: How to Master Business Forecasting* is a timely addition to the growing research on management planning and performance measurement. Criteria for superior practices are developed, including the obtaining organizational alignment and achieving significant benefits at reasonable costs.

The experienced authors include specific forecasting cases from actual practice. This book provides a lively description of successful experiences in improving management performance in both planning and control."

Dr Charles T. Horngren, Edmund G. Littlefield
Professor of Accounting Emeritus Stanford University.
Author of *Cost Accounting: A Managerial Emphasis* (12th ed), *Introduction to Management Accounting*, (13th ed), *Accounting*, (6th ed), *Financial Accounting*, (6th ed)

"This is a very useful book for managers, because its focus is on the forecasting process and not on the technique."

Professor Dr Peter Horvath,
Chairman, Horvath and Partners

"This book puts its finger on most of the important lessons I have learned from my 25 years of experience of running and using and consulting in this area, and a lot more besides. It is profound as well as practical; challenging the reader to think again about the way in which they go about doing business."

Martin Jarvis,
CEO, D1 Fuel Crops Ltd

"Sustainability in a business context is not about the here and now but about survival into the future. This is the challenge for business managers. No one can precisely predict the future, but organizations that are better prepared to weather the storms of uncertainty will not only survive but thrive.

Steve Morlidge and Steve Player have translated their many years of experience in the area of forecasting into an easily understandable and well presented text that will certainly add value to any business, and enlighten any manager in the complex art of business forecasting and performance management using leading edge tools and thought."

Aubrey Joachim
FCMA MBA, Global President, Chartered Institute of Management Accountants (CIMA); Principal Consultant, Leading Edge Change – Australia and Australasian Director, BBRT

"There are many broken processes in most organizations, and forecasting is one with a big impact. The authors help the reader discover and expose the fractures and the impact of these fractures. Their methodical approach to "healing the fractures" is equivalent to a living feedback system checking reality against assumptions and adjusting as necessary. A great way for a flexible company to minimize surprises and create solid countermeasures."

Beau Keyte,
founder of Branson Inc and co-author of *The Complete Lean Enterprise:*
***Value Stream Mapping for Office and Administrative Processes* Shingo Prize winner 2005.**

"Conducting a traditional budgeting and planning process is tantamount to a gross misuse of company resources. Enlightened firms are learning to focus on the key drivers of revenue and expense, and to plan and forecast continuously as market conditions inevitably change. This flexibility is necessary to succeed and to ensure that strategic investments are not crowded out."

Dave Martin,
CFO, Dimensional Fund Advisors

"The recent recession has made one thing clear in business – the rules have changed. No longer can companies operate in discrete and clearly defined operating timeframes. Many companies have realized that the operating parameters used in setting annual budgets in January become obsolete by the end of the first quarter. So, it is a imperative that companies develop a much more dynamic process in keeping the annual budget relevant to the changing market dynamics. Changing the annual plan targets and parameters can be a tricky effort as it is important that the overall goals and targets are not compromised as market conditions change. But rather, the path to those goals and targets must be dynamic and flexible enough to allow alternative paths for accomplishing a company's goals.

A key to a dynamic path is a forecasting process that is integrated into the fabric of the tactical decision making process for a company. The forecasting process must be able to link the sales, marketing and operations personnel so that changes in one area complement others rather than create conflict and resistance. Coordination of efforts to react to changes in market conditions is a key to success for any company in this new and dynamic business environment that we face daily."

Brian McMahon,
Assistant Controller, The Hershey Company

"Competition in business is just as intense as athletic competition.
This book shows how to use forecasting to develop a winning game plan."

Steve Pace,
CFO, Big 12 Conference

"This book perfectly demonstrates the importance of predictive capabilities for successful management in these turbulent times. In the area of Forecasting, it is the best book in the market."

Fritz Roemer,
Leader of Enterprise Performance Executive Advisory Program, the Hackett Group

"To steer the right course, companies need to adopt business forecasting methods, tools, and processes – especially during these uncertain and turbulent economic times. In Future Ready, Morlidge and Player capture this urgency and draws upon their extensive experience and cross-industry perspective to prescribe a common sense philosophy and approach to business planning and forecasting. By integrating sound forecasting practices into business decision-making, companies improve their chances of being future ready!"

Srikant K. Sastry,
Chairman of the Board,
Consortium of Advanced Management-International.
Principal, Grant Thornton LLP

"The authors have delivered a well-documented treatise on an important and often neglected business topic."

Jonathan B. Schiff,
Professor of Accounting, Fairleigh Dickinson University

"Steve Player and Steve Morlidge have seen the future of forecasting and charted a path to it. This is essential reading for finance executives tasked with leading their organizations into the world of real-time decision making."

Jack Sweeney,
editor in chief, Business Finance Magazine, founding editor Consulting Magazine

"Steve Morlidge and Steve Player both have considerable experience of the problems and issues of management control in large organizations and in this book they bring that experience to bear. To support their ideas they incorporate into the text many relevant 'real world' examples of the problems currently encountered in organizations' management control activities and they give their own 'take' on planning and control solutions. Given the extremely modest success achieved by current practices in this area, their ideas are most welcome.

This book will be valuable to middle and senior level managers, who are wrestling with the planning and control processes of their organizations. It will also have a place on MSc or MBA courses which deal with management control as a pragmatic general reader offering an alternative approach, alongside a more traditional academic text.

At one level the book can be seen as some light reading and in this form it will be 'entertaining' and thought provoking. However, this does not do justice to the book as the content is also worthy of greater attention and more detailed scrutiny; managers will definitely benefit from giving the content greater consideration. If a management team is seeking to 'overhaul' or, more appropriately, 'refocus' their planning and control processes this text should be compulsory reading for all those concerned."

Mike Tayles,
Professor of Accounting and Finance Hull University Business School;
Director, Centre for International Accounting and Finance Research

"As someone who focuses on improving business decisions I see the impact of bad forecasting systems all the time. Good business decisions require good forecasts and this book lays out the principles essential to effective forecasting."

James Taylor,
author of Smart (Enough) Systems

"This provocative and highly relevant book is a call to action for management accountants and other business professionals looking to drive business performance inside organizations. The authors view forecasting as a core business process and provide six intuitive and focused principles to master. Studies continue to reveal that CFO teams around the globe have significant gaps in their planning and forecasting capabilities, exacerbated and exposed by the global recession. This book is a solutions-oriented approach to practically filling that gap."

Jeffrey C. Thomson,
President and CEO, Institute of Management Accountants

"Probably the first entertaining book written on the subject of forecasting."

Flavio Ventacilla,
Research Associate: Business School of the University of Applied Sciences, Northwestern Switzerland

"The last twelve months have shown how volatile the business environment can be. The practical ideas in this book help us get ready to prepare for whatever comes."

Jon Zindel,
Chief Financial Officer, American Century

FUTURE READY

How to master business forecasting

Steve Morlidge

Steve Player

WILEY

A John Wiley & Sons, Ltd., Publication

This edition first published 2010
© John Wiley & Sons, Ltd

Registered office
John Wiley & Sons Ltd, The Atrium, Southern Gate, Chichester, West Sussex, PO19 8SQ,
United Kingdom

For details of our global editorial offices, for customer services and for information about how to apply
for permission to reuse the copyright material in this book please see our website at www.wiley.com.

Library of Congress Cataloging-in-Publication Data

A catalogue record for this book is available from the Library of Congress.

ISBN   978-0-470-74705-6

A catalogue record for this book is available from the British Library.

Set in 10.5 on 14 pt Garamond by Toppan Best-set Premedia Limited
Printed in Great Britain by TJ International Ltd, Padstow, Cornwall

This book is dedicated to the people in our past who made it possible to produce this book today. That began with our parents both Frank and Joyce Morlidge and Bobby and Violet Player, who lifted us and gave us a firm foundation where all success is possible. All that we reach is because they lifted us up on their shoulders.

Also, we dedicate this to our families (Sue, Lisa, Sally and Matthew Morlidge and Lydia, David, Emily, and Cole Player) and our co-workers, who sustain us and make our journey worth traveling. They give our journey meaning and joy that enriches our lives.

Work most often is accomplished by dedicated individuals diligently performing their jobs and doing so far away from the spotlight. These supporters, while often unseen, are the successful execution. Michael Player provided an outstanding example for all to follow – and he did it with wit, humor, and a genuine caring for members and co-workers that made our work special. We will honor him as we continue on the trails that he blazed.

Our hope is that this book helps you and your organization become future ready to both thrive and build a better world. We can think of no better way to bring honor and repay a portion of what so many have freely given to us.

TABLE OF CONTENTS

TABLE OF FIGURES

TABLE OF FIGURES

FOREWORD

This book fills a gap in the management literature. It translates often arcane tools and techniques into accessible language and action-based guidelines. It will help you to break free from the shackles of budgeting and learn how to manage more effectively in an increasingly unpredictable and uncertain world.

Most businesses spend a number of months each year agreeing the budget and then monitoring performance against it. In more recent times, they have updated the budget with some kind of forecast with a horizon that declines as the accounting calendar moves towards the fiscal year end. This type of forecasting has limited value. It treats forecasting is an adjunct to the annual budget rather than a core management process subject to the disciplines of continuous learning and improvement. Not only does it consume valuable time but its purpose is to help managers take short-term tactical decisions to 'meet the numbers' that, more often than not, undermine the longer-term interests of the business. Trapped in such an outmoded performance management practice, it is no wonder that the knowledge and techniques of forecasting have failed to move forward.

This excellent book makes a compelling case for treating forecasting as a core management process that enables a more adaptive organization rather than just 'fix' a glaring weakness in traditional management practice. But it is not simply about 'building a better budget'. Both authors have spent many years in the vanguard of the 'Beyond Budgeting' movement. They understand that the real opportunity for designing and implementing an effective forecasting process is not a 'better budget' with all its behavioral baggage but to continuously 'sketch the future' in a way that provides managers with a range of likely outcomes based on a variety of options. It is about building a process that not only enables decisions to be taken with confidence (such as launching a new product) but also helps organizations to respond rapidly to unpredictable events (and, as we all know, the future is more unpredictable than ever).

This does not necessarily mean that managers can better predict those events. But it does mean they can more quickly evaluate the alternative courses of action available to deal with them when they happen. This gets to the essence of effective forecasting. It is not another attempt to 'predict and control' future outcomes. Its aim is to build a process that enables managers to continuously look ahead and use all available information and practical techniques to take decisions that maximize the potential of the business.

The authors also know that no management process, no matter how well designed, can stand alone. It is part of a holistic management model within which everything is connected to everything else. Even though the book is full of useful techniques and practical advice it constantly reminds the reader that these will be of limited value if, for example, target setting, incentive compensation, resource allocation and performance measurement remain stuck in a budgeting time-warp.

This book has something for everyone. For the business leader it sets out what needs to be done to overcome the 'visibility' problem. 'Why didn't we respond more rapidly when the first signs of the credit crunch were hitting the radar screen?' is a common complaint of many CEOs. Clearly conventional approaches have not served businesses well. For the business manager it offers a methodology and a set of practical techniques to help displace the tired, old budget – an approach that they can use to steer the business in a turbulent environment. For the academic it offers research opportunities for developing new management models based on the natural sciences, particularly systems thinking. It is a book for our times.

Jeremy Hope
Cofounder of the Beyond Budgeting Round Table

Books:
Reinventing the CFO: How Financial Managers Can Transform Their Roles and Add Greater Value. Harvard Business School Press 2006
Beyond Budgeting: How Managers Can Break Free from the Annual Performance Trap (with Robin Fraser). Harvard Business School Press 2003
Competing in the Third Wave: Ten Key Issues that Managers Must Face in the Information Age. Harvard Business School Press 1997
Transforming the Bottom Line: Managing Performance with the Real Numbers (with Tony Hope). Nicholas Brealey Publishing 1995

PREFACE

'All the business of war, and indeed all the business of life, is to endeavor to find out what you don't know by what you do; that's what I called "guessing what was at the other side of the hill"'. The First Duke of Wellington

This book helps business people improve their ability to forecast the future. By improving your organization's ability to anticipate, you will be better prepared. As a result you will deliver more reliable performance and be in better shape to exploit opportunities and avoid potential catastrophes. In short, you will become 'Future Ready'.

As these words were written, we were under daily bombardment with stories of economic failure and business collapse; we have plentiful evidence of our inability to predict the future. The forecasting capabilities of governments, academics, research bodies, businesses, and other organizations have been demonstrated to be woefully inadequate. Even the British Queen got in on the act when she asked 'how come no-one saw it coming?' at a recent event at the London School of Economics (Giles, 2008). At his testimony to Congress Alan Greenspan acknowledged the poor forecasting capabilities of the Fed: 'we're not smart enough people' he said, 'we just cannot see events that far in advance. There are always a lot of people raising issues, and half the time they are wrong' (Ryan, 2009).

Business executives don't need to be told that they have a problem. 'The financial crisis has obliterated corporate forecasts' reports the CFO Magazine; 70% of respondents to their recent survey said that they were unable to see more than one quarter ahead. But, as the report acknowledged, 'abandoning the prediction game is not an option' for business executives (Ryan, 2008). A single profit warning has always been a serious matter for Chief Financial Officers (CFOs) and, they and Chief Executive Officers (CEOs) are likely to find themselves out of work after two. In any one year the 1300 UK quoted companies issue 400 profit warnings and share prices drop by an average of 20% afterwards (Bloom *et al.*, 2009). Poor profit guidance significantly shortens careers of top executives, according to recent research, and this has got worse post Sarbanes-Oxley (Mergenthaler *et al.*, 2008). Unsurprisingly, the 'ability to forecast results' was the number one 'internal concern' for CFOs according to a recent survey covering Europe, the US and Asia, ahead of such issues as 'attracting and retaining qualified employees', 'balance sheet weakness', 'counterparty risk', 'managing IT systems' and 'supply chain risk' (Karaian, 2009). Also, good forecasting has always been a major concern for operational management. Forecasts lie at the heart of the supply chain process and it is no less important for service organizations to ensure that they are able to consistently service customer demand. Again, the credit squeeze has made this even more important. Cash reserves are critical to riding out the economic storm, and for many companies, as credit has dried up, an important source of finance for R&D and other growth projects (Zhu, 2009).

Clearly, forecasting and the ability to understand risk (how far your forecasts might be wrong) is critically important to avoiding catastrophe, to managing relationships with stakeholders and to generating cash. In our view, however, the biggest value of effective forecasting lies in its contribution to steering the business; to the day-to-day decision-making that lies at the very heart of business, which is how we came to this topic. Decision-making is driven by information – without it management is no more than guesswork – and it comes in two ways. There is information about the past (actuals) and then there is information about the future (forecasts).

To demonstrate how the ability to anticipate (forecasting) contributes to decision-making – to navigating our way around the world – consider the act of crossing a road.

Without foresight, you could only proceed by trial and error, which involves doing something, observing the outcome and taking the appropriate corrective action. For example, this might involve stepping out in front of a car 50 yards away travelling at 50 miles per hour and observing that you almost get hit. The process of navigating using historical data is called *feedback control* for the obvious reason that information about the current state of affairs is *fed back* into the decision-making process. If you only use trial and error techniques to cross the road, you would be lucky to survive for a few days, even with quick and unambiguous feedback – of the sort that many organizations do not have.

The decision to cross the road involves a forecast – we ask ourselves 'will that car arrive before I have reached the other side?'. This forecast is constantly updated with new information which we use to adjust our actions; we may speed up, slow down or turn back. In fact, almost every act requires a forecast of some sort; a source of 'information about the future'. It is difficult for any organism (or organization) to survive without some sort of ability to anticipate. Most animals have to rely on the forecasting ability they were bequeathed in their genes, programmed by millennia of trial and error. We human beings are more fortunate. We are uniquely well equipped with large brains we use to build sophisticated models that enable us to project from the present into the future at will; sometimes for practical purposes (like crossing a road), at other times as a purely creative act (in science fiction literature for instance). Our 'laboratory of the mind' allows us to anticipate possible futures and to test out alternative actions before we decide what to do. This is called *feedforward* control – since we manufacture information about the potential future state of the world which is then *fed forward* into our thought and decision-making processes. This approach is less costly than learning from experience and is also safer and quicker. As human beings, we can modify our behavior by rearranging the way our neurons are organized using a process called 'thought', whereas the unfortunate amoeba has to rely on random mutation and death to improve its decision-making capabilities. 'The fundamental purpose of brains is to produce the future' says philosopher Daniel Dennett, 'they are in essence anticipation machines' (Dennett, 1991).

The good news for us humans is that we have evolved an ability to be very good at forecasting without having to think about it. The bad news is that because we have never had to think about it, we do not understand the process very well. As a result, when we try to design this capability into our organizations we often fail; forecasts are late, uninformative and unreliable.

The problems organizations face with forecasting are more serious than most people realize. First, bad forecasts are worse than no forecasts. If you have no forecast, you will at least be alert; you will always have a look out posted. A poor forecast, on the other hand, can foster dangerous complacency or misinform decision-making sending the ship on a collision course with hazardous reefs. Forecasts help us to work out what to look for – they distort our perception. If we have not contemplated that something might happen we may fail to even notice it until it is too late – which is why things are obvious in hindsight. Even worse, by the time you realize that your forecasting process has failed – as many business people have recently discovered – it is probably too late to do anything to improve it. Another challenge is that, unlike historic information which we only need to collect, forecasting information must be created; and the process of creation is likely to involve many different people in an organization, with different knowledge, experience and motivations. As Arie de Geus, formerly Head Planner at Shell remarks, 'the problem managers face is not acting intelligently in isolation but tapping all of the company's intelligence to foresee problems together' (Geus, 1997). Finally, simply forecasting better is not enough; you have to know what you can do with the information if the picture the forecast paints is not what you want, so we need to understand the link with decision-making as well.

So, wouldn't it be a good idea to understand what it takes to forecast well; to make our organizations 'Future Ready'? Perhaps it would make sense to learn from nature (including our own brains) and then find a way to apply this knowledge to our collective endeavor in organizations. De Geus concludes, 'a company is not hardwired to produce this sort of memory of the future. Managers must take specific action to produce one.'

Surely, given the importance of the process of forecasting and how long we have been at it in organizations, this knowledge already exists? There is certainly no shortage of literature on the subject. Management shelves in bookstores groan under the weight of worthy treatises on forecasting for managers (type in 'business forecast' on Amazon.com and you get over 25 000 'hits'!). Is there anything left to say?

This is what we thought when we first tackled this topic 10 years ago. *Despite the extensive literature on the subject of forecasting, what we found was that nobody seemed to have answers to the kind of practical questions that we were always being asked.* What does a good forecast look like? How far ahead should we look? What is the best way to produce a forecast? How detailed should they be? How do we measure success? How do we deal with uncertainty? We are not alone in believing that there is a huge gap in knowledge that needs to be filled. Fritz Roemer, head of the Hackett Group's Enterprise Performance Management Practice concurs: '[F]orecasting is broken in many, many companies that we see, and this is largely a result of ignorance. Nine out of ten companies simply don't really have a proper understanding of what forecasting is and how to do it well' (Roemer, 2008).

The 'solutions' touted by software suppliers and advisors to business provide only part of the answer. They promote a plethora of tools and techniques, but often with little guidance on how they can be made to work within an organizational framework, to help managers forecast more effectively. Many software companies have targeted improvements in forecasting efficiency by eliminating 'spreadsheet hell'; or promise to improve forecasting techniques by introducing 'rolling forecasts' or 'driver-based budgeting'. All these may be part of the solution, but only if they are used intelligently as part of a coherent, well informed approach.

Academics, on the other hand, seem to focus almost exclusively on a different problem: forecasting technique. This involves trying to find the best way to fit a trend to past data to help predict the future. While understanding trends is important, business people know that they cannot simply rely on the past to guide them in the future, not least because their job as managers is to make the future different to what it otherwise might be. If it isn't, why did you need managers?

The conclusion we came to was that if the solution to managers' problems did not exist we needed to create it. We set out to discover how different sorts of organizations (social and biological) and different branches of learning tackle the problem of anticipating the future. What we discovered is that few of the challenges faced by business people are unique. Effective solutions often already exist. What is missing, which is what we aim to provide in this book, is a synthesis of this knowledge and a way of communicating it in an accessible fashion to a time challenged, pragmatic business audience.

Between us we have over 50 years of hands on experience in consulting and as practicing professionals with a particular interest in forecasting in finance – revenues, profit, cash and so on, and this bias is reflected in this book. The book is, however, also useful for those that have an interest in other sorts of forecasting. The principles involved in forecasting in finance are the same as those needed to effectively forecast at an operational level, in sales and in the supply chain, so this book will be valuable for professionals in a wide range of roles. In addition, we often find that a poor, misaligned, finance process handicaps forecasting processes elsewhere in the organization and leads to other parts of the organization being deprived of the resources needed to manage their affairs effectively. 'Every living entity consumes' writes Arie de Geus in his book *The Living Company*, 'and money serves in a large corporation as the way of measuring what has been consumed. As a result of this role, when properly managed, the financing of a company becomes a governor of a living company's growth and evolution.' We are also prominent in the 'Beyond Budgeting' movement; indeed we came to the subject of forecasting because we are convinced that, for many organizations, improving forecasting processes was an important first step on the journey to eliminating traditional budgeting. Classical budgeting practice, and the mindset and behavior that often accompany it, are often *the* major barrier to change. However, providing you are aware of some of the potential pitfalls and are prepared to make some adjustments, you can do a better job of forecasting without abandoning budgets altogether.

The book is comprised of four sections, each with a different purpose, often aimed at different segments of the readership.

Section 1 lays out the problem and so will be relevant to all readers. In two parts it answers these questions:
● What is the problem with forecasting?
● How do I know if I have a problem?
● What are the benefits I can expect by improving the process?

Section 2 focuses on 'Forecasting Principles'. This provides the reader with a basic understanding of the nature and practice of effective forecasting and so provides the foundation for the mastery of forecasting. It is important for all readers to give this section their full attention. None of the content should be beyond the average manager; it assumes no mathematical or other technical knowledge or aptitude. Each of the five chapters tackles a separate theme and set of questions:
● Chapter 2: Mastering Purpose
  ○ What is the difference between a prediction and a forecast?
  ○ What is the definition of a forecast?
  ○ What are the qualities of a good forecast?
  ○ What kind of information do I need in a forecast?
  ○ How accurate does a forecast need to be?
● Chapter 3: Mastering Time
  ○ What types of forecast are there, and how do they differ?
  ○ How far ahead should I forecast?
  ○ How often should I forecast?
  ○ How should forecasting be linked to decision-making?
● Chapter 4: Mastering Models
  ○ How can I produce forecasts? What options are available?
  ○ How should I choose between them?
  ○ What are the major causes of error in forecasts?
  ○ What role does judgment play in forecasting?
  ○ Is it possible to get better at judgment and if so, how?

- Chapter 5: Mastering Measurement
  - What role does measurement play in forecasting?
  - What should I measure?
  - How and when should I measure?
  - How can I improve forecast quality?
- Chapter 6: Mastering Risks
  - Why do I need to consider forecast risk?
  - What is risk and how does it differ from uncertainty?
  - How do I go about assessing risk?
  - What should I do with risk information?

Section 3 is titled 'Praxis'. It tackles some of the issues that arise when we translate the principles outlined in the last section into practice. It is primarily aimed at practitioners – those responsible for designing, implementing and running forecast processes but it would also reward the general reader. Chapter 7 'Mastering Process' provides answers to three types of problems often encountered when we set about embedding forecasting practice into an organization:

- Theme 1: How should you design, organize and run a forecast process?
- Theme 2: In a large or complex organization with many forecast processes, should they be linked, and if so, how?
- Theme 3: Who should be responsible for running the forecast process?

Section 4 deals with transformation. This section targets those responsible for designing and implementing change in the organization, but again the content is non-technical and of general interest. The three major topics here are:

- Chapter 8: What is the best way to tackle the process of change?
- Chapter 9: If traditional budgeting practices and mindsets present a major barrier to the implementation of effective forecasting in my organization, how should I set about overcoming it, short of abandoning budgeting?
- Chapter 10: What is the best alternative to conventional budgeting?

After Section 4 and the concluding Chapter 11 you will find a Glossary which summarizes the key terms and concepts used in this book. The 30 principles of effective forecast process design are then summarized in Appendix 1.

The aim of this book has been to describe simple and practical steps that any organization can apply to do a better job of forecasting. While the ideas in this book have all been thoroughly tested in practice, the real power of the ideas comes from the fact that they are well grounded in theory. Many of the concepts have been sourced from academic work in systems science and Appendix 2 sets out some of the basic ideas, which will be of interest for the theoretically minded or inquisitive reader.

Different sections of the book are aimed at different readerships. There are other ways in which readers with different interests and learning styles can be selective about what they read. Our aim is to communicate our ideas simply and quickly so the body text is straightforward and self-contained. For readers who want to go into more detail, the main text is interspersed with 'panels' which provide reinforcement, background, illustrative examples or practical guidance. There are three types of panel:

Key Concept

This donates a critical point of importance to all readers. The other two types of panels are optional.

More

Used in panels that contain technical or practical information which enables readers to explore a topic in more detail. This includes practical tips or explanations of techniques for those involved in implementation.

Examples

Panels with this symbol contain examples, exercises or short case studies.

While the book has a strong logical thread running through it, readers will be presented with many concepts and ideas, many of which will be unfamiliar. To ensure that you do not lose the thread we will also periodically provide you with guidance which will help you orientate yourself and prepare yourself for what comes next. We use a different font, like that used in this paragraph, to differentiate this guidance from the body text.

The main audience for this book is what we call the 'thoughtful manager'. We believe that the vast majority of business people (at least those who buy this book!) are intelligent, well-meaning managers who want to 'do the right thing'. We also believe that many managers are trapped in old fashioned and dysfunctional ways of thinking. As a result they end up managing by 'rote' or out of habit. We find that those managers that are aware of this problem, and want to do something about it, are often so overwhelmed by the pressures of work they do not get time to think. Most of what these managers are offered is often no more than a palliative – the pain always returns once the placebo effect has worn off. For this audience we offer new insights into something that they might assume they already understand and some advice that will provide permanent relief. This advice is not just for forecasting practitioners. As Arie de Geus remarks, 'managers when faced with their own bad decisions, use the excuse that they were given the wrong prediction! This is an abdication of managerial responsibility; dealing with the future can never be delegated.'

Our other audience is academics, advisors and suppliers to business. There is often a large, unhealthy gap between the world of business academics and that of practitioners. We hope to be able to contribute to bridging this gap by demonstrating how 'theory' can be made practical and by identifying other areas where academic expertise may be fruitfully applied. For those closer to business we hope that this book will make your job of promoting healthy change easier. In this context Peter Senge uses the analogy of a circus trapeze artist (Senge, 1990). He argues that, however convinced managers are of the need to let go of the 'brass ring' they are currently hanging on to, they won't let go unless they can see a new ring they can cling on to. We hope that this will help those who help business people fashion the new 'brass ring'.

While reading the book you might sometimes have the feeling that we are telling you what you already know. For us that is a sign that we have managed to get to the heart of an issue and uncover a general truth. We hope our message will resonate with your experience of the real world, but not all of what you will learn is in line with orthodox management thinking. What this book demands of the general reader is an openness to new ideas and, of the practicing manager, the ability and courage to translate them into practical reality. We hope you enjoy it.

ACKNOWLEDGEMENTS

We have unashamedly mined the experience and knowledge of very many people in writing this book.

In particular, we would like to acknowledge our debt to our colleagues in the Beyond Budgeting community: to Jeremy Hope and Robin Fraser, the founders, but also to Peter Bunce, Frans Roesli, Flavio Ventocilla, Bjarte Bogsnes, Aubrey Joachim and many others who have inspired and educated us over the last ten years. We would also like to honor all of our other teachers, academic and professional, who have helped us grow; particularly Chuck Horngren, Bob Kaplan, Mike Tayles, Angela Espinosa and all the members of Stafford Beer's cybernetic family. They have enlightened the paths of our journey by sharing their insights and correcting our mistakes. Jamie Croake of American Express, Spencer Van Ness and Laura Wright of Southwest Airlines have made special contributions to the book as have many Unilever people, most notably Martin Jarvis and the Sales and Operations and Planning team, and Paul Baumann, Suzan van Dijk and other members of Unilever's Finance Academy. Fritz Roemer of the Hackett Group has also been unstintingly generous and supportive over a number of years. We would also like to thank all those who have selflessly ploughed through various drafts of this book and offered comments and criticisms, in particular, Jonathon Chocqueel-Mangan. We also offer special appreciation to Robin Baumgartner, Heather Bryce, Tiffany Wolford, and Michael Player. They continually support our efforts and diligently make sure things get done. Final thanks go to Rosemary Nixon, Jo Golesworthy and everyone else at John Wiley who has helped make this book possible.

ACKNOWLEDGEMENTS

Section I
'WHY?'

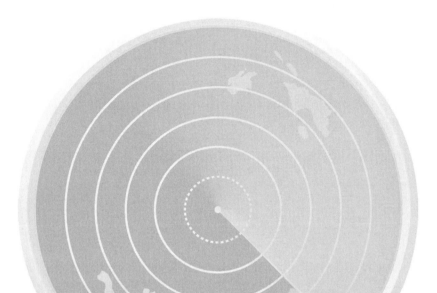

The purpose of this short section is to set out the arguments for change; for doing a better job of forecasting.

Failures of forecasting can be disastrous, and as the world becomes more turbulent and unpredictable, holding a true course and dealing with business stakeholders becomes more difficult and the risk of outright failure more real. Senior management in businesses recognizes this, and has for some time. Why is it that we seem to have made so little progress? Why do we see the same problems presenting themselves in business after business?

This section is for all readers. The first part provides a better understanding of the nature and the source of the problems of forecasting in business. In the second part readers are helped to diagnose forecasting diseases and we give guidance on potential cures. In addition, we paint a picture of the kind of benefits you can expect if you succeed in applying what can be learned from this book.

WHY CHANGE?
Everyone knows the trouble I've seen

❝Prediction is very difficult, especially if it's about the future.❞ Nils Bohr, Nobel laureate in Physics

What happens when forecasting fails – why forecasting is more important than ever – why we can't blame 'the Street' for our failures – what managers think about forecasting – how traditional management models make things more difficult – common symptoms of a failing process – remedies that don't work and one that does – what success looks like – and the benefits

Sometimes, as with the human body, you only recognize how a management practice contributes to organizational health when it fails. This is the case with forecasting; almost every economic crash or catastrophic business failure is accompanied by the lament 'how come no one saw it coming?'

The birth of an empire

We open with two such stories. The first concerns the company founded by the Italian Irish inventor Guglielmo Marconi, the man credited with the invention of the radio. He first demonstrated the ability to send radio messages across the Atlantic in 1901, but his invention shot to fame when it was used to apprehend the wife murderer Hawley Harvey Crippen, after the captain of the ship carrying him and his new partner to Canada had radioed his suspicions of their identity to Scotland Yard. One hundred years later, at what turned out to be a particularly inauspicious time, the company bearing his name was preparing to celebrate the anniversary by launching a new £0.5m website commemorating the life and works of the great man. 'We like to draw the parallel between the man 100 years ago and the company and its potential now' said Peter Crane, the man behind the project (Solomans, 2001).

The company's journey through the previous century however had not been straightforward. Marconi's company had been acquired by English Electric in the 1940s, which was itself taken over by GEC in 1968. GEC was the creation of Arnold Weinstock, the son of an immigrant Polish tailor, who, over 40 years had presided over the rationalization of the British electrical industry. Weinstock was a notoriously meticulous and cautious man, poring over the numbers of his various companies and deals in his dingy Stanhope Gate offices, surrounded by trusted lieutenants. By the time he retired in 1996, he had built up a conglomerate with profits of over £1 billion on turnover of £11 billion. More to the point, he bequeathed a cash pile of £1.4 billion to his nominated successor George Simpson.

Weinstock divided opinion strongly. To many he was simply 'Britain's best manager'. To others he was a narrow-minded bean counter who had sucked all the life out of a major chunk of Britain's industry, leaving the country ill equipped to exploit the opportunities of the new digital era.

Lord Simpson addressed the challenge of reversing this trend with gusto. He recruited John Mayo, a high flying merchant banker, sold off GEC's unfashionable defense businesses and used the proceeds of this and the equally unfashionable cash mountain to buy Marconi (as GEC was now called) a stake in the new economy.

'Simpson continued to buy telecoms assets as if they were going out of fashion' BBC business pundit Jeff Randall drily observed. 'Unfortunately for him they were' (Randall, 2001).

A bubble bursts

The second, related, story is about the poster child for the new digital age: a company called Cisco. Founded by a husband and wife team in 1986 it had, in a mere 14 years, become the world's most valuable company when in March 2000 its shares hit $80 (50 times earnings). The engine of this growth was Cisco's dominant position in the switching technology underpinning the Internet. In 1990, there were 200 000 Internet hosts. By the end of the decade there were over 100 million.

Barely a year after this peak, however, Cisco's CEO, John Chambers, was having a miserable time. On May 10, 2001 he announced Cisco's first ever quarterly loss. The loss Cisco posted for Q1 was a massive $2.89 billion on revenues down 30% on the prior year quarter, when sales had posted year on year growth of 70%. The decline was across all sectors and all territories. Over the next few months most of Cisco's competitors, customers and suppliers were to follow suit.

Chambers compared what had happened to a biblical disaster: 'this shows that a once in 100 year flood can happen in your lifetime. It is now clear to us that the peaks in this new economy will be much higher and the valleys much lower and the movement between these peaks and valleys will be much faster,' he went on. 'We are now in a valley very much deeper than any of us anticipated' (Abrahams, 2001).

The drop in the market was only half of the story, however. Based on over-optimistic sales forecasts Cisco had taken a gamble. To avoid losing sales because of a shortage of components, the company had bought stock ahead. The reason why Q1's results were so bad was that the company was forced to write off $2.25 billion of excess inventory – bringing the total inventory the company carried down to a mere $1.9 billion.

Chambers reported to analysts that visibility remained difficult. 'The suspicion remains' reported the *Financial Times* 'that visibility is fine; it is merely that management does not like what it sees' (Abrahams, 2001).

By the end of May Cisco had lost over 75% of its March 2000 value and 25% of its employees had lost 100% of their jobs.

The calm ... and the storm

On the day after Cisco's announcement, in Liverpool – home to one of Marconi's 70 odd factories – the visibility was also fine. The city was enjoying a spell of unseasonably hot weather and so management sent workers at the plant out to sunbathe on the lawns in front of the glass-fronted buildings of the Edge Hill factory. Talk was of the plane crash at the city's airport and the following day's football FA Cup Final, which featured one of the city's two big teams. What also featured in conversations was the shortage of orders that had led to this unofficial break. 'There were simply no orders going through for hardware' reported one of the workers (Daniel and Pretzlik, 2001). This did not come as a surprise to employees of the plant. In the period January to March when the plant's major customer, British Telecom, spends most of its money, workers 'usually work around the clock, seven days a week because there is a flood of work'. But this year 'work dried up – it was already quiet over the Christmas period' reported Sue Tallon, a union representative at Edge Hill.

Management only seems to have noticed this much later. On April 9, senior management gave an upbeat presentation to union representatives at the Coventry plant. It employed 1200 people but was operating at below 50% capacity. In Italy, Elio Troilli, the head of the workers' committee for Marconi plants there, says they began getting reports of a slowdown in orders at the beginning of the year.

Marconi's management was having none of this negative thinking however. On April 11, the *Financial Times* ran an article with the headline 'Marconi starts an assault on doomsayers' (Daniel, 2001). 'We have not needed to change our guidance,' Mayo said to the FT reporter. 'If we had come out each month saying "we haven't changed our guidance" people would have thought we were off our trolleys.' He based his confidence on the company's limited exposure to alternative carriers and the US enterprise market, its focus on 'solutions' rather than 'products' and its dominant position in optical networking outside the US. 'The history books will probably write that we were Lucent's nemesis. Nortel and us have taken share from them.'

The company continued in this optimistic vein. At the annual shareholders' meeting on May 15, Lord Simpson commented that while the first half of the year would be flat 'we anticipate that the market will recover around the end of this calendar year'. On June 19, he told the FT that 'we have no reason to change our view of what we said a month ago' (Daniel *et al.*, 2001).

But, when the 'flash results' came into Marconi's new Mayfair headquarters at the end of June it was clear that performance in the first quarter of the financial year was not merely weak; it was disastrous. Mayo flew back from a sales trip to Italy on the morning of Tuesday July 3 to go through the figures with Steve Hare, the Finance Director. At 6.26am on the following day, Marconi announced the completion of the sale of its medical unit to Philips, the Dutch electrical group. Fifteen minutes later the shares of the company were suspended. At 6.53pm, the Board of Marconi issued a trading statement. Sales would be 15% below the level of the previous year and profits halved. Four thousand jobs would be lost. 'Normally, at the end of June we would see a sudden uptick in performance as orders are final-ized at the end of the quarter. Instead what we saw in fact was a downturn ... it did just happen that quickly' reported Lord Simpson (Daniel and Pretzlik, 2001).

The next day Marconi shares fell 54%. They closed at 101 pence valuing the company at £2.6 billion compared to £35.5 billion nearly a year earlier. By September analysts had concluded that the shares were 'virtually worthless' (McCarthy, 2001).

By Friday evening of that same week, Mayo had been forced to resign. The Chairman of Marconi, Sir Roger Hurn, and Simpson resigned in September after a second profit warning. Steve Hare, the FD, lasted until November 2002 when he lost his job following a failure to renegotiate debt financing for the company.

Unfortunately, Lord Weinstock did not last that long. He passed away on July 24, 2002 after a short illness. 'He was the best manager Britain has ever produced' according to Lord Hanson, the industrialist. 'I think he died of a broken heart because of what happened to his company.' 'Watching Marconi slowly collapse like a great classical building was extremely painful for him,' said Sir David Scholey, friend and one time banker to Weinstock (Hunt and Roberts, 2002).

In 2005, at the end of 'one of the swiftest ever exercises in value destruction' (Plender, 2002), the bulk of what was left of Marconi was sold to Ericsson, the Swedish company, for £1.2 billion.

The world has changed, but our thinking and our tools have not kept pace

What do these stories teach us?

Clearly, growth through acquisition can be risky; most fail to deliver the antici-pated benefits and many lead to calamity. And Marconi were certainly unlucky or unwise since they bought at the top of the market. Also, the simplistic, narrow minded focus on a single financial metric, particularly when it is linked to generous financial incentives, can be, as we have discovered again recently, a recipe for disaster (Plender, 2002).

All these, and many other criticisms may be valid, but there is something more profound, more relevant to the daily practice of management, that these stories illustrate.

It is clear that our modern economies have evolved to the point that things can happen at a frightening speed. Start-ups can become huge, globally dominant corporations in a matter of a few years; for example, Google has only just celebrated its tenth birthday. Conversely, as we have discovered over the past year, institutions that have been around for a century can disappear almost overnight. Economies and institutions are now so interconnected that it can be dangerous to make assumptions about the business environment more than a few months ahead.

It follows from this that businesses have to pay more attention to the opaque nature of the future than ever before. Opting out of the global economy is not an option, and there is a limit to our ability to manage risk – the product of our inability to forecast perfectly – using tools such as insurance, hedges or diversification. If we cannot avoid business risk altogether, and it is not possible to insulate ourselves against it, we have to get better at anticipating danger – or for that matter opportunity – and responding to it, quickly and effectively. We have to become 'Future Ready'.

That is the real story here. When making decisions, we cannot rely solely on information about what has happened, we need information about what we believe might happen as well; information that we create through the process of forecasting. Equally important, we then have to build the capability to act upon this information. If we have no such information, or it is deficient or misleading, then we risk loss of opportunity, resources or, in the case of Marconi, outright failure and collapse.

Without good forecasts, businesses are horribly exposed

What is particularly striking about the Marconi case is that it is clear that the information needed to anticipate the collapse of the telecommunications market did exist over six months before their bungled profit warning. What is more, it did not require superhuman powers of detection and insight to find it. Even shop floor workers knew about it. The information must have been in company systems, but for some reason the brains in the corporation were not in contact with the brain of the corporation.

'If it wasn't brutally clear to anyone at the start of the year that the industry was imploding it should have been clear by May,' said James Heal, analyst at Commerzbank. 'They must have been on another planet,' concluded the FT (Roberts, 2001). Extraterrestrial vacations are not the only explanation for the catastrophic failure of Marconi, however. It is clear that Marconi either did not have or did not use or trust their forecasts. When asked at the annual meeting held on July 18 whether the Board knew about the poor sales figures in May, incredibly the Chairman replied 'No. We did not know it in May. It was the second month of the financial year' (Daniel and Pretzlik, 2001). Fortunately, when we are driving a car we do not wait until something has already happened before we change course, we look through the windshield. It is not recorded whether shareholders challenged

Sir Roger on his reliance on the rear view mirror to manage his business or asked why the timing of the financial year-end was relevant to managing the business.

Another telling comment was made by George Simpson. 'Normally we expect a sudden uptick in performance when orders are finalized at the end of the quarter' (Daniel and Pretzlik, 2001). Why, you might ask, are orders 'finalized at quarter end'? We often hear this kind of thing from companies who run their business by simply trying to 'hit the numbers'. Set a target, pay people to hit it (or punish them for failing) and if you succeed then assume the business is performing well. It is dangerous to run a business on automatic pilot. Manage this way and nobody is looking at where you are heading and whether you need to change course, speed up or slow down.

Whatever the reason the chronic inability of the business to anticipate the future was a major cause of Marconi's failure. With no early warning of the impending crash the painful truth revealed in the June quarter end numbers was, from the perspective of company management, sudden and unexpected. 'It really did happen that quickly' said Lord Simpson (Daniel and Pretzlik, 2001). It was not just that Marconi's business was weaker than everybody thought, or that the market had collapsed. The systems management relied upon were simply not up to the job. As a result, investors simply lost confidence in the ability of its managers to manage. Whatever you might think about the quality of Cisco's sales forecasts, it is manifestly clear that one of the reasons why the company (and its management) survived relatively unscathed was because they spotted the problem sooner than Marconi and took swift and decisive action.

In the world of business today, any company that is not able to forecast – to anticipate and to respond – risks loss (of money or opportunity) or in extreme case failure. And this is not just about what you say to the markets. Even Cisco, with its much-vaunted real time reporting systems, paid a massive $2 billion price for failing to tie operational and financial forecasting together in a sound risk management framework. Similarly, buried in the wreckage of Marconi accounts for 2001/2 are stock write-offs of £518m attributed to overoptimistic forecasts made by two of Marconi's two big US acquisitions.

There is a big difference between forecasts and prophesies

Let us be clear. When we talk about forecasting we do not mean prophesy. No one can predict the future with certainty. Our focus is the process of systematically and rationally assembling information to give managers forward visibility; visibility of likely outcomes and visibility of potential risks and opportunities.

Effective forecasting is about hard work, skill and organization, not about genius. Lord Kelvin, the foremost scientist of his generation, on August 2, 1902 solemnly informed the Chairman of the Anglo-American Telegraph Company, Francis A. Bevan, that 'I have given careful consideration to the subject, and I do not believe the shareholders of your company need be alarmed at the prospect of wireless telegraphy' (Anon, 1902). Closer to home, Alan Greenspan, ex Chairman of the US Federal Reserve and a man, when in office, widely credited with almost superhuman wisdom, was interviewed on a CBS News '60 Minutes' program broadcast on September 16, 2007. He was questioned about the sub-prime loans problem that had recently come to light. 'It does not look sufficiently severe that it will spiral into anything deeper,' he said. 'We are going to get through this particular credit crunch, we always do ... the fever will break and euphoria will come back again' (Sughrue, 2007). A year later, almost to the day, Lehman Brothers filed for Chapter 11 bankruptcy protection, and as these words are being written the world is holding its breath to see whether the unprecedented emergency bail out packages recently announced by the US and UK governments will help save the global financial system from meltdown.

The message that forecasting is within the grasp of mortals sounds like good news, which it is. All that is required is hard work, skill and organization, but this cannot be mobilized instantly. Most organizations realize that their forecast processes are not up to scratch only when it is too late to do anything about it.

One of the biggest myths in management ... 'The Street made me do it'

It is a common misconception among managers that 'Wall Street' demands that businesses accurately predict the future. This view simply does not stand up to scrutiny.

Of course, it is dangerous to generalize about anything as diverse as the 'investment community'. It is made up of thousands of people, spread all over the world, with different investment strategies and motivations all of which can change based on the prevailing market situation. However, here is a view we think is worth listening to.

In November 2002 the Beyond Budgeting Round Table held a meeting in New York. It was hosted by a financial information service company at their offices close to the site of the former World Trade Center. The guy in charge of the unit responsible for compiling the consensus forecast for Wall Street found himself (as I suspect he often does) addressing a room full of people about whom he knows very little.

Most of the room were like ourselves, slightly in awe of a man with over 30 years' experience at the center of the economic web of the most powerful nation on earth. We waited for the drops of accumulated wisdom to fall from his lips. He was talking just at the end of the 'dotcom' bubble.

This is what he told us.

He had lived through several periods of boom and bust. Although they were all different, they were also all the same; every boom sucked in people who really shouldn't have been there and who, through ignorance or hubris, contributed to their own downfall and the downfall of others.

This particular boom was characterized by an unspoken and unorganized conspiracy between senior managers of big businesses and inexperienced analysts. The senior business people need to talk up their stock price so they could make big bucks by exercising their options, and the easiest way to do this was to set expectations in the market and then deliver on them. Exactly. They did this by talking to analysts who in turn gained credibility by being seen to have access to the royalty of the business world and demonstrating an uncanny ability to predict the future. This worked well; at least it did until the bubble burst.

In the opinion of this seasoned pro, rookie analysts who had been sucked into the industry during the bubble had become mere stenographers for company leaders anxious to disseminate rosy forecasts and so put a shine on their share options.

These analysts had not exercised their most basic duty to their investors: to use their judgment. 'If you are in charge of a business and can't tell me what is going to happen at the end of the quarter then I suspect that you don't know what you are doing,' he said. On the other hand: 'if you can tell me exactly what is going to happen in a year's time then you are either a fool or a liar. You do not know what is going to happen in the future, and neither do I. What I, as an experienced analyst, want from you is a projection with some ranges around it, a good idea of what is driving the uncertainty and a convincing plan of how you are going to mitigate the risk or exploit the opportunity. I can then do something you can't do; I can go and ask your competitors the same question and based on that I will make the judgment about whether you are a good investment or not.'

So, according to this knowledgeable source, the market doesn't demand that you predict the future. It does expect that you have a good grasp of what might happen and are well prepared to deal with it. Isn't that just good, *common* sense?

Despite it being widely recognized as important the current state of the craft of forecasting is woeful

Given this backdrop it is no surprise that managers see forecasting as very important, as numerous surveys testify.

A survey of 540 senior executives conducted by KPMG in 2007 (EIU, 2007) found that over the previous three years those firms with average error in earnings forecasts of less than 5% enjoyed a 12% higher share appreciation than those with higher errors. Improving forecasting came at the top of the surveyed companies' priority list for the next three years. 'Ability to forecast results' also comes at the top of this list of the 10 most important 'Internal Concerns' for CFOs across the globe (Karaian, 2009). Furthermore, a PWC survey recorded that 65% of respondents thought the relevance of forecasting would increase over time, compared with only 5% who thought it would reduce (PWC, 2007).

One of the reasons why forecasting comes so high in the list of priorities for senior management is that the performance of their processes is so poor. According to the Hackett Group only 18% of senior finance professionals are 'highly satisfied' with their forecast process (Hackett, 2008) and it is easy to see why. On average, earning forecasts are 13% off (a fact that is estimated to knock 6% off their share price) (EIU, 2007). Another survey puts sales forecasting error in the 15–25% range (Mentzer and Cox, 1984). And industry analysts are no better, according to McKinsey (Goedhart *et al.*, 2001). What is more, the career penalties of failure have apparently increased post Sarbanes-Oxley (Mergenthaler *et al.*, 2008).

Fritz Roemer, Head of Enterprise Performance Management Practice at the Hackett Group has noticed an upsurge in interest in forecasting recently. In the past 'as long as the CFO hasn't had to declare a profit warning he thinks the process is fine, but today one profit warning involves a loss of credibility, a second the loss of the job, so the increase in interest isn't surprising'. The fundamental problem, according to Hackett, is the gap between the turbulence of the environment and the responsiveness of the forecasting process. 'The gap is widening,' Roemer explains. 'Many companies are doing nothing, but our surveys confirm that companies see the world becoming more and more turbulent. So things are getting worse' (Roemer, 2008).

The reality for many companies is even grimmer than the statistics suggest, if the scenario painted by performance management guru David Axson is true. 'Typically the sales forecast is extracted under duress from the sales organization. This forecast is then second guessed by marketing, production and finance with the result that eventually sales throw up their hands in frustration and simply say "tell me what you want"' (Axson, 2003).

It is therefore easy to see why over 70% of senior executives plan to make significant changes in their forecasting processes over the next two years, a figure which has been pretty constant since Hackett first started asking the question (Hackett, 2008). This finding is supported by a McKinsey survey entitled 'Starting Out as CFO' (Chappuis *et al.*, 2008), which found that 79% of the 164 CFOs interviewed would be making fundamental changes in the financial planning processes within the first 100 days.

However, assuming that you were one of the managers responsible for planning the changes, where would you look for help and guidance? How would you know what success looks like? And why doesn't the situation appear to be improving?

A big part of the reason is that our management systems, and the mindset that they have helped breed, are the product of a bygone era.

We have perverted the lessons learned from the pioneers of management ... and we are enslaved to our delusions

The boom in the automobile industry in the 1920s mirrored the telecoms bubble of the 1990s and General Motors was the Cisco of its day. Just like Cisco, General Motors enjoyed the boom but also suffered the bust. It was rescued by the banks and by du Pont Corporation twice in a period of 10 years. In addition, just like Cisco, GM was credited with management as well as product innovation; the modern diversified corporation with its concepts of ROI, standard Charts of Account, and the mechanisms for control of cash, inventory and production and market segmentation were all products of General Motors under the stewardship of Alfred Sloan in the early years of the 1920s.

These developments were paralleled in the world of academia. In 1922 James O. McKinsey, a Professor of Accounting at Chicago University, who subsequently went on to found the world's first modern consulting firm, wrote one of the first management books entitled *Budgetary Control* (McKinsey, 1922).

The achievements of Alfred Sloan and his contemporaries over this short period were phenomenal. Between them they almost single handedly invented much of what we call 'professional management'. 'By 1925,' Professors Robert Kaplan and Tom Johnson tell us 'virtually all management accounting practices in use today had been developed' (Johnson and Kaplan, 1987). Not only was this the template that most businesses in the world followed for the best part of the century, but it was also copied by, among others, Stalin when in 1925 he instructed Gosplan, the

Soviet Union's central planning organization, to start issuing annual control numbers rather than just advice. We've heard about the Soviet 'Five Year Plan' but make no mistake, the USSR was run using annual budgets!!

 Example

General Motors, modern management techniques and the birth of budgeting

When Sloan stepped into the top job in GM in 1923 he inherited a company created by an entrepreneur with the colorful name of William Crapo Durant. He was, in Sloan's words, 'a great man with a great weakness – he could create but not administer' (Sloan, 1967), twice leading GM into near insolvency, the last occasion being associated with a crash in the automobile market in September 1920 which left GM with a huge inventory problem (sound familiar?). It was from the ashes of this last catastrophe that modern management practices arose; they were effectively invented by Sloan himself with the help of Donaldson Brown, a man parachuted into GM from the DuPont Corporation – the largest shareholder in GM at that time.

Contrary to common belief Sloan's vision was that of a flexible, decentralized organization, which sought to respond quickly to changes and maximize returns to shareholders over an entire economic cycle. The rigid budgeting system that we have come to associate with this era of management is more consistent with the vision of McKinsey who promoted it as a mechanism for achieving centralized control. Interestingly budgeting in this form is probably the only innovation in management that has moved from the public to the private sector; McKinsey took the Federal Government's Budgeting and Accounting Act, passed in June 1921, as his model.

And, faced with the circumstances these pioneers were faced with, what they did was absolutely right. Even better, it worked … at least until the world changed.

In the pre-war world, the major problem executives faced was a problem of coordination. Without calculators, with barely more than Morse code, how do you organize the collective efforts of hundreds of thousands of people to provide consumers with products that only 20 years previously were built, one by one, in the garden sheds of a bunch of mad inventors? And produce them at prices millions could afford.

They solved the problem by constraining people. Work out, in detail, what you needed to do and how much it would cost, and then, put simply, make sure your employees did what they were required to do. Faced with a task of coordinating the actions of several hundred workers, many of whom were barely literate, the last thing you needed was flexibility. Change was a dangerous enemy that had to be captured and subdued.

Jump forward 80 years. What does the world look like now?

We still have huge businesses, which we have to organize, manage and control. But these are not the huge monolithic lumbering beasts conceived of by Alfred Sloan. They are staffed, for the most part, by well educated modern professionals who communicate using IT with a facility that would have seemed magical a hundred years ago. For sure, some of the big beasts from Sloan's era are still around, but often only because it is more difficult for them to die than it is to keep them alive. They are dinosaurs on life support.

The large businesses of today can appear and disappear within the time span of a Strategic Planning exercise. Getting big, and managing your internal affairs once you are big, is not *the* major problem any more. The problem, if you are trying to avoid becoming a twenty-first century dinosaur, is how do you deal with the voracious predators who share your patch of territory eating all the food?

Change is the problem, but we cannot deal with change by suppressing it or pretending it does not exist. The only way forward is to accept it and get good at dealing with it.

And, as business people we know that. This is why we recognize the importance of forecasting. We know now that we cannot manage businesses by remote control. We cannot just set the budgets, load up the incentive plans and let go. We cannot stick the autopilot on and go take a nap. We must steer the ship. And because the ship is so big we can't rely on a man on the top of the mast any more to tell us what lies ahead; we need technology that allows us to see over the horizon. The problem is that the radar – the forecasting process – is not working properly, and just hitting it does not seem to be the answer!

Part of the answer, for sure, is the kind of real time information systems that companies like Cisco have developed. Most companies have barely begun to learn these lessons – they are still lumbering around relying on the steam driven management processes of the industrial age.

Yet lightening fast reflexes, on their own, are not enough. Homo sapiens became the dominant species on the plains of East Africa, and subsequently the globe, not because it was quicker than a leopard, bigger than an elephant or taller than a giraffe but because it evolved a large brain; a brain that allowed it to think ahead, to anticipate and so to plan. The fact that the process of evolving from an animal with a brain the size of a modern chimpanzee to that of modern man – four times the size – took only something like 2 million years, a heartbeat in evolutionary timescales, perhaps shows just how potent this new capability actually is.

Our big challenge: to replicate in our organizations the human capacity to anticipate and so shape our destiny

This frames one of the greatest challenges facing companies in the information age: how do we build the organizational capacity to look ahead, to project our minds into the future and manage our destiny before fate manages it for us? How do we do this and in the process cure ourselves of some industrial age diseases, disentangling ourselves from our redundant legacy processes and unlearning some elements of the way we have habitually come to think and behave?

Most business people do not have time to contemplate big philosophical questions; their focus is more practical. Their concern is how do I know, before it is tested and found wanting, that my forecast process is unreliable? If it isn't up to the job, what do I do about it? And, are the benefits from an improved process worth the investment of time and resources involved? These are the questions that we will address in Part 2.

FORECASTING DISEASE the symptoms and the remedy

In the first part of this chapter we surveyed the forecasting landscape. We argued that, while the importance of forecasting is recognized, in practice it is rarely performed well, sometimes with disastrous consequences.

Common symptoms of forecasting illness ...

Fortunately for the practically minded executive, we can diagnose our industrial age forecasting diseases before they bring about complete collapse. There are telltale signs that can help you detect problems at an early stage, and from which few organizations are completely immune. Does your organization's forecasting process exhibit any of these Seven Deadly Symptoms?

SYMPTOM #1

Does your organization find it difficult to cope with unexpected or unwelcome forecast outcomes? if so it might be suffering from:

Semantic schizophrenia

Patients with this condition exhibit contradictory behavior patterns. At the root of the problem are the conflicting messages that they receive. For example, the patient may be asked for a 'best estimate' but then 'held accountable for it'. Another common example is for a patient to be asked for an update but then to be criticized for making changes to the previous forecast. Patients are also often verbally abused for producing forecasts that the recipient 'does not like' but also for forecasts which 'do not reflect the truth'.

Such contradictory demands create a 'double bind' similar to that associated with schizophrenia. Because the patient believes he/she 'cannot win' they often retreat into a delusional state, producing forecasts that minimize the cognitive dissonance induced by the conflicting signals they receive. The objective of forecasting thus becomes to reduce the amount of stress to which the patient is subject. A typical manifestation of the attempt to reduce cognitive dissonance is the question: 'what forecast do you want to see?'

The cause of this problem is thought to be prolonged exposure to traditional performance management practices, which typically do not recognize the difference between a goal and a forecast. In addition, changes or deviations are often regarded as 'bad'. The dissonance between these practices and what the patient knows should be done are not consciously recognized, thus leading to perverted patterns of thought.

SYMPTOM #2

Is there a tendency in your organization for executives to engage in protracted and sometimes acrimonious debate about what the forecast numbers should be? if so this might be indicative of:

Single point tunnel vision

Patients with this condition exhibit obsessive compulsive behavior, commonly manifested in heated debate about 'the right forecast number'. These debates can be protracted and extremely acrimonious despite the patient being intellectually conscious of the fact that it is impossible to predict the future. Indeed, the only thing that can be said with any certainty is that any forecast will be wrong and the more precisely it is stated the more wrong it will be. This is similar to the human condition of tunnel vision whereby everything that lies outside the current narrow focus of attention is thought 'not to exist'.

The irony which tends to be lost on patients with this condition is that soon after these debates finish, they often consciously move to take action leading to changes which invalidate the forecast that the protagonists have just been defending.

One cause of this pathology is believed to be the use of traditional performance management practice which encourages the mistaken perception in the minds of patients that predictability is a natural state of affairs rather than a temporary or aberrant state.

SYMPTOM #3

Is your organization obsessed with forecast accuracy? do people feel that they will be punished for 'getting forecasts wrong'? if so you might be suffering from:

Delusions of accuracy

Patients with this syndrome suffer from a delusion that it is possible to predict perfectly. Flying in the face of several thousand years of human experience, any departure from this state is regarded as being deviant behavior – at best a result of lack of professionalism; at worst evidence of dishonesty. In their private life such patients will typically go to séances or invest their money in 'get rich quick' schemes which also offer the prospect of certainty.

Patients with this problem are allergic to 'forecast error' and naturally favor lower forecast error, without any regard to the source of the error. No distinction is made between error that is the result of random fluctuation and error that may be the result of poor forecasting. As a result they may punish employees for error which is totally outside their control, for example because their results are affected by the weather or a volatile market.

 Example

Why forecast errors are inevitable

To illustrate the point about forecast errors write the letter 'a' on a piece of paper. For best results make it bigger than you normally would.

Now copy, as accurately as possible, what you have written ten times on the line below.

....

Are any of the copies exactly like the original letter? Indeed are any of the letters exactly like each other?

The answer to both of these questions will almost certainly be no.

Now imagine you were performing the same task while riding in the back of a car speeding through rush hour traffic.

> What this illustrates is that even in the most trivial and most simple process – even one where only repetition is required – there will be variation. In other words there will always be error and sometimes the error will be greater as a result of factors that are outside the control of the person performing the task.
>
> We should therefore expect any forecast – which is the result of a complex activity involving many different people, a great deal of uncertainty and incomplete knowledge – to contain error. Also, in order to make meaningful comparisons between or judgments about forecasts you need to allow for differing environmental conditions – like how far ahead you are forecasting or the inherent difficulty involved.

Patients with this syndrome often engage in wholesale and self-righteous 'correction' of what they believe are faulty forecasts. Typically, these 'corrections' make matters worse as often as they improve them but 'confirmation bias' (whereby only successful interventions are recalled) renders patients blind to their delusion.

It is thought that this pathology is caused by the absence of sound approaches to measuring error.

SYMPTOM #4

Are your organization's forecasts way too detailed? is there always pressure to provide more detail and more analysis? if so this may be evidence of:
Nervous system breakdown

This is another form of common obsessive-compulsive behavior. The cause is thought to be the impression created by exposure to conventional management practices that more data is always better; that more and more analysis will ultimately expose 'the truth'. As a result, patients with this problem forecast at similar levels of detail to that used for annual budgeting but more frequently.

Since no real life data actually exists – all forecasts are made up of (hopefully well founded) assumptions rather than facts – the result of this obsession is the creation of enormous amounts of fictional 'noise' in the corporate nervous system, which is then analyzed to create more noise.

In chronic cases management act upon these analysis. In the milder form of this disease, the analyses are simply ignored since the results are recognized as confused, misleading or simply unintelligible. Unfortunately, patients with this syndrome often interpret this rejection as a weakness in the analysis rather than a systemic weakness, and so redouble their efforts and produce even more data – ultimately resulting in a breakdown of processes or a real breakdown in the workers enslaved in the system.

SYMPTOM #5

Is your organization focused exclusively on the year-end forecast number to the exclusion of everything else? are you sometimes surprised by developments in the early part of the new financial year? if so, you need to arrange corrective measures because you most likely suffer from:

Visual impairment

The symptoms of this complaint are an inability to see beyond the year-end and blurred vision in the short term, with sufferers only able to discern quarterly chunks in the future.

Because of this lack of visual acuity, patients find it very difficult to track trends and therefore make reasonable projections. Often patients complain of 'number blindness', a complaint resulting from prolonged exposure to tables of figures set in small type, another practice which increases the difficulty of spotting trends.

The inability to see beyond the financial year-end, with visibility becoming increasingly constrained as the year-end approaches, leaves patients very vulnerable to shocks in the early months of the new year, since they do not have sufficient time to take evasive or defensive action. Where a patient does have visibility beyond the year-end, it is often unreliable, since the sufferer is often obsessively focused on the position at the year-end, to the detriment of everything else.

This problem is a common side effect of over reliance on conventional performance management systems based on the financial year.[1] It is particularly prevalent where financial incentives are tied to the achievement of annual goals.

SYMPTOM #6

Is your experience of corporate life one of being part of a well oiled machine or is it characterized by conflict, chaos and continual fire fighting? if it is the latter this is symptomatic of:

Lack of coordination

A common problem is that various organs and limbs of a corporate body develop their own nervous systems that send differing forecast signals to the different parts of the body. So, for example, the sales limbs may have a different view of the future to the operational organs which in turn may differ from that of the financial system of the corporation. As a result the patient will exhibit uncoordinated behavior, moving – if at all – in a stumbling fashion or in spasms, sometimes with different appendages apparently working in opposition to each other.

Clearly, with this complaint, the patient is unable to move about in an efficient or effective way. It is common that the patient will either be carrying too much or too little weight (stock) or in extreme cases become bulimic, violently oscillating between two states.

With so many forecasts – by pure chance – one will always be 'more accurate' than the others, but since this performance cannot be sustained, none of the competing views of the future are ever eliminated and the organization continues to suffer with double, triple (or multiples thereof) vision.

SYMPTOM #7

A particularly nasty and common complaint is associated with endemic manipulation and distortion of information. if forecasts are routinely 'sandbagged' or overhyped, even when it is clearly against the interests of the organization as a whole, then you have been infected by:
Socio-pathological behavioral patterns

A final, widespread and particularly nasty, symptom associated with chronic forecasting failure is dysfunctional behavioral patterns.

Patients will withhold knowledge until the truth becomes impossible to conceal or knowingly provide misleading information. A perverse subculture often grows up around this practice. The process of forecasting comes to be seen as a game that you can 'win' by indulging in practices that are harmful to the corporate body. For example, the rule of thumb, 'never give any nasty surprises' is used to justify consistent and deliberate biasing of forecasts, and those that are good at the politics of managing information flows can be held up as role models to be emulated. Also, patients can be practiced in the art of 'bleeding in' bad news gradually, so as to avoid recriminations. The recipients of the deliberately misleading information can unwittingly be party to their own downfall by rewarding those who lie, by mistaking falsified forecasts for 'good performance'.

Usually this pathology is associated with behavior that rewards patients for lying or punishes them for telling the truth. For example, if patients are punished when recipients react negatively to 'bad news' and rewarded when they are set less demanding targets when they hide 'good news'.

... and how we fail to make things better

Ineffective therapeutic interventions

The forecasting disease has been around for a long time. What cures have been tried and why have they failed?

The technical fix; statistical therapy

The reason for the failure of most cures is poor diagnosis of the complaint. Often the disease is treated as a defect in the technology of forecasting.

For instance a common error is to regard the cure for all 'forecasting problems' as the prescription of a better statistical method, one that provides the 'best fit' to the historic record upon which forecast can be based. If you only have a hammer, everything looks like a nail.

There are a few problems with this. The first one is that, put brutally, the fancy statistical algorithms often aren't very good. The consensus among academics is that simple extrapolation techniques (such as moving averages) generally perform as well, if not better, than the more complex ones.

The other problems with the statistically based therapy are more fundamental. The fact is that business people often cannot rely on history in the same way that someone forecasting macroeconomic trends can. First, the pace of change is such that the kind of historic record demanded by academic statisticians – at least 36 data points – often does not exist. Most major businesses and/or their markets will have undergone some sort of major structural change within the last 36 months. Even if the business has not changed, there is a good chance that accounting or reporting conventions will have, and restatements of history are usually pretty rough and ready exercises. In addition, business data, particularly financial data, is notoriously unreliable, prone as it is to manipulation, pulling sales forward, pushing costs back etc.[2]

The other fundamental problem is that for much of the time managers in business are doing or being subject to things that have never happened before, where, by definition, history is of little use as a predictor. This 'stuff', which is so inconvenient for statisticians, is called innovation. In fact, one could argue, if your management team did not succeed in making the future different from the past you should sack them. All you really need in those circumstances is a caretaker.

The upshot of this is that if you cannot rely on history to make forecasts, you have to rely on judgment, and this equates to 'unscientific' in the eyes of many academics. There is the occasional mournful debate in academic circles about the amateurish nature of business forecasting, since surveys show that judgmental fore-casting is by far and away the most popular forecasting techniques in business. We would agree that the forecasting processes used by business are poor, but not simply because they are often judgmental. We argue that there is often simply no alterna-tive to judgmental forecasting. There is, however, plenty of scope to adopt a more scientific approach to the use of judgment. This is where the opportunity lies.

Software therapy

The second kind of failed technologically based therapy involves the inappropriate application of software.

It is well known that applying an IT 'solution' without understanding the problem often simply leads to making the same mistakes more quickly and on a bigger scale – and forecasting is no different.

As a senior manager you might think that you have the right numbers but they are either not available to you or they are not available quickly enough. You might believe that the problem is that your people are either incompetent or that they are deliberately misleading you, and so need to be 'held to account' for their failings. In either case, you might decide that the solution is to introduce a fancy new piece of software that allows you to collect submissions, consolidate and analyze them. Often this approach simply ends up with 'budgeting on steroids'. Lots of numbers. Lots of gaming behavior. Lots of wasted time.

It might be tempting to blame the software industry for this, but they are com-mercial enterprises and can only sell solutions to problems that people recognize they have. It is easy, and worthwhile, to sell a piece of software that promises to 'eliminate spreadsheet hell' by using the Web to collect, collate and manage submis-sions from thousands of different contributors to a business forecast. It is much more difficult for software providers to sell a product that requires you to funda-mentally rethink the whole way in which you go about doing things. Physicians face similar problems, with patients saying 'I know I need to lose weight but don't tell me that I need to change my life style, eat less of what I like and exercise more. Just give me the pill.'

To be fair, there is a lot of talk right now in the world of business software about 'driver based' forecasting, which is very definitely a move in the right direc-tion. However, putting an engine in a horse drawn carriage doesn't make a car and some of the efforts run a serious risk of falling into the same technophiliac trap as the academic statisticians; if you only have a software hammer, everything looks like a nail.

The final problem with dipping into the 'technical medicine cabinet' as the first resort whenever you have a problem to fix is that it becomes exactly that – a fix, and you can become addicted. If the technical cure does not work the first time round you are tempted to try 'one more fix' to solve the problem. However, if the pharmacology is not addressing the root cause of the disease, there will be no relief.

Technique and technology are certainly part of the remedy, but they are not *the* cure.

Folk lore remedies

Another failed set of remedies comes from folk lore. The huckster who sold patent medicine was always able to produce someone from the audience who had been 'cured' … and they might even have believed it themselves. In casual arguments about the health risks of smoking, often someone will cite the example of a relative or acquaintance who has lived to a ripe old age and has smoked 10 packs of cigarettes a day since they were 14.

The fact is that isolated cases prove nothing, and the healthy state of any one individual may be down to any number of factors.

Similarly, we have not based this book, and the ideas in it, upon a handful of 'success stories' or any arbitrary definition of 'best practice'. Examples are helpful to illustrate or to gain deeper understanding of a point of principle but on their own case studies are not enough.

No one ever cured an illness by showing the patient a picture of someone who is healthy.

A counsel of despair …

Not everyone falls for the 'technological fix' or the 'folk remedies'. Some seem to believe that it is not possible to forecast well because of fundamental flaws in the human psyche.

With a shrug of the shoulders, they will say things like 'it's all about judgment', 'you can't buy experience' or 'there is no point doing anything until we get people to stop being too optimistic/sandbagging'. Another common one is: 'you will never change sales people; they will always …' (insert appropriate prejudice).

While these fatalistic comments reflect genuine challenges, all too often they become an excuse for not trying, or, worse, a justification for manipulation of a forecasting process in the name of compensating for the perceived weaknesses.

... and the cure

We believe – in fact, we know – that it *is* possible to change, and that the cure we are searching for is KNOWLEDGE.

The name we give to useful knowledge is 'science'. It is useful knowledge because it has been systematically assembled from logical first principles, tested, and found to be robust; a basis for informed action. According to a recent KPMG survey 'it is those companies that tackle forecasting as a science that are the ones that are getting it right' (EIU, 2007). Without this knowledge, we will fail to grasp the nature of our relationship with the future and what we can do to influence it. It is because we do not understand the 'science', that we place blind faith in technological fixes and folk lore.

Adopting a 'scientific' approach does not mean that judgment and learning are irrelevant. Our knowledge needs to be both theoretical and practical. You can be the best pastry chef in the world but if you have no grasp of the properties of eggs and how they respond to heat, your soufflé will always come out as a soggy mess. On the other hand, you cannot consistently make good soufflés without a lot of practice. How happy would you be if you were treated by doctor who had a good scientific training but no practical experience or vice versa?

We believe that we have been living in the 'snake oil' era of forecasting, but that we have the knowledge to do much better. Theory without being theoretical. Practical but more than mere technique. This combination will give you the ability to master forecasting and so better navigate the organization through turbulent times.

The even better news is that you can get instant benefits from almost any increase in your knowledge. Any bad habit abandoned and any improvement in forecasting health will be rewarded with tangible benefits, with little extra cost apart from that involved in acquiring, practicing and deploying the knowledge.

What does success look like?

Imagine this.

It is the first Tuesday of the new month. It is 2pm and you have just received your monthly forecast briefing pack, bang on time, so you now have half a day to digest the content before your regular monthly meeting.

All the normal stuff is there, but you first dive into the section marked 'changes since last month'. The process is so well grooved now that most of what you saw last month will not have changed much – so it is like finding out about what is happening in the world by glancing at the headlines of a newspaper rather than diving straight into the stock quotes. One of the first things you look for is the forecast reliability indicator since this tells you whether your process is working well and whether there are any alarms about to go off. The rest of the pack is very familiar and easy on the eye. There are a few tables with key statistics but there are also many graphs and pictures that quickly give you a sense of trend. In particular, you look at the risk charts that reveal how much reliance you can place on your central forecast by showing 'a bandwidth' around it and several alternative medium term scenarios.

The Wednesday morning meeting has all the usual suspects: colleagues from sales, marketing operations as well as finance. The atmosphere is relaxed and congenial, but that is because everybody knows the drill and his or her own part in it – there is no need for excessive formality.

The meeting starts off, as usual, with a quick review of the last month. People are open; where there have been failures to anticipate events people are willing to admit shortcomings and oversights – there is no blame because everyone knows that some sort of error is inevitable in forecasting. Openness and candour are important if you are to properly understand what has happened and learn what this means for the forecast process and what implications this might have for the future of the business. In many cases, because problems and opportunities have already been flagged the meeting is simply informed of the corrective action already taken.

The second part of the meeting usually involves one member of the team presenting the results of a 'deep dive' into an issue that cropped up in the previous meeting. Relentless curiosity and skepticism are qualities that have proven to be valuable. Most months throw up something that does not feel right or needs further investigation to get a proper understanding about what is going on.

Finally, you come to the most important part of the meeting: actions. Discussions about 'what needs to be done' take account of the 'gap to target' but strategic goals and competitive performance trends often override gap closing considerations. In addition, it may be that a completely unforeseen set of circumstances demands swift response, which might mean putting a contingency plan into action. However, things are normally under control so the team often does no more than reshape the existing plan. This involves rescheduling activities, perhaps stopping some and starting others in response to the changing outlook and an evolving understanding about their effectiveness.

After two hours the meeting finished with a review of the meeting itself. What went well? What could be done better? What will you do differently next month?

... and what are the benefits?

What kind of results might you expect by improving your forecasting process? Ask yourself these questions:

- If you were able to consistently produce forecasts that were neither optimistic nor pessimistic, and with a small level of variability, by how much would you be able to reduce stocks? 5%? 10%? In one major multinational business which suffered from persistently optimistic forecasting this number amounted to over $500 million, more than enough on its own to justify the investment required to improve forecast processes.

- How much product is thrown away or discounted because it is out of date or obsolete? By how much might you be able to reduce the cost of obsolescence? 50%?

- In a service business, better forecasting means improved use of resources and better customer service. How much would you be prepared to pay to improve this by 2% or 5%? What is more, there is evidence to prove that by improving forecasting organizations can and do improve customer service *and* reduce stocks at the same time.

While there will be efficiency benefits, the real value lies in enhanced effectiveness.

- Better forecasting means that decisions are better informed. There is an increased chance that the right things will be done at the right time: fewer last minute panics, fewer times when the business has to slam on the brakes. How much time and resource would be saved by avoiding doing things in a hurry or by not needing to abort part completed projects?

- Better forecasting helps organizations enhance what the US military calls 'situational awareness' and so helps a business spot discontinuities early. What value would you place on improving the agility of your organization? What costs would be avoided if you were able to spot problems early and put appropriate contingency plans into effect? What opportunities might you be able to exploit?

- By anticipating better and responding more quickly the performance of your organization will become more predictable, less prone to shocks and surprises. What value would you place on that?

- Finally, good forecasting demands and so fosters effective teamwork and collaboration. What other spin-off benefits might there be and what are they worth to you?

Whatever number you come up with we are confident that it will be a big one – certainly big enough to reward the investment of time in reading this book. There is little cost; the journey on which you are about to embark does require application and discipline, but nothing that is beyond the vast majority of readers.

If this sounds like it is for you then read on.

• • • • •

You should think of the next five chapters – section 2 of the book – as being like a Sunday afternoon hike in the hills; it starts off gently and then gradually gets a little steeper. The hill might slow you down a little but climbing it doesn't require any special aptitude or training. If you are unfit, you might find yourself breathing a little hard in the later chapters, and your legs might ache on Monday morning, but for an investment of four hours or so, and perhaps a little bit of practice, you will have made an enormous step towards acquiring the knowledge needed to enhance your organization's forecasting performance. At the end of Part 2 we will take stock and prepare for the next leg of the challenge.

The next chapter is 'Forecasting 101'. The content is technically undemanding but you might find that it challenges many of your current assumptions about what forecasting is and what is required to be good at it.

• • • • •

Another story ... but with a happier ending

 Example

On September 11, 2001, just 6 months after the bursting of the telecoms bubble, two jet liners flew into the World Trade Towers in downtown New York. In the process the Head Office of the American Express Corporation was severely damaged, and along with the office went a whole set of assumptions about the future. 'Basically we didn't have a head office, the place was in turmoil and we were left sitting at our desks in alternate locations without even calculators and wondering "what does this mean for our business?" ' says Jamie Croake, VP of Planning.

But instead of the total loss of control and collapse that the jihadist terrorists undoubtedly hoped for, the experience gave urgency and focus to an initiative that had been on the stocks in AMEX for a few months: Planning Transformation. Over the next two or three years AMEX learned that not only was it possible for a business to operate without the traditional panoply of fixed plans but that there was a better way of doing things …

We will return to the AMEX story later.

SUMMARY

In an increasingly turbulent world the ability to anticipate, even if only a few months ahead, can mean the difference between survival and failure. In addition, if managers fail to demonstrate an understanding of the dynamics of business performance investor confidence can be seriously undermined. As a result, senior executives in business place an increasingly high priority on improving their forecast processes. The record of business, however, is not good. One reason for this is that the traditional management model, based on the concepts of budgeting, has not kept pace with the demands of the times. Budgeting is based on the assumption of predictability rather than the reality of change. As a result, we do not have a process legacy that helps us forecast well or a mindset that helps us deal with change and turbulence. The inadequacy of current processes and thinking is manifest in a set of failure symptoms that are endemic in organizations. Technological fixes are no cure; the remedy has to be based on a sound conceptual understanding of the purpose and nature of forecasting. The benefits of getting it right are considerable, both in terms of improvements in efficiency and effectiveness.

KEY LEARNING POINTS

Seven common symptoms of forecasting illness

SYMPTOM #1 Semantic schizophrenia: confusion about the aims, purposes and characteristics of good forecasts.

SYMPTOM #2 Single point tunnel vision: an unhealthy obsession with a particular forecast number.

SYMPTOM #3 Delusions of accuracy: the mistaken assumptions that it is possible to be perfectly accurate and that lower errors are representative of better forecasts.

SYMPTOM #4 Nervous system breakdown: misguided attempt to improve forecasts by going into more detail and analyzing forecasts obsessively.

SYMPTOM #5 Visual impairment: the failure to provide enough forward visibility and discern trends in performance.

SYMPTOM #6 Lack of coordination: the tendency to generate a proliferation of competing forecasts.

SYMPTOM #7 Socio-pathological behavioral patterns: the unwitting encouragement of behavioral patterns that are damaging to the forecast process and to the health of the organization as a whole.

'Fixes' that don't work
1. The application of IT without understanding
2. Blind faith in sophisticated statistical forecasting techniques
3. Simplistic remedies based on incomplete and selective use of case studies.

Enhanced capabilities from improved forecasting
1. Better anticipation
2. Better situational awareness
3. Greater responsiveness
4. Enhanced coordination
5. More relevant analysis of performance.

Potential benefits
1. Lower stocks
2. Less obsolete stocks
3. Better customer service
4. Lower costs
5. Better use of resources
6. Fewer shocks
7. Quicker to exploit opportunities
8. More predictable performance
9. Enhanced teamwork and collaboration.

NOTES
1 Frederic Vester, the German systems scientist, has speculated that planning first started when humankind made the transition from hunter-gatherers to farmers, since this activity required that they think a year ahead (Vester, 2007). It is not clear why the position of the earth in relation to the sun should still be the primary driver of planning in twenty-first century corporations, but it clearly is.

2 Many managers are unaware of just how much judgment is involved in the preparation of financial statements, and how this judgment can become biased if pressure is applied (as it often is) to come back to a number such as a profit target or a forecast. According to *CFO magazine* nearly half of finance executives feel under pressure to adjust results (Durfee, 2004). Given what we know about the variation and inevitability of error, we should therefore be very wary if there is no difference between forecasts, targets and actuals.

Section 2
PRINCIPLES

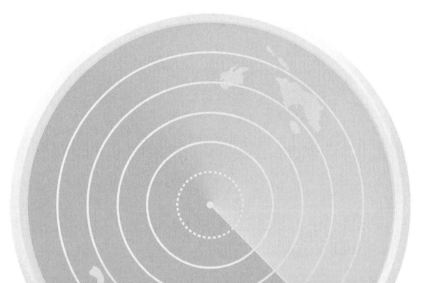

The purpose of this section is to lay the logical foundations for forecasting.

We start by addressing the question 'why do we forecast at all?' Armed with a sound grasp of the purpose of forecasting, we work from first principles: we demonstrate what needs to be done to create a sound process and how to do it.

Specifically you will discover:

- why an understanding of time, particularly response times, is important;
- what techniques you can use to create forecasts and how you choose between them;
- why measurement is critical to successful forecasting, and how to do it well;
- why an understanding of risk is important, and how to use this knowledge to better exploit opportunities and protect your business from loss.

This section is aimed at any manager who wants to acquire a solid grasp of the principles of good forecasting. This will include practitioners, but also recipients of forecasts, potential leaders of change and any other manager in search of answers.

By the end of this section, you will have all the knowledge to design a process capable of delivering a reliable forecast.

Chapter 2

MASTERING PURPOSE
– the Cassandra paradox

'There is absolutely no inevitability as long as there is a willingness to contemplate what is happening.' Marshall McLuhan

'He who lives by the crystal ball soon learns to eat ground glass.' Edgar R. Fiedler

Why a good forecast might not be a good prediction – the purpose of forecasting – how it differs from budgeting – the definition of a forecast – and how it differs from a target, a plan and a budget – the five qualities of good forecasts – the implications for forecast process design

PREDICTIONS: 'WHO NEEDS THEM?'

There is something deeply paradoxical about the way we human beings relate to the future.

Throughout history, we have tried to 'divine the future'. A stunning array of divination techniques have been, and still are, used by different cultures. In fact, there are more professional astrologers alive today than there are professional astronomers.[1] Prophets feature prominently in our written histories. For example Greek legend gives us the Oracle of Delphi and in the story of the siege of Troy Cassandra famously dispenses her doomladen (and correct) prophesies. Her personal tragedy is that her predictions are ignored, because Apollo cursed her after she spurned his advances.

'Illusory certainty is part of our perceptual, emotional and cultural inheritance,' says the psychologist Gerd Gergerenzer. 'It can provide us with images of the environment that are useful, although not always correct, as well as feelings of comfort and certainty. Throughout history humans have created belief systems that promise certainty such as … astrology and divination, systems in which people find comfort' (Gigerenzer, 2002).

 More

Divination techniques
Some examples of techniques used for divination that we do not recommend for business forecasting:
Spatulamancy: by examining skin, bones and faeces
Moelosophy: by examining moles as a guide to character and the future
Ophalomancy: the number of knots in the umbilical cord
Heptoscopy: the liver, popular in Babylonia but not with Caesar (apparently it was the technique used to produce the warning 'beware the ides of March')
Scapulomancy: by observing the cracks on shoulder bones burned in fires
Dilitiriomancy: by poisoning birds
Aachnomancy: as in Mambila Spider Divination
Plasromancy: using turtle shells.

In everyday life, human beings seem to have a deeply seated need to 'know what is going to happen' in order to help us cope with the fear of uncertainty and ambiguity. Business life is no different. When senior managers ask for a forecast, what they need is a tool to help them cope with an uncertain future. Often however what they want and expect is 'a prediction'.

WHY IT IS IMPORTANT TO UNDERSTAND THE DIFFERENCE BETWEEN A FORECAST AND A PREDICTION

Contrary to what many people might believe, a forecast, if it is to be an effective management tool, does *not* have to be a good prediction of the future. In fact, most of the time, we should be happy that the future turns out different to that which has been forecast. To illustrate this point consider an example.

Imagine that you are running a small start-up business that is going through a rough patch; your customers are all large businesses who do not seem to understand cash flow and care even less about your predicament. You visit a fairground and see a small booth. The sign outside advertises itself as 'The Oracle of Delphi. She guarantees to predict the future' and the best bit: 'or your money back'.

You go into the booth and a lady, dressed in flowing eastern robes, tells you: 'I see problems ahead. You will meet a tall dark stranger with a limp carrying a briefcase (this sounds rather like your bank manager). He talks to you and you start weeping.'

This sounds like very bad news. Your bank manager has already made a few threatening noises about your overdraft. How can she know these things? 'Tell me more' you demand.

Her hands hover over the crystal ball again. 'I see a calendar on the wall. I see some numbers. Yes … it is the 10th of November, and the clock …' she sways at this point as if to faint … 'it is ten past ten'.

Oh no! You have an appointment to see you bank manager next week at 10 o'clock! This is a disaster! 'What' you ask the soothsayer 'can I do about this? I am going to be ruined!'

'Nothing my friend' she says. 'It is your fate. Nothing can be done … and in any event, I have a reputation to uphold. Didn't you see the notice outside – I don't want any warranty claims!'

You have at least two possible reactions to this. 'Wow! She's really good! I thought I was in trouble – now at least I know it. I must recommend her to my friends.' Or 'Shoot! What was the use of that?' A practical business person, we would suggest, is more likely to choose option number 2.

What is the point of this silly story?

It is this. We might *think* that we want to 'know the future', but in reality we only want to know the future in order to be able to do something about it. In other words, we want to *change* the future to make it more acceptable to us. In this case, you either want to find a way of raising some cash from another source quickly or put extra effort into getting your major customer to pay up. Visit the office; demand a check in your hand – that sort of thing.

In other words, *a perfect prediction is perfectly useless.*[2]

This is the Cassandra paradox: if the Trojans had not ignored Cassandra, if they had taken steps to avoid the tragedies that she prophesied (looking the wooden gift horse in the mouth for example), then she would have failed to give accurate predictions. By prophesying she becomes a poor prophet and would not have become the romantic, tragic figure of legend.

What businesses need are forecasts not predictions.

A prediction is a statement of what will happen. A forecast is a statement of what you think will happen, based on certain assumptions about the world – assumptions about the external environment and about your own future actions and those of others. In other words, it is the very fact that the forecasted future might not come about – because the assumptions might be wrong or have been changed – as a result of decisions you make based on forecasts – that makes forecasting useful.

 More

Predictions, Forecasts and Assumptions

It is important to appreciate the difference between a forecast and a prediction.

Often people will use the word prediction and forecast interchangeably. The Oxford English Dictionary defines a prediction as a statement about the future and a forecast as a conjecture, part of the process of thinking and planning in advance. We think that this is a good distinction; predictions claim to be authoritative whereas forecasts are always conditional. Here are the definitions that we will use:

Prediction   a statement about the future based on insight (scientific or supernatural) into the workings of the world

Forecast   a projection based on assumptions about the future state of the world.

Assumptions play a key role in forecasting. They have the same relationship to forecasts of the future that facts have to the present reality. We cannot make a judgment about a forecast without understanding the assumptions that have been made. This is of great practical significance, as we shall discover.

This apparently simple statement has profound implications for the way we think about forecasts, the way we build them, how performance is measured and the way we behave in response to a forecast. We will explore this further over the next chapters. Before we do that, let us delve a little deeper. We will use an analogy that we find helps people reorient their thinking about forecasting.

FORECASTS: WHY DO WE NEED THEM?

Stop someone in the street and ask him or her to word associate with 'forecast', they will most likely come up with 'weather'. This is only natural since we use this kind of forecast every day.

We will give you another kind of forecast. The forecast made by the navigator on a sailing boat.

What do these forecasts have in common (apart from the fact that the weather is a big input into the navigator's forecast)? We suggest that one thing they have in common is that (unlike the prediction made by Madame Delphi above) we are likely to want to take action based on the forecast. In the case of the weather forecast we might want to take an umbrella with us or cancel our plans for the sailing trip at the weekend! In the case of the forecast from the navigator, we might decide to change course.

In what ways do these actions differ?

Two uses of forecasts: to help plan for the future or to help shape a different future

Well, in the case of the weather forecast our actions are *in reaction* to what we think is going to happen in the future. We will hope to avoid getting wet or, if we are planning a sailing trip, the risk of being put in a perilous situation. In the case of the forecast made *while* sailing however, we are not simply reacting to what we think might happen in the future; *we are seeking to change the future.* By tacking to port, we are avoiding the rocks that we otherwise might have hit. In other words by reacting to the forecast, we are invalidating it. Our reaction to the forecast means that it *is no longer an accurate prediction.*

In business, we do have examples of the first kind of forecast. For example in running a supply chain, we make forecasts of future demand of say, one litre bottles of Coca Cola, in order to make sure that we produce or procure enough stock in order to satisfy customers. However, in business many of the most important forecasts we make are of the second kind; where we forecast the future in order to make it different to what it otherwise would be. Therefore, if the forecast sales of Coke began to fall behind Pepsi, or earnings forecasts are coming in below analysts' expectations, the management of Coca Cola might beef up their advertising campaigns or promote the product more heavily. *They forecast the future in order to make it different.*

This has profound implications for the way in which we forecast. Implications that we do not always fully appreciate because our thinking is confused. We are confused because we do not understand the difference between prediction and forecasting. We are confused because we fail to appreciate that the purpose of a forecast is to drive action, and in informing action we might invalidate the previous forecast we have made. The source of confusion, in business at least, is a legacy of the tool that, for nearly 100 years, has been the default management process: the budget.

How a budgeting mindset is a handicap

Most business people are steeped in the practice of budgeting, a practice which often starts with some sort of estimate of future outcomes. In budgeting, this estimate is converted into an instrument of control since the objective of budgeting is to make the budgeted outcome come about. In this scenario any deviation from budget – the initial estimate – is therefore 'wrong'. So unlike forecasting (where we forecast in large part to make the future different from the forecast) in budgeting we plan for a desired future in order to make it come about. In other words, *forecasting and budgeting have completely different purposes.* Unfortunately, however, we often come at forecasting with a budgeting mindset. So, the first step in developing a healthy forecasting capability has to involve tackling the source of confusion head on.

DEFINITIONS

A way to start the process of eliminating confusion and building up a coherent body of knowledge is to set out some clear definitions.

Let us start with the definition of a forecast, and keep our example of a ship's navigator in mind.

Look at Figure 2.1 – it shows a typical sailing scenario.

The sailboat in this example starts from A. Before it sets off we make a plan; in this case the plan shows a zigzag pattern, and those of you who know anything about sailing will know that this is because it assumes that the wind will be coming from the north, and a sailboat cannot sail directly into the wind. What happens next happens all the time in sailing – and in business for that matter – something changes which screws up the plans. In this case the wind blows from a

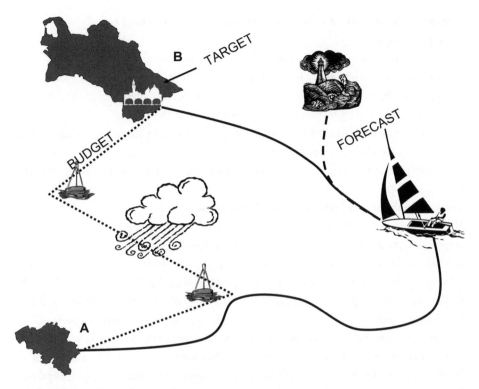

Figure 2.1 Forecasting in business is like navigating at sea.
When sailing, you project the future in order to make decisions – to change or to remain on course.

different direction. It is now coming from the west, which blows the sailboat off course.[3]

In a traditional budgeting system, this change will be treated as a variance and the 'classical' response to this is 'get back on plan'. We know that this often does not make sense since the assumptions on which we based the original plan are now faulty. The change in the environment has rendered the budget obsolete, and if we 'got back on plan' sailing the same course, we could end up taking twice as long as needed. Instead, we need to plot a new course. To do this we need a forecast to help us work out what we need to do differently, so the skipper says to the navigator 'where are we heading?' The navigator shouts back 'we are heading towards the rocks by the lighthouse … bear to port (left) quickly'. As a result the skipper quickly tacks (changes course) away from the wind, thereby missing the rocks and heading towards the original target (B).

This brings us to our first definition:

Forecast: a description of where we think we are heading, based on current assumptions

In other words a forecast is a likely future actual outcome.

In the case of a business, the assumptions used to produce a forecast will include those about the business environment, the likely future impact of things that we did in the past, and the things that we plan to do in the future.

This seems sensible; but it is not enough. We need to know more than simply where we are heading; we need to know where we want to go and what we have to do (differently) in order to get there. We need to introduce two new terms: target and plan.

Target: a description of where we would like to be

If there were only one thing that you could take away from this book it is this: *targets and forecasts are not the same.* As Fritz Roemer says 'a forecast is what the future will look like, a target is what the future should look like. This is a huge difference.' Indeed, he argues that 'you should expect that the forecast will not be in line with the target in a turbulent world. The real value of forecasting is that it provides us with the ability to proactively manage the gap' (Roemer, 2008).

In a conventional, budgeting style performance management system, a target is usually expressed as a single, fixed point, say '4% growth in the 2008 financial year' or '\$100m profit'. In the sailing analogy, it would be port B, which might be expressed as a map reference. Those of us in the Beyond Budgeting fraternity recommend expressing targets in relative terms: 'better than the competition' or 'better than in the past'. In other words, we are saying that in business you are not sailing to a fixed des-

 More

Budgets and targets

Any form of budget is in effect a target; an expression of what we would like to happen rather than what we think will happen. Therefore, an overhead budget is a target – in this case one that we would not want to exceed. In practice the management of a business requires taking into account a whole range of targets, and the more of them we have the more difficult will be the task of meeting them all, and the greater the risk of perverting or destabilizing the whole system.[4] We will return to the issue of target setting in Section 4.

tination; you are in a race! It does not matter for the purpose of this discussion, however, whether you use relative or absolute targets – the definition holds.

So, if a forecast is what we think will happen and a target is what we would like to happen, what is a plan?

The whole business of performance management is littered with sloppy definitions which lead to sloppy thinking and the word 'plan' is a good example of this. Sometimes the word is used interchangeably with 'forecast', sometimes it is used to express a desired outcome – in effect a set of targets. The definition we will use in this book is precise and unambiguous.

Plan: a set of related future actions designed to reach an objective
and

Planning: the process of defining a set of future actions with the aim of achieving an objective
A plan is a set of actions; a set of actions which can, but need not necessarily, be quantified. In the sailing example it would include the course we take, the sails we use and so on.

When we forecast we base our forecast on two things. First, we need to estimate the impact of those things over which we have no control – the impact of external events (the weather) plus the anticipated outcomes of actions to which we have already committed ourselves (we are on a eastward course and it will take us 400 yards to change course). Second, we need to take account of the likely future impact of actions to which *we have not yet committed ourselves* – our plans – in this case the effect of the tacking maneuver.

Steering the ship towards the intended goal is therefore made up of selecting appropriate actions – that is the process of planning.

At the point when we select, hopefully we will have 'closed the gap' between our forecast and our target. Often, however, the moment we complete a planning exercise something changes: either in the outside world (the environment) or in our estimate of the likely outcome of our own actions. As Figure 2.2 illustrates, we are therefore in a state of perpetual replanning with no end. The frequency and the extent of the replanning depend, among other things, upon the rate of change in the environment and in our knowledge. To quote Stafford Beer, a cybernetic guru: 'plans should continuously abort' (Beer, 1979). Again, this differs from conventional budgeting – since this involves fixing plans for a year.

So, to complete the picture, what is the meaning of the word 'budget'?

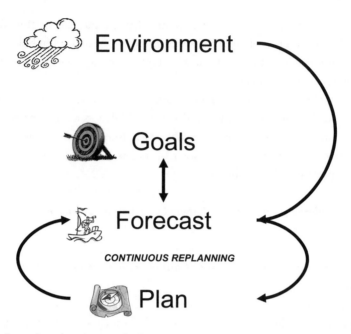

Figure 2.2   Forecasting and continuous replanning.
A forecast is the link between external reality, our aspirations and the plans we put in place to bring our aspirations about.

Budget: a sum of money allocated to an activity or action to which an organization has committed itself

For the answer, we have to go back to the original meaning of the word 'budget'. It is derived from the French for a leather purse: 'bougette'. The term is thought to have come into commercial use since it was used to describe the money that early merchants gave a captain of their ships in order to trade for spices or whatever. In other words it is a financial constraint that was a consequence of there being no ability to transfer money to fund opportunistic purchases. Translating this into modern day business, at the point that you commit to a project – whether it be building a house, digging a tunnel, making an advert – you will have an idea of what you want and how much it is going to cost. So it makes sense to create a budget (a constraint) in order to make sure that costs are controlled and the scope of the project doesn't creep. However, to fix a budget before you have any idea what you need to do – against plans that will, and need to, change – does not make sense. By doing so you constrain yourself unnecessarily, reduce flexibility and increase the chances of failure. This is the position that businesses who rely purely on budgeting to manage their finances often find themselves in.

These four definitions provide us with the building blocks we need to get started. The next step on the road to designing a sound forecast process is to specify what qualities a good process should have.

'A GOOD FORECAST': A SPECIFICATION

Five qualities of a good forecast

We are not fatalists, we have established that *the reason why we forecast is that we need to make informed decisions.* Decisions that lead to action, whether that action is to make a change in the business to respond to a forecast, to invalidate a forecast, or to communicate something to an outside stakeholder about a forecast.[5] If that is the purpose, process design should follow from it.

So, exactly what qualities should a good forecast process have? There are five, which are described by the mnemonic **TARAC**.

A good forecast needs to be:

T = Timely
A = Actionable
R = Reliable
A = Aligned
C = Cost Effective

A good way to remember this is to arrange the letters in reverse order so that they make **CARAT** – the measure of precious materials.

Timely

The first requirement of a forecast is that it is timely. That is, in time for appropriate action to be taken.

The frequency and speed of forecasting should be related to the speed of change of key variables

First, let us consider the frequency and speed of forecasting. It makes little sense to have a process which produces a forecast every month but spend (as is often the case) most of the month producing it.[6] It is something that Martin Jarvis, former leader of Sales and Operations Planning at Unilever has frequently encountered. 'It is very easy for businesses to get stuck into doing this at such a detailed level that they don't have time to take decisions before the next forecast cycle comes round' (Jarvis, 2008). The only justification for producing a monthly forecast is that the business changes materially in a month. If it takes two weeks to produce then at least half the value has disappeared – perhaps more because it takes time to assimilate

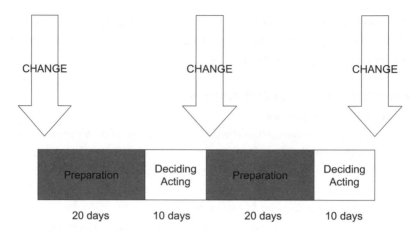

Figure 2.3 The forecast cycle.
For a forecast to be useful, it needs to be available in good time for meaningful action to be taken before events change. In this example, 2/3 of the month is given over to preparing a forecast that will soon be superseded; so much of the effort is wasted.

the forecast and decide to take action. If you are going to forecast monthly then you need a process – a process that involves production of a forecast, analysis of it AND action – that takes a fraction of that month (see Figure 2.3). This is not such a daunting prospect; in reality different things change at different rates and different scales. Not everything need be reforecast every month.

 **Example**

Freeing up management time at AMEX
Releasing time for more productive work was a critical part of the raison d'être of AMEX's planning transformation. With the traditional process, 'we basically started with something that we called "the march of the thousand spreadsheets". We spent six or seven of the eight days of our regular cycle collecting and consolidating spreadsheets, which meant a lot of late nights and all nights,' says Jamie Croake. 'And it never came to the right answer so we had to do it over and over again, and by the time we had finished the information was stale – out of date. This meant that our planning teams spent on average 83% of their time trying to keep up with the spreadsheets and only 17% of their time on analytics; working out what was actually going on and what we could do about it' (Croake, 2008).

The need for visibility is driven by the time it takes to respond

The second point refers to the horizon. If it requires 18 months to launch a new product then you need at least 18 months' notice of a gap in your product portfolio. If it takes two months to change prices and product cost is heavily dependent on the price of a certain commodity then you need at least two months' visibility of commodity prices.

We will learn more about these issues in the next chapter: 'Mastering Time'.

Actionable

The detail which a forecast should contain depends on the nature of decisions that need to be taken

In the context of what has been said before about the relationship between forecasting and decision-making this might sound like a statement of the obvious. However, it is worthwhile thinking a little more deeply about the implication of the word 'actionable' in the context of forecasting.

Assume it were possible to forecast the revenue of a business 'top down' using a graph showing two years' worth of history and a ruler. Indeed for many businesses, this simplistic approach often yields more 'accurate forecasts' than sophisticated 'bottom up' forecasting systems. Why not forecast like this all the time and throw out the expensive software?

The reason that we do not forecast this way, even though we may not be aware of it, is that while a forecast which simply says 'growth will be 3%' could be perfectly accurate, you can't do anything with the information. What you need to know is 'why isn't it 2%?' or more pertinently 'what do I have to do to make it 4% or 5%?' In other words, *only forecasts that are based on an explicit set of assumptions are actionable.*

You might think that this is a stupid example. People would not be so crass as to forecast in a way that was not 'actionable'.

Well think again.

Why we shouldn't use conventional accounting data structures

A majority of forecasts are prepared using a standard accounting chart of accounts, which classifies revenue and expenditure by type: gross revenue, materials, overheads and so on. While this might be helpful to establish *what* you have received money for and spent money on, it does not tell you anything about *why*. If you do not know why things have happened in a particular way in the past then it is difficult to make them happen in a particular way in the future.

Taking a simple example: say the profit forecast looks poor, and travel and hotel expenses look high. Simplistically you might say that 'in order to meet our profit targets we need to stop all travel this quarter'. However, if the travel was associated with the implementation of a major revenue generating project then one of two things will happen – either you lose the contract and profit drops or travel and hotel expenses don't change and you miss your profit target. Because the chart of account does not reflect the causal structure of the business, it cannot produce information that is actionable.

Example

Gary Crittenden, former CFO of American Express says 'in my opinion, the key lesson is to cut out detail and focus on the key drivers. Under the old system, it took one business unit alone eight weeks and hundreds of person-days to assemble the bottom up forecast. This made doing meaningful business reviews and timely investment analysis almost impossible. Managers had believed that all they needed to know was the cost of adding or eliminating an employee. However, they found that these numbers only had a 5 per cent effect on the net figures. What they needed to identify were the volume drivers, those that influenced 80 per cent of the numbers. This turned out to be only fifteen lines on the profit and loss statement' (Hope, 2006).

In our view, the use of the chart of accounts for forecasting is one of the main reasons that businesses under pressure go into 'head count reduction mode'. They simply do not know where the levers are that they can pull, so they attack the thing that is most visible in the accounts – people costs. Jobs are lost and departments reorganized without any real understanding of the impact on projects, customer service and ultimately revenue.

How more detail leads to worse forecasting

Another consequence of using the chart of accounts is that managers can easily get overwhelmed with detail. Much of that detail is irrelevant and it slows the process down. 'Many companies use accounting consolidation engines to collate their forecasts and approach forecasting as if they were preparing their year end returns,' observes Roemer, 'this accounting mindset is killing forecasting in many businesses we see' (Roemer, 2008).

In addition, increasing the level of detail often leads to increased forecast error. This may seem counter-intuitive, because there is a widespread belief that 'holding people accountable' will automatically improve accuracy.[7] In fact the naïve assumption that 'more is better' is plain wrong. Indeed more often than not, more detail means higher errors not higher accuracy.[8] Arie de Geus describes the detailed forecasts produced by the accounting profession in particular as 'useless but compelling' because of the false sense of precision and predictability that they help create (Geus, 1997).

In summary, the main requirement of a good forecast is that it should be actionable. This means that it should have the *minimum amount of detail required to provide management with a clear understanding of what is driving future performance*. This will include the causal factors underlying trends and the incremental impact of plans put in place to change those trends. Only by providing management with actionable information will they be equipped to change the future.

We will learn more about how to create actionable forecasts in Chapter 4: 'Mastering Models'.

Reliable

Often managers complain that their forecasts are 'inaccurate'. What exactly do they mean?

Reliability is the most desirable quality for a forecast, not accuracy

As we have already seen, perfect accuracy – zero error – is not attainable in any kind of process. It is even less likely when the process concerned (forecasting) is based on speculation about what *might* happen rather than measurement of what *has* happened. But this is not a hopeless situation; we argue that we do not need accuracy from a forecast process – we need *reliability*. By reliability, we mean forecasts that are *accurate enough* for our *purpose*: decision-making.

This means that how we define 'reliability' will depend on our purpose. If we are captaining an oil tanker in the open seas, we might be comfortable using our radar to plot our course to, say, within 100 meters, five miles ahead. On the other hand, if we are berthing the boat in a dock, inches count (and radar is not capable of delivering the required precision).

What does this mean in practice for forecasters in organizations?

Reliable forecasts are unbiased – free from systematic error

First, this means that forecasts have to be *unbiased*. We know that any forecast will never be perfectly accurate; there will always be errors. While it is unrealistic to expect zero errors, we can demand that errors be evenly balanced – that is, there should be approximately as many positive errors as negative errors. Therefore, on average, the error is zero, and on average, we will have the right information on which to base a decision.

It makes no sense to have any other goal for accuracy. It is therefore somewhat shocking to discover that not only are biased forecasts tolerated, they are often encouraged. For example, people may be praised for coming in above a revenue forecast or below an expense forecast. Even worse, in our experience very few companies explicitly define what a 'good forecast' is. A company will often have accounting manuals with many chapters devoted to the definition and treatment of an accounting provision and absolutely nothing to define 'a good forecast'. 'Making a good forecast is a science in itself' says Bjarte Bogsnes of StatoilHydro. 'In accounting we have thick manuals, well documented procedures and detailed audits to check the quality. In forecasting we have next to nothing' (Bogsnes, 2009).

All forecasts will contain variation (unsystematic error) but a reliable forecasting process will keep this variation at acceptable levels

The second feature of a reliable forecast is that the errors (the level of variation) should be within tolerable limits *for the purposes of the decision we need to make* (see Figure 2.4). So for our oil tanker, plus or minus 100 meters is acceptable in the open sea since we will use this to make course changes that we can effect within five miles. When berthing that tanker, we need a greater degree of precision.

Shockingly few companies routinely measure forecast accuracy. Of those that do, few set targets, and those that do tend to set arbitrary targets (e.g. plus or minus 5%) irrespective of the inherent difficulty of forecasting. So for example, we find the same target applied to small units operating in volatile markets and large units operating in very stable markets. 'Mastering Measurement' is the theme of Chapter 5.

The further ahead you look the greater the chance that your forecast will be affected by more than random variation; in time it is inevitable that events will differ significantly from the assumptions you made when you made your forecast. The words we use to describe this kind of forecast error are 'risk' and 'uncertainty' and mastering this aspect of forecasting goes beyond effective measurement. 'Mastering Risk' is the subject of Chapter 6.

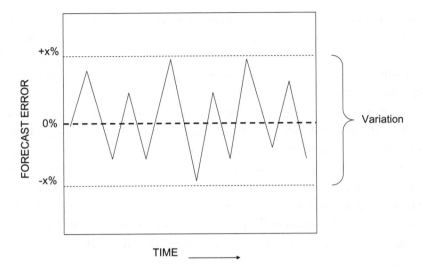

Figure 2.4   Every forecast will be wrong; there will always be some error.
A good forecast is unbiased, as in this example: there will be roughly as many positive errors as there are negative errors. In addition, the range of errors – the variation – should have no material adverse effect on decision-making. A forecast is reliable if there is no bias and the level of variation is tolerable.

Aligned

The fourth characteristic of good forecasts is that they are aligned.

Different forecasts need to be aligned where coordinated action is called for

No one would like to be a passenger on a sailboat where every crewmember had his or her own forecast. At best they would waste a lot of time arguing about 'who was right', at worst they might be taking completely incompatible decisions. Yet this is the state which we observe in many businesses. Where this occurs, it is almost certain that everyone responsible for a forecast will be able to point to his or her forecast being 'more accurate' at some point over the recent past. And where does that leave you?

'A man with one watch always knows the time. A man with two is never sure'

Segal's Law

The disconnect between volume and value forecasting is a common form of mis-alignment in many businesses. Martin Jarvis sees this as a major missed opportunity. 'Aligning forecasts of value and volume creates a win for the financial community because their forecast is more solidly based on what is really happening in the business. For operational managers the win is that their forecasts are made more visible and are taken more seriously. This makes it easy to spot and drive out the bias that is so costly and the problems and opportunities which are a huge hidden source of value' (Jarvis, 2008).

It is difficult to have sympathy with those who argue that 'I have to produce my own forecast because theirs (Sales/Production/etc.) is always wrong'. Arguably, it is better to have one wrong forecast that you use and improve, rather than multiple forecasts that only serve to confuse people and generate completely unproductive debates. 'Having one set of figures (OSOF) has helped us be more confident about the basis on which we run the business,' says Richard Sciver former VP Finance at Unilever Poland. 'Too often in the past everyone was second guessing everyone else so nobody was really sure where we were heading' (Morlidge, 2005).

How to align forecasts produced for different purposes needs to be carefully thought through

What is tricky, however, is to keep forecasts aligned when they have different purposes. For example, a CFO might wish to use a forecast to communicate to investors while a division of the same business might want to use the same forecast to allocate resources and the Supply Chain Director to plan production. Each of these different purposes might require differing horizons, levels of detail, accuracy and so on. The solution to this problem is presented in Chapter 7 'Mastering Process'.

Cost Effective

Finally, a forecast should be cost effective.

The value derived from a forecast should be greater than the cost of producing it

Again, you might say, a statement of the obvious. Why then is it the last item in our specification rather than the first?

We offer three reasons:

1. If you do not know what you are producing forecasts for – that is you do not do anything different as a result – you should question whether you should be forecasting at all, or at the very least question the way you produce forecasts. In particular, those businesses that treat forecasting as a rebudgeting exercise should question the value their efforts are adding.

2. You should not manage your forecast as if it were a transactional process. Each forecast process will be unique, perhaps only in a minor way, because the fore-

cast context will differ from business to business. Therefore, standardizing processes and reducing costs – while they may be desirable and appropriate – should not be the primary goal. The primary aim should be to build an effective process, and only when this has been achieved should cost be a consideration.

3. We believe that if you follow the guidelines set out in this book you WILL end up with a cost effective process. It will be effective since it will be designed around decision-making and the management of risk. It will be low cost because we advocate less detail, faster process times, the elimination of unnecessary analysis and the reduction and perhaps even elimination of budgeting. If on the other hand, you simply supercharge your existing budgeting process with sophisticated database and workflow tools you could well end up with an expensive and cumbersome monster.

· · · · ·

This chapter has tackled the fundamental question 'what makes a good forecast?' It has not been complex or difficult to understand but we hope that it has given you food for thought. Perhaps things that might have seemed confusing in the past are now a little clearer. The next chapter continues in the same vein. Forecasting is, by definition, about the future: about time. The second fundamental question we need to tackle is 'how far ahead should we forecast?' A deceptively simple question, but one that many clever business people have struggled with, and which has big implications for the design and operation of forecast processes. Fortunately, if you string your thoughts together in the right order finding answers is not too demanding.

· · · · ·

SUMMARY

A common misconception is that a forecast is a prophesy, a prediction of what *will* happen. In business, however, one of the main reasons we forecast is to project what might happen 'if'. That is, given a set of assumptions about the world but also planned future actions. If the forecast outcome is undesirable, managers can change their plans, and in so doing they invalidate the previous forecast. The purpose of forecasting is therefore to support decision-making, to help create the future rather than to predict it. In practice, forecasting is often confused with budgeting, which has a different primary purpose: that of setting targets – its currency is aspiration not expectation. Whereas a forecast is a statement of what we think will happen, a target describes what we would like to happen. As circumstances change, forecasts and targets will be pulled out of alignment and it is the existence of these gaps that stimulates decision-making. It follows that the most important quality for a forecast is that it is actionable, which means it provides information useful for decision-making. The information needed for this is likely to be different in nature and less detailed than that required for budgeting purposes. It also needs to be available in time for decisions to be made, which makes speed in the production of forecasts important. Also, decision-making demands forecasts that are reliable (accurate enough) rather than those which are perfectly accurate, and when organizations are interdependent, forecasts need to be aligned. Cost effectiveness is important, but less so than the other four qualities.

KEY LEARNING POINTS
What a forecast IS NOT
A prediction: since the purpose of business forecasting is not to foretell the future but to change it.

A commitment: since forecasts need to change to reflect changes in the environment and in management actions.

Precise: it is neither possible nor necessary.

Definitions
- Target: a description of where we think we are heading, based on current assumptions.
- Forecast: a description of where we would like to be.
- Plan: a set of future actions designed to reach an objective.
- Planning: the process of defining a set of future actions with the aim of achieving an objective.
- Budget: a sum of money allocated to an activity or action to which an organization has committed itself.

Five characteristics of a good forecast (TARAC)
- **T = Timely:** available at the right time
- **A = Actionable:** containing the right sort of detail
- **R = Reliable:** accurate enough: for the purposes of the decisions to be made. Which means that they should:
  - Be unbiased
  - Have acceptable variation
- **A = Aligned:** with other stakeholders (who are likely to have different purposes)

- **C = Cost Effective:** which is likely to follow if the other characteristics are present.

Design criteria

- **Detail:** sufficient to inform decision-making related to the purpose, but no more
- **Cycle time:** short enough to allow time for decision-making between updates
- **Frequency of update:** matching the rate of significant change in the forecast
- **Length of horizon:** sufficiently long to allow effective response but no more
- **Level of accuracy:** sufficient for effective decision making: no systematic bias and acceptable variation
- **Number of forecast processes:** one for each purpose
- **Relationship with forecasts prepared for other purposes:** closely aligned where coordinated action is required.

NOTES

1 According to Gallup (quoted in Geus 1997), about 26% of the American public believe it is possible to predict the future. Ronald Reagan famously used the astrologer Jeane Dixon to help him run the country.

2 This is an exaggeration to make the point. Some, but not all forecasting – especially that we are concerned with – *is* concerned with prediction. See p. 67 for more.

3 The analogy of sailing is a good one for management, and one that we will return to again. Managing any kind of organization involves acts of helmsmanship in the face of an unpredictable and changing environment. Plato was the first to make this analogy when describing the art of good government in *The Republic*. When Norbert Weiner was looking for a word to describe the 'science of communication and control' he borrowed Plato's term (Kubernetes) when he coined the name 'Cybernetics' (Weiner 1948). Cybernetics is, in our view, the source of the science that underpins this book. For those that are interested in finding out more about this misunderstood, and sadly somewhat neglected, field of scientific enquiry there is a short appendix at the back of this book.

4 This might seem like an obvious statement, but it is not something that contemporary management practice takes into account. Some seem to believe that target setting *is* performance management. See Seddon (2008) for examples of how the target driven approach to management has helped destroy performance, professional standards and morale in the British public sector.

5 In fact, if we consciously 'do nothing' that is a decision as well.

6 According to the Hackett Group only one-third of companies are able to produce forecasts in 10 days or less. What is more, the length of time taken is highly correlated with

managers' satisfaction. Only 9% are dissatisfied with processes completed in 10 days or less, but this rises to 83% for processes that take over 30 days (Hackett, 2008).

7 A cynical interpretation of this statement is that it is a euphemism for 'I need somebody to blame (other than me) when it goes wrong'.

8 Providing that there is a good correlation between the individual data elements, forecasting using extrapolated aggregated data avoids summing the error of low level forecasts.

Chapter 3

MASTERING TIME –
delay and decision

❛All is flux, nothing stays still. Nothing endures
but change❜ Heraclitus 540–480BC

> *How forecasting and response times (time lags) are linked – why an understanding*
> *of response times helps us predict – the nature of time lags in business – how to*
> *determine forecast horizons – the different types of horizon – the difference between*
> *strategic, forecasting and operational horizons – how often we should forecast – why*
> *it is important to have flexible processes for resource allocation – the relationship*
> *between forecasting and the decision-making life cycles – how we can confuse a decline*
> *of performance with a decline in knowledge*

WHY FORECAST?

Have you ever thought why we need to forecast at all?

If we can react to events quickly, we do not need to forecast

To answer this question we will return to our nautical analogy.

First, if you are the captain of a super tanker in the open sea do you need to
forecast? Most definitely. Without sophisticated radar and navigation systems it
would be too dangerous to sail such ships. But if you are in a speedboat, do you
need radar? Is navigation difficult? No. Why not? What is the difference?

The most obvious difference between a speedboat and a super tanker is their
maneuverability or agility. But what do we mean when we use these terms? Agile and

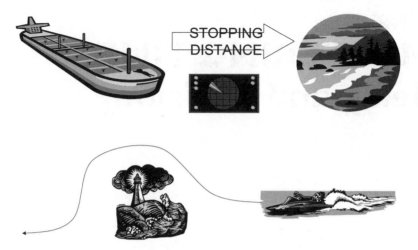

Figure 3.1 We only forecast because we cannot react.
Forecasting is essential whenever there is a significant time lag between taking action and that action having an effect, as in the case of a super tanker.

maneuverable are terms we apply to systems where there is a small time lag between taking a decision and that decision having the necessary effect.[1] A super tanker, which is not agile, will take miles and perhaps hours to change course significantly or to stop, whereas with a speedboat we would measure the same things in seconds or yards. If we cannot change immediately, we need to plan ahead. In other words, *the reason why we forecast is that we cannot react quickly enough* (see Figure 3.1).

Forecasting in business involves us supplementing and formalizing the forecasts we derive from our senses

This is of course a simplification. Technically the pilot of the speedboat is forecasting, but not formally – he is using his eyes and brain – and good sailors have a highly developed capacity to anticipate; for example a dinghy sailor will look for ripples on the surface of the water (lead indicators) to help anticipate gusts of wind which could destabilize or capsize the boat. Also he/she is not reacting instantaneously – there is a reaction time which is determined by the capacity of our nervous systems.

The point is this … a formal forecasting process is not necessary in this case because the 'forecasting systems' hardwired into our bodies are able to provide an *adequate* level of control. If we had a very agile vessel and our nervous systems were *not* adequate then we would have to supplement or replace them – as we have done to a large degree in modern fighter planes.[2]

Today's large organizations are much more like super tankers than jet fighters. While there are things we can, and should, do to improve their agility (like decentralizing decision-making authority), some form of formally structured process of generating foresight will, most likely, always be required. This is particularly the case with publicly quoted companies where external stakeholders are very intolerant of sloppy navigation or unscheduled detours.

So, put at its simplest, the need to forecast is determined by an inability to respond, specifically because of the existence of a lead time between taking a decision and the decision taking effect. Control engineers call this time lag the 'latency' of the system.

In the case of the super tanker, since it takes three miles (or 21 minutes) to stop, you need to have a good forecast at least three miles (or 21 minutes) ahead; two miles is insufficient and five is probably superfluous. But unfortunately in real life we need to do more than simply look ahead – we need to be able to do something with our 'fore-knowledge'. In systems with long lead times, decision-making can become complicated, particularly when you are trying to respond to an unstable environment. Let us illustrate this with another familiar example.

The complexity of the actions needed to respond to unpredictable change in even the simplest systems can be overwhelming

At some time in their life most people will have taken a shower where the shower controls are not very sophisticated. This is typically because the control knobs are located some way away from the showerhead. Therefore, when you turn the dials it takes a couple of seconds for the effect of the change to register at the showerhead. Adjusting the shower so that it is the right temperature can be a tricky business and most of us end up dangling our hand in the water until it is safe to step in.

This is similar to the situation we are faced with in business except that:

(a) unlike a shower, where the input temperature of the water is usually pretty constant, the business environment is dynamic and unpredictable;

(b) we have many 'controls' in a business, each subject to different time lags which we operate simultaneously;

(c) we don't have the option of 'standing outside' until the 'temperature' is comfortable!

In fact, even in a simple system like a shower, if we are impetuous or clumsy in the way we make interventions in the system, we can easily end up making things worse: creating a system that is more volatile and unstable than if we had simply done nothing.

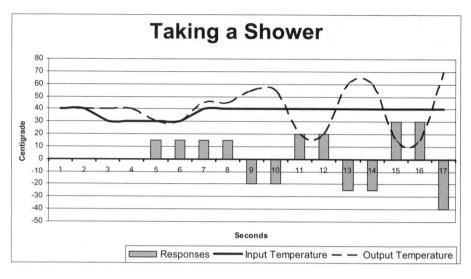

Figure 3.2 How lead times can induce instability.

 Example

How time lags can lead to a loss of control of the future

To demonstrate how easy it is to make things worse consider the example of my shower at home. Its controls aren't engineered very well but also for some reason it is plumbed in so that it is very sensitive to any other piece of equipment in the house which draws off hot water. So if you are unlucky enough to be taking a shower when the washing machine is on, the temperature drops whenever the machine starts a fill cycle.

With my shower system we are dealing with a number of uncertainties; I don't know when the washing machine's fill cycles will start and finish and by how much it will affect the temperature of the incoming water. I also don't know what effect turning the shower controls a half turn will have and I don't know how long it will take for my action to have an impact.

I am sure by now you will have a good idea what it is like trying to have a shower in these circumstances; but if you don't some typical results are shown in Figure 3.2.

A comfortable temperature is 40 degrees centigrade plus or minus five degrees and as you can see the input temperature (the solid line) is originally set correctly. Unfortunately, the washing machine has a fill cycle that lasts four seconds and when that happens the input temperature drops 10 degrees, but it takes two seconds for the drop in input temperature to be registered at the shower head. I can use the shower control to regulate output temperature, but unfortunately this has a lag of two seconds as well.

After two seconds the washing machine starts but this drop in temperature doesn't register until the fourth second. The shower is now slightly too cool so I turn up the hot water supply. This is slightly misjudged – I increase the temperature by 15 rather than 10 degrees, but while the input temperature is still 30 degrees (as it is in periods seven and eight) this is tolerable. However the effect of the fill cycle on the washing machine (from the sixth period) hits the shower head in period nine, which, combined with the impact of my earlier intervention, sends the temperature soaring to 55 degrees. In panic I turn the shower knob the other way (a reduction of 20 degrees this time) but, after a lag of two seconds, this has the effect of bringing the temperature down to a chilly 20 degrees to which I overreact … and so on.

What is happening here is that we are attempting to reduce the difference between our actual and the target temperature but changes that happen in the time it takes for our interventions to have an effect result in an *increase* in the difference.[3] In these circumstances a very minor change in the environment can create extreme oscillation in performance.

It is difficult to effectively control a modern organization of any scale or complexity without a formalized process to anticipate and respond to the future

This example is simplistic but it makes the point. What this illustrates is the negative consequences of failing to anticipate changes in the environment and the delayed impact of decisions taken either in response to, or in ignorance of, those environmental disturbances.

Economies and industries are, however, many hundreds of times more complex than the most sophisticated piece of engineering equipment, and the difficulties of measurement are formidable. In our view this means that any business, once it gets beyond a certain level of complexity, will be lucky to survive and prosper in the longer term, without a well thought through approach to anticipating the future.

More

The science of System Dynamics and its contribution to understanding economic instability

The reason why economies exhibit cyclical behavior is partly attributable to industries with long lead times like capital goods and construction industries (and the banks that lend to them). For example, new building is commissioned at a time of boom but it is completed and comes on stream in the down cycle. By adding to the stock of unwanted property, it effectively makes the downturn deeper. It is also tempting to speculate whether the cycles of retrenchment and restructuring familiar to many who have worked in a mature business might be the result of similar causal patterns.

Systems Dynamics is a branch of applied systems science which applies control system modeling techniques to human activity systems. These techniques have been applied not only to businesses but also to cities and at the scale of the whole planet (Limits to Growth – The Club of Rome (Meadows *et al.*, 1972)[4]). In complex systems the results of the interaction of multiple feedback loops can lead to counterintuitive results (so-called 'unintended consequences').

Let us now explore some of the consequences of this analysis for the design of forecasting systems.

HOW FAR AHEAD SHOULD WE FORECAST?

We can now begin to answer some of the questions that we posed in the preface.

The length of the forecast horizon needed is determined by decision-making lead times – and so will vary between and within businesses

In any business we have a wide array of actions we can take to help 'steer the ship'. Some of these actions can be executed quite quickly (e.g. a change of price). Other actions may take a long time to put into effect – for example launching a new product or exiting from a territory. The logical consequence is that the forecast horizon should be related to the longest lead time in the business. So if the longest lead time is the 12 months it takes to launch a new product then the forecast horizon should be at least 12 months.

More

Time lags and driving

Highways provide a good example of how decision-making lead times are taken into account in design. Ideally roads should be designed to take account of 'decision sight distance', the sum of the time taken to decide whether a hazard exists, the reaction time of a typical driver and the braking distance itself, which is influenced by the design speed of the road and the incline.[5] If visibility on the road is less than the decision sight distance then the risk of an accident is increased. Most companies have forecast processes that fail this design criterion.

What this means is that there is no 'right' horizon for forecasting; it will be based on the particular organization and the nature of the decisions it makes. For example, a business in the capital goods industry should be routinely looking two years ahead. In fashion and retail businesses the forecast horizon may be less than a year. One thing is for sure: the conventional calendar year focus of traditional planning and budgeting makes no sense at all. For a start, it is wrong to impose a 12-month horizon. Second, in practice, when we budget in the autumn we might be looking 15 months ahead but in late summer, before the budget cycle starts we might only have four months' visibility.

Example

Forecasting and time at StatoilHydro

An example of an intelligent approach to forecast design is provided by StatoilHydro, the Norwegian oil company. It has decided not to impose a standardized forecasting horizon on its business because it is made up of an upstream exploration business that operates with very long lead times, and a retail business with very short horizons that is supplied by a refinery business which has lead times somewhere in between. Indeed, each of these businesses has units with very different lead time characteristics.

***Since we need be able to respond continuously, rolling forecast horizons
are necessary***

From a theoretical point of view then, if our 'longest lead time' is 12 months we need, at all times, a 12-month horizon. This is what we call a 'rolling forecast': a forecast where the horizon 'rolls forward' such that there is always a consistent level of visibility.

This differs from the conventional approach where the length of the horizon expands and contracts depending on when the forecast is conducted. Bjarte Bogsnes of StatoilHydro compares this approach to driving a car. During the budgeting cycle we shine a strong light into the future 'then we turn off the high beams and start driving into the next year with low beams only. At the beginning of the year our lights illuminate all four quarters ahead. As we drive on and the quarters pass, the low beams get gradually covered in mud and become weaker and weaker ... but we do not mind as long as we can see until year end ... Is this a safe way of driving in the dark?' Most businesses we know of who have introduced rolling forecasts[6] adopt a horizon that is longer than a year (see Figure 3.3); American

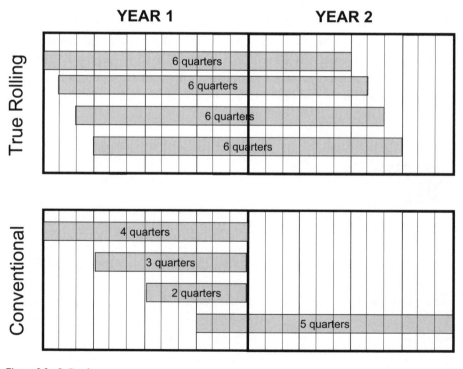

Figure 3.3 Rolling forecasts.
Unlike conventional budgets, true rolling forecasts have a consistent forecast horizon, irrespective of when a forecast is made.

Express uses five quarters, Tomkins and New Zealand Telecom, Tomkins and Unilever Canada 18 months.[7] This might not sound like a big change, but in fact, an 18-month rolling forecast, updated every quarter, can increase visibility by a factor of three over one with a fixed annual horizon.[8]

More

Why a pure rolling horizon might not be necessary

Are we advocating that at all times and in all circumstances, we should work with a pure 'rolling horizon'? Not necessarily. Why?

The reason for this is that we take decisions in response to new information. In practice we will have lots of information about the near horizon, and this information is likely to change rapidly. Providing this information is relevant to the decisions that we might want to make, it therefore makes sense to refresh our view of the near horizon frequently. In the far horizon, however, our knowledge is likely to be less clear. We will have less information and what information we have is likely to have less certainty attached to it than information in the very near future. As a result we will not want to refresh our longer term horizon at the same frequency as the shorter term.

Another factor is that there are usually a limited number of things we can do which change things in the short term. In the longer term we have many more options – we have the opportunity to deploy 'long lead time' actions now, but also, closer to the time we have medium and short term actions at our disposal. We are therefore unlikely to want to make decisions which affect the far future with the same frequency that we make decisions with a short term impact. 'Wait and see' may be the best tactic.

In practical terms if you forecast the short term on a monthly cycle, then the longer term horizon might only be refreshed on a quarterly cycle. You are left with a pattern that looks like a 'mini concertina' as shown in Figure 3.4.

How, you might ask, do I decide what is 'the longest lead time' action? Where should we draw the line?

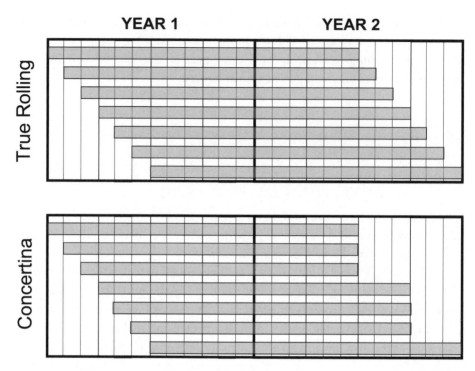

Figure 3.4 A concertina forecast horizon.
It may not be necessary to have a strict rolling forecast.

Business forecasting fills the gap between operational horizon where management can only respond and the strategic horizon where a business has sufficient time to reposition or restructure

It is useful to divide the attention span of an organization into three chunks. Each chunk has different characteristics and is associated with a different set of purposes. We call the short term the 'operational horizon'. Here we use forecasting to decide how we are going to react; what products we are going to manufacture or services we will provide; where and when. In this horizon, we use forecasting rather as we use short term weather forecasts. Because we have little or no ability to change the future our forecast *is* an attempt to predict.

The long term is the 'strategic horizon'. In this horizon, we are relatively unconstrained so the management process is about making choices. We can choose 'what business we are in', in what countries, using what facilities, and with what kind of

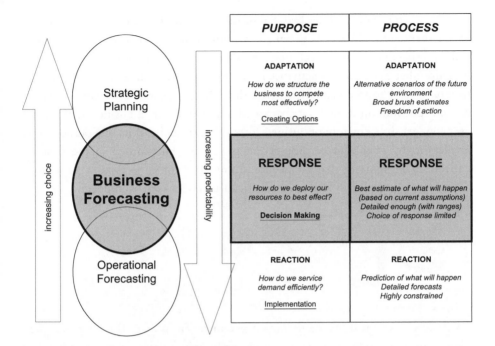

	PURPOSE	PROCESS
Strategic Planning	**ADAPTATION** *How do we structure the business to compete most effectively?* Creating Options	**ADAPTATION** *Alternative scenarios of the future environment* *Broad brush estimates* *Freedom of action*
Business Forecasting	**RESPONSE** *How do we deploy our resources to best effect?* **Decision Making**	**RESPONSE** *Best estimate of what will happen (based on current assumptions)* *Detailed enough (with ranges)* *Choice of response limited*
Operational Forecasting	**REACTION** *How do we service demand efficiently?* Implementation	**REACTION** *Prediction of what will happen* *Detailed forecasts* *Highly constrained*

increasing choice

increasing predictability

Figure 3.5 Three different types of forecasts.
Business forecasting – the subject of this book – differs from Operational and Strategic forecasting.

organization. Within limits, the future is what we choose to make it. We should not attempt to forecast *a* future, but we may forecast a set of possible futures from which we can choose (see Figure 3.5).

Our concern is the medium term, which we call the 'business horizon'. We chose this name because, while the short term primarily concerns those that are required to deliver goods and services, and strategy is primarily the job of senior management, the business horizon usually involves the entire organization in some fashion. Over this time frame we can 'steer the ship' but we have certain constraints; the goals that have been chosen, the product portfolio and business infrastructure which we have been bequeathed all constrain our ability to act. The point is that the process of 'looking ahead', and what one does with that foreknowledge, is fundamentally different from the other two horizons. Unlike the short term we have choice, but that choice is circumscribed. We can steer, but unlike in the strategic horizon we have limited options. Managing in the business horizon is about making trade-offs.

Where you draw the lines between operations, steering and strategy is a matter of judgment, and will vary between and within businesses depending on decision-making lead times. It is critical, however, that you *do* make these distinctions and recognize that management activities in the three horizons differ fundamentally in their purpose. The process used to manage them therefore has to differ. Unfortunately, it is not uncommon to see strategy carried out as if it were a business forecast but over a longer time horizon; or business forecasting treated as if its sole purpose were prediction. In particular, because action is possible but limited in the business horizon, it is important that the freedom to move is not unnecessarily constrained by arbitrarily imposed inflexible management practices such as budgeting.

 More

Time and military strategy

Arguably, time has been the dominant parameter in military thinking over the last century, starting with the Blitzkrieg philosophy of the Germany Army. In the US military, the ideas of John Boyd have become influential.

Boyd was a remarkable man, the archetypal maverick. He started as a fighter pilot in the Korean War and graduated to be a legendary instructor at the Nellis Airbase of 'Top Gun' fame (he was known as 'Forty Second Boyd' on account of his boast that he could beat any other pilot in a simulated dogfight within 40 seconds – he never lost). On his own initiative (using 'stolen' computer time) he developed the Energy/Maneuverability Theory, the first scientific formulation of aerial combat. During a spell at the Pentagon, Boyd subsequently used the E/M Theory (which as the name suggests was predicated on the merits of maneuverability – the ability to change course quickly) to help develop what became the F-16 and F/A 18 aircraft, in the face of opposition from the defense establishment. After studying military strategists from Sun Tzu (author of *The Art of War*) onwards he went on to develop a comprehensive theory of warfare, built on the concept of the OODA Loop. OODA stands for Observe-Orient-Decide-Act.

Boyd contended that the combatant (whether a single soldier or a whole army) that was able to move around the OODA loop (or decision cycle) the fastest would emerge victorious. His thinking stimulated the US Marines to redefine their military doctrine based on the concept of 'maneuverability warfare'. Boyd has also been credited with helping to draw up the plan of attack that proved so successful in the First Gulf War.

Boyd's thinking revolved around the use of time. In combat this involves speed (speeding up the OODA loop by reducing lead time) and it is interesting that he regarded those that helped develop the Toyota Management System as kindred spirits. The TMS is founded on the concept of eliminating waste ('muda'), and time is one sort of waste. By eliminating wasted time the production process is speeded up and becomes more responsive to consumer demand – thereby creating a 'supply chain based on customer "pull" rather than producer "push".'[9]

In our view an important role of forecasting is to help us understand the impact of time on our business and to use the knowledge to maximize agility.

HOW FREQUENTLY SHOULD WE FORECAST?

An unthinking approach to forecasting, which is all too common in our experience, would have us reforecast every element of the forecast, every cycle. We have already suggested that it makes sense to reforecast or 'refresh' the shorter term horizon more frequently than we refresh the longer term horizon. But in order to make good design choices we have to more specific. Let us explore the issue of forecast frequency in more detail using our super tanker analogy again.

Different elements of a forecast need to be refreshed at different frequencies

If our super tanker is sailing the southern Pacific Ocean how often should the navigator 'refresh' the forecast? Although it is probably wise to have someone on bridge at all times, the captain would probably not be expecting much other traffic in that part of the ocean, nor the need to execute any delicate or complicated maneuvers. As a result the navigator would probably not be expected to update the forecast very frequently.

On the other hand, when passing through the English Channel where up to 40 ships can occupy the same narrow strip of water at any one time, en route to Rotterdam – the world's second busiest port – navigational finesse is critical. The forecast may have to be updated every few minutes – because the super tanker has so little maneuverability any change in the traffic patterns ahead is potentially disastrous.

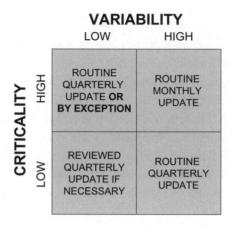

Figure 3.6 Forecast updates.
Showing how the degree of variability and the degree of materiality to decisions might interact to determine the forecasting cycle.

In principle, the more rapidly an important forecast variable changes, the more frequently we should refresh the forecast. The criterion of importance is the likelihood of a change in the variable concerned affecting a 'steering decision'. Whereas in a traditional 'budgeting' style process all variables are automatically reforecast, the approach to forecasting we advocate differentiates between 'critical variables' which are frequently refreshed (perhaps more often than before) and 'non critical variables' which are refreshed infrequently. Perhaps the results might look something like Figure 3.6.

Adopting a more discriminating approach to forecast frequency speeds up the process and reduces the effort involved in forecasting but there is another important benefit. As we discussed earlier, it is impossible to eliminate random variation from any process. Therefore, if we reforecast unnecessarily it is likely that we will inject noise into the process, which in turn could generate spurious analysis and, worse, unnecessary action.

On the other hand, forecasting too infrequently – a common problem in business – can be just as damaging. A key finding of a recent Hackett Group forecasting survey (Various, 2008) was 'a stunning mismatch between forecasting approaches and the markets in which firms operate'. Of the 20% of companies who reported that their business could change significantly within a month, 80% used a quarterly forecast cycle. The fact that businesses do not forecast frequently enough is not a new insight. The performance management system Alfred Sloan set up in General Motors before World War Two relied heavily on frequent forecasting.[10]

Example

How Southwest Airlines has incorporated volatility into their forecast design

The best example we have seen of rationally scheduling forecast updates comes from Southwest Airlines. Different parts of the forecast are updated on frequencies ranging from quarterly to daily; fuel typically comprises a third of the costs of operating an airline, and top line revenues are also very volatile, not least because of the flexibility in pricing that modern airlines have. The ability to update forecasts, as when key parameters in their business change, enables Southwest to be spectacularly responsive to changes in their business with the minimum of bureaucracy. See Figure 3.7.

	Economic Relevance	Variability	Speed of response	Update Frequency	Forecast Horizon
Revenues	High	High	High	Daily	Month
Labor Costs	High	Low	Medium	Twice monthly	Six months
Fuel Costs	High	High	Medium	Weekly	Quarter
Maintenance Spending	Medium	Medium	Medium	Twice monthly	Six months
Advertising Spending	Medium	Medium	High	Monthly	Six months
Aircraft Ownership Costs	Medium	Low	Low	Quarterly	Year
Airport Rates and Charges	Medium	Medium	Low	Weekly	Six months
Other Operating	Medium	Medium	Medium	Twice monthly	Quarter

Figure 3.7   How Southwest Airlines schedules forecast updates.
Forecast updates take place at different frequencies, depending on the volatility of the variable and the economic relevance to the business. (Reproduced with permission).

THE ANATOMY OF A DECISION

So far we have glossed over the issue of 'steering' in business; perhaps the analogies with sailing have made it sound rather straightforward. In fact, the process of 'steering' a business is usually a complex task. There are three reasons for this:

1. The constraints on resource allocation
2. The range of options
3. The nature and implications of time lags.

Decision-making and resource allocation

We have already established that the purpose of forecasting: to 'help steer the ship'. By providing information about the likely future position we can decide either to do nothing different or we can change our plans and so 'change the future'. When sailing this might involve moving the tiller and raising or lowering different kinds of sails.

If we did not have the ability to make these changes – perhaps because the tiller was fixed in one position or because we only had one sail – there would be little point in forecasting; we would go wherever the current took us. Clearly this is absurd; no one would set sail without the ability to shape their destiny. And yet, because of the constraints placed on the manager by conventional performance management systems, *this is the position in which many businesses find themselves.*

In order to effectively steer a business we need a flexible process for allocating resources

How exactly do you steer a business? You can only do this by 'doing something different'. Doing something different usually involves some combination of:

- **Stopping** an existing activity
- **Starting** a new (unplanned) activity
- **Speeding** up a planned activity
- **Delaying** a planned activity
- **Changing** a planned activity.

If we are in a race – as businesses operating within a competitive environment surely are – what we would ideally like is to *choose* the best action from a range of possible activities.

Whatever change we make we have to transfer resources – money or manpower – away from one activity/part of the business to another. Just as any kind of physical activity involves an expenditure of energy, so any kind of activity in business requires the expenditure of money. The problem is that, unlike our body which has a number of clever ways of transferring energy to where it is required at the right time, conventional business performance management practices such as budgeting often make it very difficult to make such changes.

Budgeting constrains our ability to reallocate resources

As anyone who has ever participated in the process will know, once agreed a budget is often treated as an entitlement to spend by the recipient. Attempts to cut budgets are resisted fiercely and come the end of the year there is often a rush to spend it since annual budgets can create a 'use it or lose it' mentality. If the future turns out exactly as you expected this lack of flexibility in resource allocation does not present a problem, but in these circumstances you don't need to forecast either!

Managers may be in the fortunate position of having surplus, unallocated budgets, and so have some room for maneuver, but from a total business perspective this can be severely suboptimal. It is akin to that of a General who wants to mount an attack in 'sector 1' but has allocated one tank to each of his 10 sectors and only has one left over for himself. Before he can mount an attack, he has to persuade sectors 2 to 10 to release their tanks, perhaps to find that they have already committed them to their own local small scale skirmishes.

 Example

Dynamic resource allocation at Telecoms New Zealand

Telecoms New Zealand, a provider of Internet, data, voice mobile and fixed line services, quickly learned this lesson.

Between 2003 and 2005, they introduced a rolling 18-month forecast process, but at first, while they were updating their forecasts on a quarterly basis, resource decisions (and the incentive scheme) were still locked into the annual cycle. 'You might say that's pretty obvious but it really wasn't at the time,' says Marko Bogoievski CFO during this transition. 'People liked to think that they were making more dynamic decisions on a daily basis. But when we looked at our operating and capital expenditure processes we realized that once they were locked into the annual plan they were really difficult to change or move between business units. Now we have done away with the old delegated authorities and given business units decision-making authority within reasonably tight operating bands based on return-on-invested capital criteria. They are free to make choices providing they stay within those bands' (Hope, 2006).

The inescapable conclusion is that in order to make the process of forecasting worthwhile you need to create the capacity to *allocate resources dynamically*. For many businesses, this is a dramatic change in the way of doing business. To be clear, we are not advocating that organizations be more quick to cut budgets – many businesses are already well practiced in this 'art'. What we *do* advocate is creating an ability to move resources around the organization, in real time, to exploit opportunities and mitigate threats as they emerge. How to go about this is outside the scope of this book, but while we do not underestimate the challenges involved, there are many examples of even large and complex businesses having successfully made the change from which implementers can learn and take heart (see panel below).

 Example

Dynamic resource allocation in Unilever and AMEX

In Unilever's Polish Foods business, forecasting and dynamic resource allocation goes hand in hand. 'We call it resource allocation, but these formal words just describe how we go about exploiting opportunities in the market place' says Richard Sciver, former VP Finance (Morlidge, 2005). Forecasts are updated every month based upon current assumptions about the business, including assumptions about what projects will be run and when. Projects include advertising campaigns, promotions and new product launches. The decision to commit to most of these projects is, however, only made a few weeks prior to the start of each quarter based upon up-to-date knowledge of what is happening in the marketplace, an assessment of the likelihood of success of each project and an understanding of how much money is available to invest, derived from the forecast.

Artur Magolewski, former Financial Controller, explains: '[T]he funds allocation process runs on a quarterly cycle. Four months before the start of the quarter Business Teams come up with proposals and one month before the start of the quarter, after extensive discussions they are approved. I say approved, but in practice this means 99% approved. We always leave ourselves the flexibility to react to what is happening in the market place – so if there is a need we change plans on the go.' Marketing people, who traditionally jealously guarded their budgets, see the benefits: '[W]e always have base "budgets" for long lead time activities, such as advertising. But on top of that we always have a pool of money which is "free" and can be allocated to activities with the most promise, which is great,' says Monica Rut, Brand Team Leader.

The aim of the business is to maximize growth, within an overall profit constraint, and the results have been stunning. In 2005, the year before this approach was introduced, business performance was static and stuttering. Within a matter of months the business was growing at a rate of 7%. One of the reasons for this spectacular turnaround is that the business managed to replace the zero sum game of traditional resource allocation process, where one party can only increase their allocation of resources at the expense of another, with a win-win game. Because total investment available is driven by top line growth, everyone stands to gain if resources are invested in the best place. Defensive behavior around budgets has disappeared, '[I]n the past it was a constant fight to stop marketers holding sleeves – which they did because they were always expecting budgets to be cut,' says Magolewski. Another benefit is that insights about successes and failures are now shared more openly and resources flow freely between business units.

At AMEX, according to Jamie Croake one of the biggest benefits of their Planning Transformation was the better visibility it gives to senior leaders of the business. 'They are now able to make decisions about investment and strategy a lot earlier than they could in the past. We have been able to trigger investments a lot more frequently, which give us an enormous amount of flexibility' (Croake, 2008).

The book written by Anand Sanwal, based to a large degree on his experience of introducing IO (investment optimization) into American Express is a good source of more information about dynamic resource allocation practice (Sanwal, 2007).

Budgets should only be 'fixed' at the point of commitment

The picture we have painted – of plans in a perpetual state of flux – may sound chaotic. But to reiterate the point we made in Chapter 2, once a commitment has been made to a project or a set of activities – and you have a reasonably clear idea of what it is going to cost over what period of time – it makes sense to create a budget in order to make sure that sufficient resources are available to execute it. This doesn't mean things cannot be changed, but that changes will be more difficult to make, and if changes are made there will probably be negative consequences (wasted resource etc.). The problem with the conventional approach to budgeting is that we effectively commit – (lock resources in place) too soon and thereby unnecessarily constrain the range of options – or flexibility – available.

The conventional practice of resource budgeting simplifies the task of management, which is probably a major reason why it persists. Certainly, once the constraints of fixed budgets are dispensed with, businesses can be faced with a problem: the problem of overwhelming choice. For example, American Express has to deal with about 5000 live projects at any one time.

The new role of planning: the continuous process of whittling down a wide range of options to a point where a commitment to act is made ...

The truth is that, once the artificial constraints of budgets are removed, almost any business has a huge range of things it could do. It isn't infinite, since resources are not infinite, but it is certainly well beyond the capacity of any single individual to contemplate and make resourcing decisions about in a rational fashion. What makes dealing with the excess of choice even more difficult is that knowledge of the options available is spread through the organization – much of it is in the heads of employees, many of whom might not even appreciate the possibilities themselves until they are asked.

In our view, the role of planning is to structure the process of change; the process of exposing what can be done, deciding what is to be done, and mobilizing the resources to ensure that it is done. Planning is about producing plans which constantly change, not about creating *a* plan which does not. Planning is a process that helps expose options and then reduces them to a set of feasible alternatives that are capable of being acted upon swiftly.

Decisions and time

... but before we can choose an option we first have to create it

The problem of choice has other facets. Sailors have a limited number of well defined actions to choose from. The impact these actions have may vary depending on the weather or the tidal conditions but the act of choice is fairly clear cut. When you decide to tack you will know precisely what impact the maneuver is likely to have on the course of the vessel, how long it will take to effect and everyone knows exactly what is involved – you simply have to execute. But decision-making in business is not so straightforward. Every decision is unique; if you are to steer the business effectively you will need to estimate what impact each action will have and how long it will take for this to be manifest. Furthermore each intervention has to be created, and the process of creation itself involves a time lag. This means that every purposeful act has a life cycle that has to be managed.

'The way to get good ideas is to get lots of ideas and throw the bad ones away.'

Linus Pauling

The life cycle of a business decision usually has five stages:

The life cycle of a decision
1. **Assessing options**
At the beginning there is an almost infinite amount of choice of what can be done. The set of ideas is limited only by your imagination. Generating new ideas may sound easy but it is not. The task of mobilizing the latent creativity of their people is often a problem for organizations, but it is outside the scope of this book.[11] Assuming that you have some ideas, the first step is to assess which of them have potential. Ideas can be rejected altogether or 'kept in mind' as options for future consideration.

In practice some of the actions we take in business will be similar to actions we have taken in the past and so require limited original thought. Others will be completely novel. But whatever the source of the idea, at this stage in the process we have not yet decided what action we will eventually take – if any.

2. **Assessing feasibility**
The next phase involves crystallizing ideas into something sufficiently tangible for you to be able to assess whether you have, or can acquire, the technical capability required and whether it makes sense from a financial and business point of view. This may involve building prototypes, experimentation or pilots.

At this stage in the process you have greater clarity about what is possible but you will not yet have determined what is necessary; you do not yet have clarity about the *likely outcome* of the decision-making process.

3. Capability

This stage is where you make plans, which involves working out how best to achieve a given objective by breaking it down into practical, implementable steps. As we have discussed, this involves making a selection from a set of feasible options and then working out the steps required to execute the activities selected.

By this stage you have more clarity about what you are likely to do and how to go about it. That uncertainty which remains should be limited and capable of being quantified.

4. Making commitments

At some stage in the decision-making process you will commit to action. Commitment involves allocating resources in a way that, while not necessarily irrevocable, can only be reversed with significant financial penalty. At this point you might want to create a budget for the project or the activity.

At this stage, you know what the action you have taken is and you are reasonably certain about the resources required. There may, however, remain great uncertainty about the impact of the decision that you have just made.

5. Execution

Finally, having made a decision, it will need to be implemented. Once implemented there will be an impact, which may be temporary or permanent in nature and more or less in line with that anticipated. The uncertainty about this impact will only begin to be resolved once the process of implementation has commenced. As a result of what you learn you are likely to have to revise your assessment of the future impact.

More

Managing an innovation funnel

All decisions pass through these five stages, but not all projects do. In a healthy process, we should expect to have many more ideas than we do projects undergoing feasibility testing, more projects in feasibility than are planned and so on. A good process should be competitive; poor projects would be weeded out – in fact even projects that succeed in passing through all the stages of the process may be changed, perhaps out of all recognition. A good process will always 'improve' good projects. In addition, particularly in a fast moving or uncertain environment, it makes sense to build options. Projects may 'sit' in the feasibility stage for some time, but since they are 'partly cooked' they are capable of being activated quickly if circumstances change. For these reasons the process we have outlined is often described as a 'funnel' process; the initial stage captures good ideas that are then channeled into a small number of executable projects. Many companies build a formal 'stage gating' process to formally manage the stocks and flows of projects through the funnel. Projects are documented and systematically tracked through their life cycle with transitions from one stage to another having to pass through a decision 'gate'. Particularly for large companies which have to manage complex interrelated projects, this makes a lot of sense. As with any process, however, it can easily become bureaucratic, so discretion should be exercised. See Figure 3.8.

Every decision that you make requires you to go through these five steps, implicitly or explicitly. To that extent all decisions are the same. How does this tie in with the forecasting process?

We need to manage a dynamic portfolio of options, at various stages in their life cycle

The implication of the decision making life cycle is that at any one time there will be decisions at different stages about which you have different levels of knowledge.

Figure 3.8 The innovation funnel.
Showing how executable projects are distilled from ideas.

Some would be still in the ideas or feasibility stage where you can only guess at the likely outcome; others might be in execution and you will know a great deal about these. Given this variation it is important that there are clear rules about when and how an activity is included in a forecast. For instance, once something enters the 'planning' stage there is probably enough certainty and clarity to make a sensible estimate for the purposes of forecasting. But how should we treat projects in 'feasibility' or even 'ideas'?

This is a fundamental forecasting problem. In the short term you have a great deal of knowledge, not just about what you are going to do but also about the likely environmental conditions. At the far end of the horizon, you can only speculate about the environment and might have only a vague idea about what you might do. The 'loss of knowledge' as we look further into the future we call 'forecast decay' (see Figure 3.9). You know you will be taking some action in, say, 12 months' time, but you do not know what. The problem is that if you do not compensate for forecast decay by making some assumptions about activity at the far end of the forecast horizon, then you are effectively forecasting inactivity. Since the result of inactivity is usually negative there is therefore a risk that the forecast will look 'bad' and you will be spooked into unnecessary 'corrective action'.

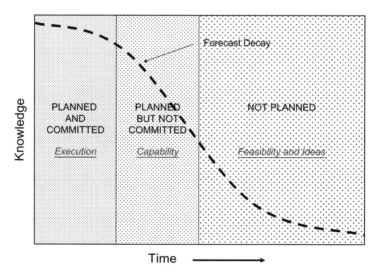

Figure 3.9 Forecast decay.
Knowledge declines the further ahead we look; we have to be careful that we are not misled by this.

We will discuss how to deal with the phenomenon of forecast decay in the next chapter, 'Mastering Models'. But first we need to explore some other implications of the decision-making life cycle.

Different types of decisions have different lead times

While it is true that all decisions can be seen as having a life cycle made up of five sequential steps, in other ways they can be very different. One of the most obvious ways in which decisions differ markedly is in the length of time between different stages of the life cycle. In other words they will have different lead times.[12]

Some routine decisions, where the logistics are simple and we have previous experience, might proceed swiftly from one stage to the next. Larger strategic decisions, each of which is unique and with significant implications for the future, will take much longer. In fact, some strategic decisions could spend years in the ideas or feasibility phases before detailed plans are crystallized.

Sub horizons will hold different types of detail relating to different types of decisions

In practice this means that while you might have a high degree of confidence in the shape of your activity plans six months out for long lead time projects, it might be that for shorter lead time projects, looking more than two months ahead may be pure speculation. You have plenty of time to respond to changes in the environment, so it makes no sense to lock yourself into a fixed plan prematurely. Traditional planning and budgeting systems, however, tend to demand the same level of detail across the whole annual horizon, irrespective of decision-making lead time. This type of traditional process wastes time[13] but also carries the risk of making resource commitment decisions too soon, thereby reducing flexibility. It may therefore make sense to treat short, medium and long term resource allocation and forecasting processes differently, using different forecasting and resource allocation processes (and perhaps with different organizational responsibilities) for different horizons.

The best way of improving responsiveness to an unknown future is to shorten lead times

To take this line of argument one step further, while it is true that having a good forecasting process allied to an efficient dynamic resource allocation process will increase organizational agility, a more cost effective way to increase flexibility might be to compress decision-making lead times. In many organizations more time is consumed by laborious decision-making processes around the planning and commitment steps than in the actual act of execution. This is particularly the case in organizations with bureaucratic budgeting processes. Sometimes, reallocating budgets in response to changing needs can take as long as setting them in the first place. If the process of idea generation is continuous, resource allocation decisions made frequently, firm commitments made only when necessary and the organization is aligned around them, then decision-making lead times can be collapsed dramatically. This increases flexibility and simplifies planning (and forecasting) processes.

In conclusion, in order for forecasts to be useful we have to be able to act upon them. In other words we need to be able to change the future. To do this effectively in the first instance we need, as far as possible, to be free from unnecessary constraints such as those imposed by budgeting, at least in its classical form. We then need to understand and to handle the complexity of a dynamic resource allocation process since only by changing the way in which money and manpower is deployed can we change what we do and so shape the future. Because of the range of options open to business, our resource allocation process needs to be sophisticated. Among other things it demands that different kinds of decisions be handled in different ways. This presents a number of new conceptual challenges which we have alluded to but also a number of practical forecasting problems that we will address in the next chapter.

$$\bullet \quad \bullet \quad \bullet \quad \bullet \quad \bullet$$

The next chapter deals with how the content of forecasts – the numbers – should be produced. It might be tempting for readers to skip or skim this chapter. If your forecasts are based on judgment you might believe that there is nothing we can contribute. Alternatively, you might think that this is a highly technical subject, relevant only to professional forecasters and statisticians. The next chapter is harder work than the previous two, but we strongly recommend that you do not jump over it. Judgment in forecasting is unavoidable, but it is often exercised very poorly. A little understanding of why this is can help you make big improvements. Mathematical routines are also a common feature of forecasting, but it is essential for technical managers to understand what they can and can't do for you. Professional forecasters sometimes have a poor grasp of the business they are attempting to model and so need help to make good choices about the technique to use. Also some familiarity with the process will make you a better and more discriminating consumer of forecasts; all too often managers are hoodwinked or seduced by technical gimmickry. With a little understanding, even the most innumerate manager can learn to intelligently question and challenge forecasts.

$$\bullet \quad \bullet \quad \bullet \quad \bullet \quad \bullet$$

SUMMARY

Forecasting involves understanding and managing lead times; if we were able to respond instantaneously to events then we would not need to forecast. In business, however, time lags – the delay between making a decision and the effects of that decision – are often long and the range and number of different possible decisions can make the situation very complex. As a result, in order for an organization to reliably achieve its goals and maintain stability it needs a formal forecasting process which takes time lags into account. It follows that the length of the forecast horizon should be a function of the lead times of those decisions that we choose to use for steering the business and that the horizon be 'rolling' rather than fixed. The 'steering' horizon will differ from the horizons associated with different kinds of decisions, specifically strategic (longer lead time) and operational (shorter) decisions. Since decisions are driven by information, forecasts need to be updated at the same frequency as the relevant information changes. Also because the resources are needed to enact decisions, an organization's resource allocation process should operate at the same frequency. Decisions have a life cycle that starts with an idea and ends with an executable project and it is important that the relationship between this life cycle, resource allocation and forecasting is well understood and defined, particularly towards the end of the forecast horizon, since the further forward we look the less information we are likely to have about future plans.

KEY LEARNING POINTS

- Operational forecasting: takes place in the time horizon within which there is little scope for change.
- Business forecasting: takes place when it is possible to steer the business within the constraints of the existing goals, scope and structure of the business.
- Strategy: a process of exercising choice over the scope, goals and structure of the business.

Definitions

- Decision-making lead time: the time between taking a decision to do something and the impact being manifest. Business forecasting involves estimating the impact of all those decisions which allow a business to change course.
- Forecast horizon: the period of time in the future covered by a forecast.
- Rolling horizon: where the length of the forecast horizon is held constant. In principle the length of the horizon should be determined by the longest decision lead time.

- Concertina horizon: where the length of the forecast horizon varies depending on the phase in the forecast cycle.
- Forecast decay: the degradation of forecast quality resulting from a decline in knowledge about planned future activities towards the end of the forecast horizon.

The life cycle of a decision

- Assessing Options: where ideas are generated and crystallized into potential projects.
- Assessing Feasibility: where potential projects are tested for practical and economic feasibility.
- Planning: where activities (projects) are specified and ordered in time.
- Commitment: where irrevocable commitments of resources are made to an activity (project) or set of activities, resulting in the creation of a budget.
- Execution: enactment of a decision.

Design criteria

- The length of the forecast horizon: the longest decision-making lead time.
- The need for sub horizons: the existence of decisions with a significantly shorter lead time.
- The frequency of forecast update: the frequency should be based on:
  - Volatility: the rate of change
  - Materiality of changes to decision-making.

NOTES

1 Agility is not just a function of the lag between decision and effect. The length of time it takes to recognize the facts, assimilate them and to take decisions based on them are additional factors that affect agility or maneuverability. See the discussion of the OODA loop in this chapter for more.

2 In fact, the Eurofighter cannot be flown without electronic controls. In order to make it very agile it is designed to be unstable: the human nervous system cannot operate quickly enough, unaided, to keep it in the air.

3 In systems terms, by changing the controls on the shower we are trying to apply negative feedback (to eliminate the gap to target), but because of the time lags, it is being experienced as positive feedback – which increases rather than reduces the gap. In 1868 Maxwell demonstrated mathematically how time lags could destabilize a system, and so explained why some steam engines exploded. The example used here has similarities with

the 'Beer Game', a simulation used to demonstrate the interplay of imperfect information and time lags in a supply chain. Typically the system will become unstable, often exhibiting a so-called 'bullwhip' effect. See Senge (1990) for a description.

4 The 1972 'Limits' report famously predicted economic decline and environmental problems in the early part of the twenty-first century. At the time it was published it was severely criticized and largely disappeared from public consciousness. In November 2008 (Turner, 2008) it hit the headlines again when academics claimed that subsequent economic developments had largely vindicated the predictions.

5 In practice, other factors such as the actual speed of a vehicle, its mass, road conditions, the amount of alcohol in the driver's bloodstream and so on influence actual braking distances.

6 According to the Hackett Group (Various, 2008) about a third of companies have rolling horizons and most of these are longer than four quarters.

7 The UK charity Sightsavers now uses a three-year horizon. This matches the typical length of its relief projects (typically involving the surgical correction of glaucoma), thereby allowing them to be more effectively managed.

8 A fixed year-end horizon may provide an average visibility of only six months.

9 Robert Coram has written 'Boyd – The fighter pilot who changed the art of war' (Coram 2002), a gripping biography of a fascinating but deeply flawed man. Tom Johnson and Anders Brohms describe how Toyota learned about the management of time (from Ford) in their book 'Profit Beyond Measure' (Johnson and Brohms 2000). The military doctrine of the US Marines is set out in MCDP 1 'Warfighting'.

10 In his memoirs (Sloan, 1967) he commented: '[T]wo things were involved, first the art of forecasting and second shortening the reaction time when a forecast proved wrong, which can be expected to happen even in the present day of complex mathematical forecast technique ... Adjustment will be made from month to month in such a manner to eliminate the extreme peaks and declines that have heretofore been characteristic of the industry.'

11 While it is creative, ideas generation need not be an art; it is something that can be managed. 'What If', a UK based agency specializing in ideas generation has published a number of books about how to stimulate and exploit new ideas which we recommend to any reader wishing to discover more about this. For example see Allan *et al.* (1999).

12 It is sometimes surprising to discover how little management know about lead times in their business, and what the consequences are for them. For example, we witnessed a very senior manager demanding that advertising be cut three weeks before the year-end in order to meet a profit target, not realizing that advertising slots have to be booked and paid for three months in advance. Another example is of a company that focused all of its management activity on 'delivering the quarterly numbers', failing to recognize

that because of lags in the business and revenue recognition rules there was very little that could be done in anything less than six months.

13 A business one of us worked in insisted that sales people forecast promotions to the end of the year, despite the fact that their customers only committed to run them three months ahead. As a result they were forced to waste a lot of time guessing what promotions their customers might take and then a whole load more time afterwards explaining to the accountants why they had got it wrong!

Chapter 4

MASTERING MODELS:
mapping the future

❝The map is not the territory.❞ Alfred Korzybyski
1879–1950

> *What a model is – why we cannot predict without models – different types of models – their strengths and weaknesses – how to choose which one to use where – forecasting trends and discontinuities – how forecasting combines the use of different types of models – why we can't avoid judgment in forecasting – and why it is the primary cause of bias – how to deal with forecast decay*

What do catching a ball and weather forecasting have in common?

Any kind of prediction requires a model

Most of the science upon which weather forecasting relies has been in existence for a few centuries but that does not mean that it is easy to produce a forecast. Indeed, modern weather forecasting uses some of the largest supercomputers in the world to perform the complex numerical calculations required. This involves taking input values from a range of locations (like wind speed and air pressure) and feeding them into the system which subsequently produces a set of outputs: predictions about the temperature, likelihood of rain and so on, for many points on the globe for a period of time in the future. But what is it that sits 'in the system' which allows us to produce a prediction? It is a model; one which takes the output of centuries of scientific endeavor and distills it into a set of mathematical equations.

More

Why perfect prediction is not possible

As we all know weather forecasts are not perfect, even though the basic science has been well understood for centuries and there are few parts of nature which have been more extensively studied. In fact, weather forecasts are usually accurate for the next five days or so but their performance falls away sharply after that. The reason for the fundamental unpredictability of weather forecasts – indeed, the unpredictability of *nearly all* real world systems – was discovered by a meteorologist called Edward Lorenz. What he discovered has subsequently come to be called 'Chaos Theory' (Gleick, 1998).

The fact upon which Chaos Theory is built is that most natural systems are highly nonlinear; this means that their output does not vary proportionately to their inputs. Weather systems are nonlinear, as are economic systems. Doyne Farmer, Los Alamos physicist turned entrepreneur and complexity scientist, demonstrates what this means by comparing the task of catching a ball with that of trying to catch an inflated balloon when the air is let out. Perfectly deterministic systems, if they are nonlinear, can behave like the balloon – in ways that cannot be predicted. This is true *even if we know everything about them*. Unpredictability can take the form of sudden shifts in behavior – the so-called 'tipping points' popularized by Malcolm Gladwell[1] (Gladwell, 2002). For instance in the recent financial crisis it seems like the failure of Lehman Brothers was the key discontinuity: Jim O'Neill of Goldman Sachs described it as the 'game changer' before which 'his forecasts were panning out OK' (Giles, 2008).

You might think that this makes forecasting a futile exercise. Even though a system is fundamentally unpredictable, if you can forecast with confidence a little way ahead this can be of enormous benefit. Short run weather forecasts are very valuable and Farmer has used his understanding of complex systems and non-linear physics to build models which are able to predict short run movement in stock prices. After a 10 year collaboration with UBS, the Swiss banking group, Farmer sold the 'Prediction Company' to them in November 2005 for an undisclosed fee. Fortunately most of the systems we are attempting to forecast in business are a good deal more predictable than the stock market.

Well, catching a ball involves a model as well.

The input into the model comes from our eyes rather than a set of scientific instruments. Among other things, we assess how far away the thrower is, how big and how heavy the ball is, how much force has been applied to it and its trajectory. If the ball is light, we might even take into account the wind (meteorological parameters). These factors will then be input into a model that we carry around in our head, one that is 'hardwired' into our genetic makeup[2] that we have been using and improving since kindergarten. Based on the output from our mental model – a forecast of the likely future position of the ball – we will move in a particular direction at a specific speed with our hands held out in a particular way. We also work out how to brace ourselves so that in the process of catching the ball we do not hurt ourselves or allow it to bounce out of our hands.

Few people appreciate that the process of catching a ball – something that seems so simple and straightforward – can only be replicated by machines using sophisticated models based on Newton's Laws of Motion and Universal Gravitation.

 More

The models we use when we exercise judgment

Scientists believe we learn to catch a ball using something called the 'catching heuristic'. A heuristic is like a simple program[3] – a 'rule of thumb' – that we use (usually subconsciously) to accomplish some task. In this case the heuristic involves looking at the angle of the ball and moving in a way that keeps the angle constant; a routine that ensures that the catcher's trajectory coincides with that of the ball. Human judgment, sharpened by millions of years of evolutionary experience, relies heavily on heuristics; for instance, the 'gaze heuristic' probably evolved with hunting activity. Heuristics can be extraordinarily effective in many situations but in others, these simple routines can lead to us making systematic errors in judgment; what scientists call 'cognitive bias'.

All forms of forecasting – and all purposeful actions involving some form of forecast – rely on models. Any purposeful action requires 'if this … then that' reasoning; as in 'if I am late home from work this evening then (because I have a model of my partner's psychology in my head) … .' Most of the models we (and other living creatures) use, whether we are catching a ball or making an estimate at work, are not mathematical in form (for instance it is unlikely that a dog catching a Frisbee will be doing $f = m.a$ sums in its head) but they are models none the less.

What exactly is a model?

A model is a simplified representation of the world constructed for a specific purpose

A model is a simplified representation of reality. Because a model is a *simplified* representation of the world it will never be 'perfect'. It can only make predictions based on 'what it knows' about the world, which will never be complete. As a result we cannot select models based on whether they produce a perfect prediction – they never will. The criterion has to be: does it produce forecasts that are useful (*good enough*) *for our purpose*?

More

How to build a model

Building a model first involves selecting an aspect of reality that is of interest for the purpose of the modeler. By implication, this involves ignoring aspects of reality that are not of interest. Second, and this is particularly important for physical models (as in ship design for instance), the scale of the model may be physically changed to make it possible to study the phenomena of interest. Finally, particularly in scientific models (such as scientific theories which are a particular type of model which has been rigorously defined and tested), the inputs to the model and often the model itself may be expressed in mathematical form to allow forecasts (outputs) to be made with precision. So a model could be something used to forecast the weather, estimate whether we have enough time to cross the road, calculate where a ship is likely to be in one day's time or study the effect of wind flow over a car body shape. A model (more likely a set of interconnected models) is also used to estimate the economic outcome of a series of activities in a business.

A map is a good example of a model. It takes an aspect of the real three dimensional world, reduces it to two dimensions, changes the scale and eliminates or distorts some aspects of the world, accentuates others and converts it to a symbolic notation. All mapmaking involves this procedure, but the 'model' (map) produced at the end will differ depending on the purpose for which it is to be used. So, a map that is useful for a mountaineer will be hopeless for a motorist or a railway maintenance engineer, because they have different purposes (see Figure 4.1). Try walking around London using the London Tube map; it is a masterpiece of clarity for subway travelers but only by completely distorting the geographical position of stations, so it offers poor guidance to pedestrians.

To produce a good business forecast we need to use the right kind of model

What has this got to do with business forecasting?

In the last chapter, we looked at the role of time in forecasting. The only reason why we forecast at all is that we cannot react quickly enough; because of the delay between the decision to take action and that action taking effect we cannot steer adequately. This delay means that, if we want to affect future outcomes in a (reasonably) predictable way, we have to take likely future conditions into account. Specifically, we need to know what the world would be like if we took no action, and the likely outcomes (and timing) of those actions. By definition, *we do not have facts about the future, so we have to make assumptions*; which is where models come in.

The deliberations about 'purposes' and 'time' in the last two chapters help us design an appropriate *structure* for our forecasting process – the level of detail we need, what period of time should be covered and so on. We now turn our attention to the *content* of our forecasts. This involves working out how we estimate the likely future outcome, bearing in mind our design criteria: TARAC: Timeliness, Actionability, Reliability, Alignment and Cost Effectiveness. As we have discovered, making any kind of prediction – i.e. populating our forecast with content – involves selecting the right model. This is the task to which we will now turn.

TYPES OF MODELS

Forecasting is a process: a model is used to transform a set of assumptions about the world (input) into a forecast (output)

Forecasting is a process, one that involves the manufacture of estimates of future outcomes. Just like any other kind of process it first needs a set of inputs. In the case of a forecast process, these will be assumptions we make (see Figure 4.2). The

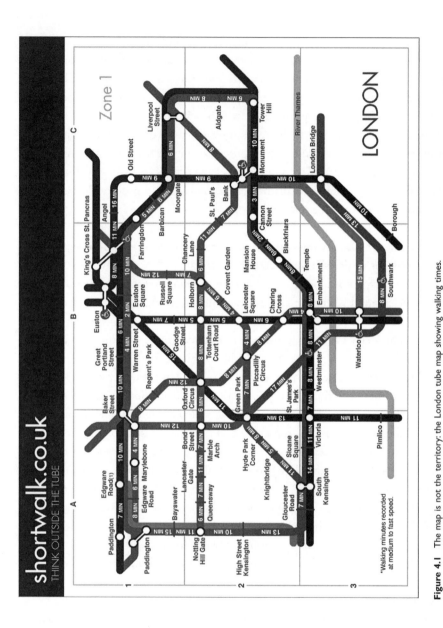

Figure 4.1 The map is not the territory: the London tube map showing walking times.

This is a good example of how models can distort aspects of reality but still be useful. Look at the Central Line running horizontally across the map from Bank to Notting Hill Gate. Notice how 'Tube space' differs from 'walking space'. (Reproduced with permission.)

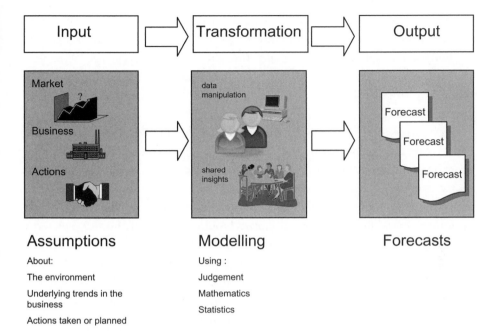

Figure 4.2 Forecasting as a process.
Shows how models transform assumptions into forecasts.

assumptions may include outside world phenomena such as inflation, market growth, or commodity prices or they could be the output from another forecast process. For instance volume forecasts might form an input into a cost forecast that in turn feeds a profit forecast. Like any manufactured 'product', the output of the process – a forecast – has to meet certain quality criteria (TARAC). In between the input and output sits a transformation process. In a food factory, it might involve an oven or a packing machine. In the case of forecasting the transformation process comprises a model.

There are three types of models we can use to build our forecasting process: often in combination

There are three types of models we can use to produce a forecast. At one extreme, we have the kind of model that we use when we catch a ball; one where the model is hidden because we manipulate the relationships between inputs and outputs (that is the forecast) in our head. We call this kind of forecasting *judgmental*, because judgment is the word we use to describe the process of manipulating implicit mental models. For reasons we will discover later, *we will never avoid the use of judgment in business forecasting.*

At the other extreme, we have the kind of forecast modeling that meteorologists use; based on explicit *mathematical* models. Much of what we forecast in business we understand well enough to make this the modeling approach of choice. Mathematical models can be complex but they need not be – multiplying sales volume by price is a simple mathematical model used extensively in business forecasting.

In between these two forms is what we call *statistical* forecasting. When we use statistical models to project into the future, we are not trying to establish and model the nature of relationships between variables – for example volume and numbers of people employed. Like judgmental forecasting, we simply use prior experience to project into the future. Unlike judgmental forecasting however, the modeling we use is mathematically based. We use statistical routines to identify historical patterns of behavior and then use these to extrapolate into the future.

All three of these approaches have a place, and all but the most simple business forecast will probably use all three types in combination. To forecast well we need to make good choices about what kind of model to use where, and we can only do this if we understand the relative strengths and weaknesses of the three approaches.

 Key Concept

Trends and discontinuities

The future – which is what we are trying to anticipate – always has two components – trends and discontinuities, and the interplay between the two is a recurring theme in this book. Although most systems are nonlinear, natural systems are often configured in a way that makes them relatively stable, within limits.[4] This manifests itself as 'trends': patterns of past behavior that repeat themselves. Trends are forecastable ('a trend is your friend' forecasters are told) – more or less well, depending on the modeling technique we use. Indeed if there were no trends, forecasting would not be possible at all. However, if the future was always like the past, forecasting would be easy – which it is clearly not. Discontinuities (also called 'structural breaks' by econometricians) describe those occasions when the future is not like the past – either because there is a change in trend or because the situation becomes chaotic (without any apparent pattern). Discontinuities represent novelty, and novelty is very difficult to forecast, particularly if the source of novelty is outside the business. Business forecasts should always recognize the likelihood of novelty – a forecast that is based purely on an extrapolation of trends will always be fallible. However good we are at forecasting trends and anticipating some discontinuities, we need always to be open to the possibility of novelty we have not anticipated – a theme we will return to later.

Judgmental models

Judgmental models are the most commonly used in business forecasting

Despite the disapproval of the professional forecasters in academia, the majority of business forecasting and budgeting processes rely on judgmental techniques. 'Usually forecast modeling is done in the head of managers,' says Fritz Roemer of the Hackett Group, 'and when these are the most experienced and knowledgeable managers in a business, working within a good process, we often find very high levels of forecast accuracy' (Roemer, 2008).

In most businesses sales forecasts, cost budgets and project cost estimates will be based on the judgment of an individual or a group of individuals, rather than a mathematical or statistical model. Judgment may involve the straightforward process of making an estimate (e.g. $x) or by applying a judgmental uplift or inflation factor to a historic number (e.g. x% less). Very often, high level forecasts are derived from low level judgmental forecasts. So for example, a cost budget will typically be built up from judgmental forecasts for individual line items – salaries, travel, training costs and so on. As we mentioned earlier, it is common for forecasts to be adjusted, and almost always this is done by applying 'judgment' rather than using some kind of mathematical procedure.

The attractions of using judgmental forecasting are obvious.

Judgmental forecasting is cheap, quick, and is able to deal with complex and novel situations reasonably well …

First, at least on a small scale, it is cheap and quick. The act of compiling a forecast simply involves adding up all the estimates of all the individuals responsible for elements of the forecast.

Second, it exploits the knowledge and skill locked up in the heads of maybe hundreds of employees. Knowledge and skill which will have taken many hundreds of man-years to acquire and which might be impossible or very costly to model in any other way.

Because of the sophisticated modeling capabilities of the human brain, judgmental forecasting can cope with novel or unusual circumstances in a way that mathematical or statistical approaches cannot. Human beings do this, usually unconsciously, by drawing on similar experiences from their past – perhaps experience from outside their professional life – and applying this understanding to the new context. Those with a good mental stock of relevant historic knowledge we call 'experienced'.

Finally, if an individual has come up with a forecast for her/himself then they are more likely to understand the forecast and be committed to it.

There are, however, a number of significant disadvantages to judgmental forecasting ...

... but it can be cumbersome when carried out at scale ...

While on a small scale, judgmental forecasting might be 'easy' and 'quick', in large and complex businesses the task of compiling a judgmental forecast can be formidable. For many businesses, the forecast process may involve the 'invention' of millions of pieces of data which then have to be collected in a structured fashion. The difficulty of the task is compounded by the fact that, because of interdependencies between different elements of the forecast, the collection process often cannot be run in parallel; it has to be sequential in nature. Thus the estimated cost of 'A' might be dependent on the cost of 'B' or the volume of 'C'. In these circumstances, changes to one of the parameters of the forecast may require the process to be repeated – and since there are limited 'economies of scale' in judgmental forecasting, the second forecast will not take significantly less time than the first. As a result, it is common to find incoherent or incomplete judgmental forecasts because there is not the time or the will to recast the forecast to accommodate the latest change.

It is this problem that the software vendors tackle with web-based 'workflow' and collaboration software products.

... and it is dependent on the expertise of the 'modeler'

Second, not everyone contributing to the forecast will be experienced or knowledgeable. Many large organizations have a high throughput of people through jobs and the level of organizational restructuring activity in business can quickly render historically acquired knowledge out of date. Even where forecasters do have requisite knowledge, they may not have the time or the information necessary to produce a good forecast when required.

Also, because the 'models' on which judgments are made are in people's heads it is more difficult to learn from experience – that is to 'improve the model'. In addition, because the model is not explicitly stated, managers do not know whether judgment is being applied consistently, that is, whether the 'same model' is being used all the time. By the same token it is difficult to determine whether one person's judgment is better than anyone else's and why. So judgmental forecasting processes are often characterized by unproductive arguments about 'who has the right number'; a debate which is usually left unresolved, and leads to the phenomenon of multiple competing forecasts.

More

The art of assumption making

A good way to improve the quality of judgmental forecasts is to ensure that forecast assumptions are explicitly and clearly stated. This not only helps the recipients make sense of the forecast, it also provides the basis for learning. When a forecast is 'wrong' we can more easily identify the reason (the false assumption) and make corrections. Assumptions need to explain the reasoning used, so a bald statement such as 'share growth 3.2%' is not adequate. 'We have assumed that the rate of growth will slow from 4 to 3.2% because of saturation in the target market' is much more useful. 'You can only improve a "model in the head" when the assumptions are made transparent,' says Fritz Roemer. Unfortunately, 'there is often a huge deficit in this area and as a result organizations often struggle to learn and improve' (Roemer, 2008).

In addition, there is overwhelming evidence that judgmental forecasts are prone to certain types of forecasting error.

This might not be a big problem if the errors were random errors – that is, they simply increased the level of variation. Unfortunately judgmental processes are chronically prone to systematic error, which is they are very often highly biased.

The major drawback of judgmental forecasting is that it is highly susceptible to bias
The biggest problem with judgmental forecasting is that it is often highly biased; that is, they display consistent patterns of positive or negative errors.

Sometimes these patterns of bias can be the result of what we call design errors; the forecasts may be biased because we use the wrong information or ask people to do the wrong thing. Therefore, for example, if we use cost budgets as a basis for a forecast we should expect the results to be biased. Because cost budgets set a limit on expenditure, we should expect to see many more examples of 'underspend' than 'overspend'.

More often though, bias in judgmental forecasting is a result of three factors: inherited or conditioned patterns of human thought, traits associated with man as a social animal, and the nature of the performance culture in many organizations. The three main sources of behavioral bias are cognitive, social and motivational.

Cognitive bias is the result of a failure to process information logically
As we have seen, when we use our judgment, we are using a special sort of model – a heuristic. The heuristic may be something that we have acquired through personal experience. However, human beings have a large shared legacy of heuristics, a product of our common evolutionary history.

Heuristics form part of our so-called 'System 1 thinking' repertoire – which is fast, automatic, effortless and implicit. This contrasts with 'System 2 thinking' that is slower, conscious, explicit and logical (Bazerman, 2006). Before Herbert Simon's work on bounded rationality in the 1950s (Simon, 1957) academics assumed that managers used System 2 thinking. In fact, Bazerman tells us 'the frantic pace of managerial life suggests that executives rely on System 1 thinking' particularly when they are under stress, perhaps even more than the executives themselves realize.[5]

Heuristics are useful and often surprisingly powerful. Indeed, under many circumstances they have proven to be more effective than so-called rational decision-making mechanisms (particularly if we can 'train' them as we do when we learn to catch).[6] On the other hand, they are prone to systematic error, a fact that leaves us human beings with a set of mental 'blind spots' which are collectively called 'cognitive bias'. According to Dan Ariely, this means that we are 'predictably irrational' (Ariely, 2008).

The heuristics most commonly involved in biased managerial decision-making are the 'Availability Heuristic' and the 'Representative Heuristic'. The Availability Heuristic leads us to overestimate those things to which we ascribe a greater significance, perhaps because they are related to recent or frequent events or for some reason carry emotional impact. The Representative Heuristic can cause systematic error because we apply inappropriate pre-existing mental categorizations to phenomena.

Bazerman identifies 14 types of cognitive bias that impact managerial judgment, all of which have been repeatedly validated experimentally.[7] The table below lists them along with some examples of how they might distort judgmental forecasts.

BIASES ATTRIBUTED TO THE AVAILABILITY HEURISTIC		
BIAS	DESCRIPTION	EXAMPLE
1. Ease of recall bias	The tendency to overestimate the impact of those events which are easy to recall	The assumption that what has just happened will happen again – poor estimation of risk. Giving more weight to colorful anecdotes than statistics.
2. Retrievability bias	The tendency to overestimate the impact of events deemed to be more likely (according to our existing mental models)	The failure to appreciate the importance of shelf position on sales of consumer goods (an important factor in consumers' search repertoire)
3. Presumed association bias	The tendency to overestimate probabilities because of false attribution of causality to events	If sales peaked after an intervention last time – assume that the same will happen next time (ignoring the effect of random chance)
BIASES ATTRIBUTED TO REPRESENTATIVE HEURISTIC		
4. Insensitivity to base rates bias	The tendency to misestimate probabilities because of failure to frame the question properly	Overestimating the chances of success of a product – due to failure to give appropriate weight to the probability of failure
5. Insensitivity to sample size bias	The tendency to ignore sample size when making judgments	Placing undue weight on low sample survey/ anecdotal data

BIAS	DESCRIPTION	EXAMPLE
BIASES ATTRIBUTED TO REPRESENTATIVE HEURISTIC		
6. Misconceptions of chance bias	The tendency to expect random phenomena to look random, even with small sample sizes	Forecasting based on extrapolation from data which looks like a pattern (but which is in fact random) –'overfitting'
7. Regression to the mean bias	The failure to appreciate the consequences of averaging as the sample size increases	Attributing causality to an intervention when it was simply the result of random variation around an average
8. Conjunction fallacy	The tendency to attribute a higher probability to a subset of occurrences than to the whole	e.g. 'sales people always sandbag their forecast' yet 'our forecasts as a whole are unbiased'
BIASES ATTRIBUTED TO OTHER HEURISTICS		
9. Anchoring	The tendency to make judgments by reference to a benchmark (which may or may not be relevant)	Forecast constructed by reference to target or previous forecast resulting in underestimation of variation
10. Conjunctive (and disjunctive) events bias	The tendency to ignore cumulative probabilities	Underestimation of the difficulty of large complex projects such as innovations
11. Overconfidence bias	A tendency to overrate our ability to successfully tackle medium to difficult problems	Unjustified confidence in our own judgment – so fail to seek out information to support forecasts
12. Confirmation bias	The tendency to seek evidence which confirms beliefs and ignore that which doesn't	We remember when we have correctly spotted bias in the forecasts of others but not when we fail ourselves (justification for adjusting forecasts)

BIASES ATTRIBUTED TO OTHER HEURISTICS		
BIAS	DESCRIPTION	EXAMPLE
13. Hindsight bias	The tendency, after the event, to overestimate our ability to successfully estimate an outcome	Overly critical judgment of the forecasting efforts of others (justification for adjusting their forecasts)
14. The curse of knowledge bias	The tendency, when judging the actions of others, to overlook information available to us but not them	Overestimation of the sales of innovations – ignoring the fact that we know more about the product benefit than consumers

 Example

An example of overconfidence bias

Here is a simple exercise that illustrates one of these cognitive biases:

FINISHED FILES ARE THE RESULT OF YEARS OF SCIENTIFIC STUDY COMBINED WITH THE EXPERIENCE OF YEARS

How many times does 'f' appear in this sentence? Take no more than five seconds, counting them only once. Then record your answer and write down how confident you are that you are right (between 0 and 100%).

Typically, respondents express confidence levels of about 90% but only about 1/3 get the answer right,[8] and that third are no more confident than those that get it wrong.

This is an example of confidence bias.

Source (Armstrong, 1985)

Social bias originates from the behavior of groups

There are many good reasons why business forecasting should be organized as a social process involving groups of people working together.

First, forecasting often involves many parts of an organization's activities so it is unlikely that any one person will have the requisite knowledge. Second, the process of collaboration increases understanding and promotes buy in, increasing the chances that the forecast is acted upon, and that any deviation from the forecast is spotted quickly.

On the other hand, groups do not automatically produce better forecasts than individuals. Indeed, new biases are often introduced when people work together in groups. A well known example of this is 'groupthink', a term that has been applied to the decision-making of advisors to President Kennedy during the Bay of Pigs fiasco. 'Groupthink' describes the tendency of groups to conform, which can lead to hasty, irrational decision-making or collective blindness to an obvious or uncomfortable truth.[9]

We would all like to believe that we are intelligent, independent minded adults exercising free will. In practice, most of us are heavily influenced by the views of people around us. It is very difficult to swim against the tide and if people do not share our opinion it very often leads us not only to question whether our own judgment is correct but to change our mind.

 More

The desire to conform

A famous experiment by Solomon Asch, which has been replicated many times, demonstrates how powerful the need to socially conform can be. The experiment required subjects in a room to match a line with one of three unequal lines. All but one person were stooges who had been briefed by Asch to give the wrong answer. All participants were required to give their answers verbally with the subject last. Even under these conditions, where there was no apparent reward or penalty involved, only 25% gave the right answers all the time (Asch, 1955).

This tendency to suppress 'deviant' opinion is exacerbated by the tendency for businesses to be organized around teams, teams that have a common purpose such as the Board of a company. Even when people are not formally organized into groups characterized by a high degree of social conformity we tend to seek out individuals holding similar views and opinions to ourselves and so reduce the chances of 'deviant' opinions being aired.

Unfortunately, the obvious solution – allocating the task of forecasting to a single individual – will not necessarily improve matters. It is an unavoidable fact that the knowledge needed to build a good forecast for a business may be spread around the organization. In addition there is a lot of evidence that groups are capable of making better decisions than individuals, even (arguably especially) when the individual involved is an expert.

More

Why experts fail and what to do about it

One of the most surprising findings from decades of research into forecasting is that, beyond a minimal level, expertise in a particular subject is of little value. 'Do not hire the best expert you can – or even close to the best. Hire the cheapest expert,' recommends forecasting guru J. Scott Armstrong (Armstrong, 1985). This is probably because experts are more susceptible to overconfidence bias than those of us who know we are ignorant. Partly in response to this, companies such as Hewlett Packard, etc. have experimented with prediction markets.

Prediction markets are a way of harnessing the knowledge of a large number of people and, in the process, cancelling out whatever bias an individual or small group of individuals might have. Typically the participants are given a small amount of historical information about, say, the sales of a particular product, and a small amount of 'play' money which they use to place 'bets' on future outcomes. It is claimed that a large number of apparently 'ignorant' people do a much better job of forecasting than conventional approaches, but if this is true it is difficult to see how this approach can be used extensively in business forecasting given the nature and scale of the forecast process and the speed at which it is conducted. To find out more read *The Wisdom of Crowds*, by Joseph Surowiecki (Surowiecki, 2004).[10]

What is the answer? Be aware of the pitfalls and design and run the process in a way that promotes evidence over opinion, surfaces dissent and discourages blind conformity. Proper measurement practices will also help to expose systematic bias in judgment (see Chapter 5).

More

How to foster dissent and mitigate the effect of social bias
One way in which dissent might be surfaced but without triggering unproductive debate or conflict is to capture them in 'range forecasts'. Making dissenting views visible in this fashion legitimizes dissent in a constructive way as well as enhancing the organization's 'situational awareness'. See Chapter 6 for more.

The most common form of behavioral bias is motivational bias

The third, and perhaps the most significant, source of systematic error is 'motivational bias'. This is introduced when, consciously or otherwise, people are incentivized to forecast a particular outcome. It may be one that they stand to benefit from in some way, or which they think other more powerful people would prefer, rather than the outcome that they believe is most likely.

We have already touched on this when we noted the tendency of forecasts to match targets. There is often a range of pressures – explicit or implicit rewards or punishments – that drive bias into judgmental forecasting.

Many executives will be familiar with statements like these:
'My boss wants to see a forecast coming back to target.'
'If I don't show 4 per cent growth in sales I will be crucified.'
'If I disclose that sales will fall short of target my marketing budget will be cut.'
'If I forecast beating my target it will be increased.'
'This forecast is unacceptable, you must do better.'
'The only kinds of surprise I want to see are nice ones.'
These quotes illustrate some of the gaming routines that take place around targets and resource allocation that are responsible for driving bias into forecast processes. The distortion introduced by conventional performance management practice into forecasting behavior could be manifest in systematic overforecasting (positive bias) or underforecasting (negative bias). For example:

Factors driving positive bias (systematic overforecasting):
- If a revenue forecast in line with or exceeding a target is treated as 'good performance'.
- If a revenue forecast below the target is treated as 'bad performance'.

- If more resources are allocated to those that overstate their resource requirements.
- If resources are reduced as a result of revenue forecasts being below target.
- If resource budgets for year 2 are based on resource forecasts in year 1.
- If priority in allocating a scarce resource (say stock or production capacity) is driven by a revenue forecast.

Factors driving negative bias (systematic underforecasting):
- If revenue targets in year 2 are based on performance in year 1 (particularly if financial incentives are involved).
- If an increase in a revenue forecast is treated as 'good performance'.
- If a reduction in a revenue forecast is treated as 'bad performance'.

It is clear from this analysis that many of the behaviors regarded as being 'positive' in the context of budgeting introduce bias into forecasts. Dealing with the tension between budgeting behavior and effective forecasting practice is a theme we will return to later.

These are obvious examples, but motivational bias can infect the forecast process in far more subtle ways. For example, because of our training or a personal investment in the business or an endeavor we might want to attribute a shortfall in sales to the weather rather than to distribution failures. As a sales person, we might have a motivational bias to see every issue as a sales issue, which can be solved through investment in customers rather than perhaps being a quality issue that can't. If we have made a heavy investment in a project either financially or emotionally, we might be reluctant to acknowledge the results are not what we would like them to be. Everybody gives more credence to facts that confirm their prejudices or legitimize their desires.

In addition systematic bias can be introduced when managers perceive that the *motivation of other people* might be affected by the forecast. For example, there may be a fear that if a forecast is in excess of a target people will stop trying, or that if it is too far below people will give up.

There is little doubt that motivational bias is the biggest problem with judgmental forecasts, and probably business forecasting as a whole, since so much personal and financial capital often hangs on forecast outcomes. *This tendency to bias is deep-rooted, and can persist even when its existence is acknowledged.* One reason for this is that *many performance management practices promote systematically biased behavior.*

Bias is particularly pernicious because it can change suddenly and without warning
One of the most common challenges to the promotion of the ideal of 'unbiased forecasts' comes from those who believe that it is easy to detect bias (though this is

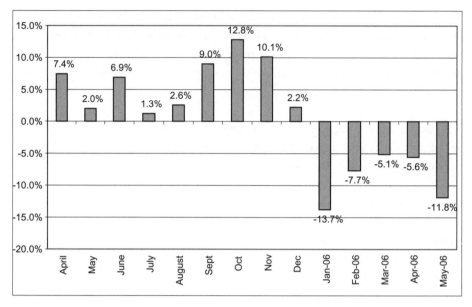

Figure 4.3 A run chart.
An example to demonstrate how bias can change unpredictably. The shift in bias may be associated with motivational bias which has 'changed polarity' due to a change in target at year end.

a form of reasoning bias – misplaced confidence) and therefore right for them to adjust for it.[11] Even if it were true that people were good at spotting bias, which we doubt, the strategy of 'adjusting for it' only works if patterns of bias are consistent.

In practice, however, patterns of bias can change quickly and unpredictably (see Figure 4.3). For instance, patterns often flip when people in key roles change, or because of the time of year. They also often change around period ends and budgeting and target setting cycles, since these are significant events in the process of judging and rewarding performance. Ill advised attempts to compensate for bias, coupled with the tendency for the polarity of bias to suddenly switch can have disastrous consequences. For example, you may consistently add 4% to forecasts to compensate for negative bias only to find that the next set of forecasts flip to being, say 6%, too high for reasons that you could not have foreseen. Instead of your forecast being pessimistic to the tune of 4% (if you had not chosen to adjust) it is now 10% too high. How many profit warnings have their origin in this kind of behavior?

Judgment will always be part of forecasting in business; so forecasting in business will always run the risk of bias. Because we cannot change the way our brains are wired up, we have to design forecast processes with built in safeguards, checks and balances so that they are less prone to infection by bias. We will return to this subject later in the 'Mastering Measurement' and 'Mastering Process' chapters.

Mathematical models

The second type of forecast model is the mathematical model.

Simple mathematical models are used in virtually every forecasting process

We use simple mathematical models everywhere. For instance, most businesses forecast volume and price separately in order to generate a forecast of revenue. They may well forecast different elements of price separately (list price, discounts, rebates and so on) to reflect the fact that not all elements of price vary proportionately with volume. Structuring forecast models in this way has obvious benefits for decision-making (steering) purposes since different elements of price represent different 'levers' that can be pulled to affect future outcomes. Most businesses who produce physical goods will use a mathematical forecasting model based on the standard 'bill of material' and anticipated raw material prices to forecast direct costs (see Figure 4.4).

Until recently businesses exclusively used judgmental methods to forecast so-called 'fixed costs' but the advent of activity-based costing techniques has led to an increasing interest in mathematical modeling in this area. This is usually described as 'activity' or 'driver'-based forecasting and is based on the assumption that there are reliable mathematical relationships between, for example, the level of business, the type of activity associated with the business, the amount of time needed and

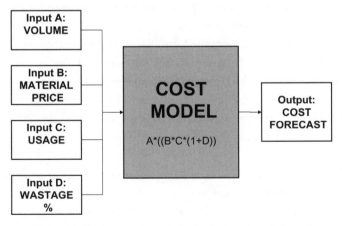

Figure 4.4 Product costs: an example of a simple mathematical model.

the number and cost of people employed. Many businesses also use sophisticated mathematical modeling to forecast volume,[12] perhaps factoring in the effect of weather on the size of the market or advertising on market share.

Example

Driver-based models at AMEX

The introduction of driver-based models was a key element in the Planning Transformation at AMEX. Whereas before, the Corporate Office team was faced with the task of collecting and consolidating thousands of spreadsheets, they now have a web-based system that requires no more than eleven models. 'We already knew from our experience after 9/11 that it was possible to produce forecasts with models, it didn't need to be a "bottoms up" exercise,' says Jamie Croake. 'Then we used the back of an envelope, but now we had a central team and they went to each of the business units and asked them to tell us what they would do if they had to forecast every line in their Profit and Loss account with a driver and an algorithm. Now, having implemented them in our tool, it not only gives us a more streamlined process, it also gives us more confidence in them because the models have been standardized. Before, people could build forecasts in whatever way they wanted' (Croake, 2008).

Mathematical models address some of the weaknesses of judgmental forecasts: first, they are free from motivational bias

A mathematical model is not immune from bias, for example the impact of volume on costs in a business could be systematically misestimated. But once bias has been detected it can be corrected by changing the parameters of (or inputs to) the model. This process of improving the model in this way – so that it better fits reality – is a process of *learning*; and because mathematical models use explicit assumptions and procedures this process of learning is relatively easy.[13]

Second, reforecasting is quick and easy – and because patterns of causality are explicit there is a clear link to action

Another benefit is that, once a mathematical model has been set up, it is quick and easy to generate forecasts. A mathematical model can often be designed to forecast nonfinancial as well as financial metrics. The process of constructing a mathematical model can also help to expose good 'lead indicators' – those features of, or inputs into, a model that have a strong causal link to important output variables – which can be incorporated in the routine performance measurement process.

 Example

Systems dynamic models at Symbios Inc.
Another example of mathematical modeling is the use of Systems Dynamic modeling in Symbios Inc., a supplier to the IT and telecoms industry. They found that statistical, judgmental techniques and simple driver models failed to cope with the turbulence generated by the lead times characteristic of their industry. 'During revenue shortfalls we'd beat up the marketing and sales groups and get some more design wins to fill the revenue hole next quarter. Of course, this never worked because of the long delays and probably caused more instability. The model (we now use) helps people understand the dynamics, stabilizing the business, increasing the efficiency of the organization and boosting growth' (Sterman, 2000).

However, mathematical models can be complex and time consuming to build ...
On the other hand, the process of constructing a mathematical model can be very time consuming and costly, not least because specialist software may be required. In addition, models can quickly get very complex, which not only means that the model is difficult and time consuming to construct and validate, but it may be difficult to make sense of.[14] In these circumstances it may be difficult to decide what action to take. In addition, a process producing confusing or counterintuitive results is unlikely to command the confidence and commitment of users.

... and they do not cope well with novelty and change
The other major drawback of mathematical models is that modern businesses change frequently and this high 'maintenance overhead' can lead to models falling into disrepute or disrepair. Also, by their very nature mathematical models cannot cope with novelty – you can only rely on those models which have been validated

against the historical record and it is only worthwhile doing so if the phenomena being modeled persist or recur in the future.

Statistical models

Given a reasonable amount of historical data, we can use the third type of model: a statistical model. Statistical models employ extrapolation techniques to generate forecasts.

Simple statistical models are widely used and often outperform more complex ones

The term 'statistical' can scare people, but statistical models can be very simple and easy to understand. For instance if, say, overheads have been constant at around 8% of revenue for some time, then it might be reasonable to use this to forecast costs. Also, as we have already mentioned, simple techniques often out-perform more complex ones (Armstrong, 2003).[15] There is a huge array of clever software programs available now and those forecasters with enough knowledge to be overconfident in their own ability can fall into the trap of overcomplicating statistical forecasting. As forecasting guru J. Scott Armstrong says: 'it is your choice: you can learn the fox trot or you can learn to tap dance in scuba gear' (Armstrong, 1985).

 More

Where to look for more information about models and modeling

Many of the 25 000 books on business forecasting in Amazon's catalogue that we referred to earlier are treatises on statistical forecasting. Despite the amount of shelf space given over to the genre, statistical approaches are often not well understood or widely used in business. Perhaps this is because of the amount of advice available, and the complexity of some of the approaches offered, which can be overwhelming. We suspect most readers will be thankful that we will not be attempting to provide guidance on statistical forecasting techniques here. Instead, we highly recommend the Wharton University website 'Principles of Forecasting' as a resource for those needing to delve into this topic in more detail (Various, 2009).

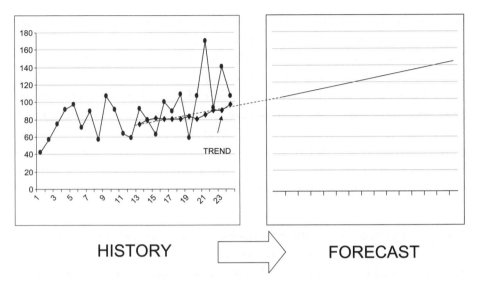

Figure 4.5 A simple statistical model.
This example shows a simple linear extrapolation from a time series.

Statistical routines are often the only way we can forecast complex patterns of behavior

There are, however, many applications where the use of sophisticated models is rewarding. For example, they are commonly used to forecast sales of high volume products and services. There are a large number of software products on the market that apply a range of complex algorithms to historical data in order to predict sales and such techniques can achieve high levels of reliability. In addition, like mathematical models, once built, statistical models can be run quickly and at low cost. They are also (almost completely) free from motivational bias and, if based on recent history, can adapt to changes in the behavior of the system (see Figure 4.5). Furthermore, they are usually easier to construct than mathematical models since you are only looking for the existence of patterns in data that repeat themselves; you are not trying to understand *why* they recur.[16]

Statistical techniques can be dangerous in the hands of the ignorant, and the quality of data that is required for their use may not be available

A significant drawback, however, is that statistical modeling often requires a good deal of skill. Sophisticated software tools may be required to carry out the analysis and a high degree of technical competence is needed to ensure that these tools are applied in the right way for valid statistical inferences to be drawn. Clever tools in the wrong hands can be dangerous. It is easy for an unskilled practitioner to produce credible looking results which are in fact spurious.

Part of the skill required of modelers involves making judgments about whether the available input data is of sufficient quality. In business it is often deficient. Academics typically demand at least 36 pieces of data before they have enough confidence to extrapolate. Many businesses would find it difficult to source this much data at all, and what is available is often 'corrupted' by restructuring, restatement, variable accounting periods and other such phenomena. In practice this often mean historic data has to be 'cleaned' up to remove or adjust for all potentially misleading data, a laborious process which often requires extensive use of judgment.

The major drawbacks with statistical modeling are that they are a poor guide to action and they also cannot cope with novelty

In addition, statistical modeling is a 'black box' technique. Because we are seeking to establish relationships, not to explain causality, it is often not possible to explain the results derived from a statistical model. This may make it difficult to determine what action to take, and as with complex mathematical models, a lack of understanding or the existence of confusing or counterintuitive results can undermine confidence in and commitment to the forecasting process.

Finally, statistical models also cannot cope with novelty or change. By definition they are based on the assumption that 'tomorrow will be like today'; they forecast trends, they cannot forecast discontinuities. Since discontinuities are a common feature of economic systems, not least when they are the result of management action *in response to* forecasts, this restricts their use in business forecasting. They also cannot assimilate domain knowledge – useful insights about the situation from managers and analysts.

The conclusion: there is no 'silver bullet', the choice of model requires the exercise of judgment

It is clear that there are a range of techniques that can be used to produce a forecast. Each approach has strengths and weaknesses. What they have in common is that none of them will produce 'perfect' forecasts – there is no 'silver bullet'. However, some will be better than others depending on the context in which they are used.

How do we decide what kind of technique to use and when? Are there guidelines to help people choose the right approach to adopt in a particular set of circumstances? We think there are.

GUIDELINES FOR MODEL CHOICE

In choosing a suitable modeling approach, the starting point has to be an appreciation of the strengths and weaknesses of the various approaches

Judgmental forecasting works well in circumstances where what is being forecast is either very simple or well understood, so more sophisticated models are unnecessary, or when circumstances are so novel or complex that mathematical or statistical modeling cannot cope.

Mathematical models work best when the situation is well structured and repetitive or where it is important to properly understand the mechanics of the process for the purposes of steering.

Statistical models work best where there is adequate historical data and the causal structure of the system is either not understood or it is not necessary to understand it – having a good 'result' is all that matters.

What further guidance can we give?[17] Again the navigator on board our super tanker will come to our aid.

Often we will use different models for forecasting 'momentum' and 'interventions'

For the captain of the super tanker the purpose of a forecast is to help him or her to make a decision about whether to change course and speed. The navigator will probably start the forecast process by taking into account the effect of momentum, which is huge because of the size of a super tanker. The momentum of the vessel is the delayed result of decisions taken in the past, and if the captain does not choose to do anything different, the momentum of the super tanker will determine where it ends up.

We can observe similar phenomena in business. In a mature business, a large percentage of the sales volume may be driven by well established patterns of customer behavior. Decisions about investment in buildings, machinery or organization made years ago, and which cannot or will not be changed frequently, may be the primary determinant of the organization's cost structure. 'Looking at the trend is always the base line for understanding forecasts,' says Artur Magolewski, of Unilever Poland, 'and Moving Annual Totals is a good tool for doing this' (Morlidge, 2005). On the other hand, in new businesses or highly dynamic marketplaces, perhaps very little about the future structure of revenues and costs can be safely inferred from what went on in the past.

Having established the impact of 'momentum' the navigator needs to work out the impact of planned decisions on the direction or speed of the craft. Let us call these planned changes 'interventions'. In business, intervening is what managers do, and in the last chapter we explored how interventions – decision-making – affected the forecasting process. Interventions may just hit the top line of the business – for instance when we offer an extra discount to sell more product – or they could just affect the cost base of the business – such as a training initiative or restructuring an organization. Often however an intervention affects multiple lines of the Income Statement or the Balance Sheet. For example, the launch of a new product will obviously have revenue and cost implications, but may also involve significant investments in advertising, machinery, stocks and so on. Some interventions may be similar to those that have been made in the past. Often, however, they will differ, perhaps only because the context – the state of the market, competitors' activities and so on – has changed.

It is clear that these two components of a forecast – momentum and interventions – differ significantly. We therefore advocate using different forecasting approaches for each.

Example

Forecasting momentum and interventions at Unilever
Unilever's Canadian business has adopted a novel approach which has proved to be very successful. Momentum and interventions that have already been committed are managed through a streamlined, highly automated process that runs without any need for management. Instead, management focuses their attention on uncommitted interventions. As a result the business now runs a process with a rolling 18-month rather than a fixed annual horizon, but using a third of the time and resource.

Mathematical or statistical models are most often used for momentum forecasting
Since momentum is the result of historical acts, our purpose of decision-making does not require that the momentum forecast be actionable. We do not need to forecast it in any more detail than is necessary to provide a prediction of the outcome that is reasonably accurate (and timely, aligned and cost effective). Since forecasts are often more reliable if they are less detailed, high level statistical models are well suited to momentum forecasting. If 'momentum' is the product of the interaction

of a number of factors which vary independently, however, it might be necessary to build a number of more detailed statistical models. If the system is well understood and stable, then mathematical modeling may be preferred.

 More

How to choose the right level at which to forecast
In an ideal world we would use a high level statistical model to forecast momentum, but this may not be possible. For example momentum may be a product of multiple variables whose patterns of behavior are weakly correlated; overhead costs might be driven by inflation, volume or cost efficiency improvements – all of which might be trending in different directions at different rates. In this case a high level statistical model is unlikely to yield good results. Another good example is working capital; stocks tend to be driven in part by sales volume, debtors wholly by sales revenue and creditors by total (i.e. product and non product) cost, so in this case a mathematical model would probably be the best option. Choosing the right level of aggregation for momentum forecasting is a matter of judgment. Use common sense based on your understanding of the drivers of momentum business but only disaggregate momentum forecasts further when the results are not fit for the purpose – making good decisions. But beware of falling into the accountant's trap of disaggregating forecasts purely in order to make someone 'accountable' for every element of the forecast.

The general rule for momentum forecasting is: do the minimum amount of work necessary to generate a forecast that is 'accurate enough'.

What about forecasting interventions?

Since interventions are more likely to be 'novel', judgmental forecasting is often the most appropriate approach
What do we know about interventions and what are the consequences for the choice of a forecasting model?

First, most interventions are the result of a decision to change course. As a result, we want to know if we commit to a particular intervention what the outcome will be. Will it result in an outcome that is consistent with our goal or do we need to amend it, supplement it or do something completely different? So, the incremental impact of the intervention needs to be made explicit. In the competitive world of business, it is unlikely that any two interventions will be exactly the same. If the structures of the interventions are similar, the business context may be different, so a different outcome should be expected.

These qualities mean that, as a rule, forecasting interventions is more likely to involve the use of judgmental techniques. In effect forecasting the impact of an activity is like preparing a business case: if I do A I anticipate that the outcome will be B.

 Example

Learning how to make more effective interventions at Unilever Poland
While every intervention is unique, in most businesses a significant proportion of interventions will be similar enough to ones that have been used before for things learned from the one intervention to be applied to another. The best organizations find ways to share experiences, perhaps by keeping a 'library' of the results of previous interventions, and they use these to extract learnings – 'what worked and what did not and why'. In this way not only will forecasting improve; so will performance.

In Unilever's Polish Foods business, an 'after the event' evaluation of all interventions is part of the formal activity approval process. In addition, business unit heads are encouraged to share their experiences with their peers informally every quarter. 'We review what went well and what went wrong. By listening to the experience of others we can improve the quality of our activities, which everyone benefits from because this grows the top line and creates more money for investment,' says Monica Rut, Brand Team Leader (Morlidge, 2005).

The second quality of activities is that they have a life cycle; they all pass from ideas to feasibility, then planning to commitment, and finally to execution.

A major issue with forecasting interventions is that our knowledge of detail 'decays'
towards the end of the forecast horizon
We learned in the last chapter that a consequence of decisions having a life cycle is that you can experience 'forecast decay' – the deterioration in the quality of forecasts

towards the end of the horizon as a result of the deterioration in our knowledge about interventions. By definition, we have facts about those interventions that are in the process of being executed. We also know what we have committed to, and what the incremental impact is likely to be. Interventions in the planning stage will usually lead to a commitment (or at least we have to assume that they will). Projects in the feasibility and ideas stages may not happen at all, and if they do we can only speculate what they will look like and what impact they will have.

Clearly, it is straightforward to make sound judgmental forecast assumptions for projects in the planning, commitment and execution stages. But what should we do with projects in feasibility and ideas? There are three options.

We can accept 'forecast decay' ...

The first approach is to exclude them from the forecast altogether. Since one can only make guesses about the impact of such interventions, arguably it is wrong to contaminate the decision-making processes with the result of speculation, particularly if it concerns high impact, long lead time projects like innovations. If one of the purposes of forecasting is to prime the innovation process, it is important to be able to distinguish between the absence of projects and the absence of information about projects. On the other hand, failure to make any assumptions can mislead decision-makers. For instance the feasibility and ideas stages of short lead time projects may impact the medium rather than long term forecast horizon, thus making the consolidated forecast difficult to interpret.

... another approach is to 'fill in the gap' in our knowledge based on an assessment of probable outcomes ...

If you decide to include an estimate of the impact of early life cycle interventions in the forecast, there are two ways of doing it. First, it may be possible to make some assumptions about the likely impact and probability of success based on previous experience. Therefore, for example, you might discover that only 50% of projects in feasibility ever see the light of day and that on average they only deliver 30% of the revenue growth first envisioned. Armed with this knowledge you can make some reasonably robust assumptions based on the current state of the early stages of the funnel.

... or by using a mathematical or statistical model

The second approach is to model the rate at which projects will flow into the planning stage. This works well if the historic record shows that they follow a predictable pattern, perhaps because the interventions concerned are numerous and repetitive in nature. For major, completely novel, interventions such as new product innovation, it is probably unwise to make sweeping assumptions in this way.

There is extensive literature on modeling techniques, so in this chapter we have focused on giving guidance on how to choose the right model and how to overcome practical problems managers might face in implementing their choice. Before we leave the topic there are two more problems worth discussing.

Problem: How do we decide what to treat as 'interventions' for the purposes of forecasting?

Every day in every business managers make decisions. Many will involve making changes to existing plans and each of these could be treated as an intervention for the purposes of forecasting. An obvious merit of this approach is that each intervention is treated (quite correctly) as an investment rather than a cost; the accountant's distinction between capital and revenue has led to an unhealthy focus of attention on those expenditures that happen to end up on the balance sheet to the detriment of those that do not. For example, a company like Unilever will typically invest 10 times as much on advertising and promotion as on capital, but only the latter will appear on the balance sheet. AMEX calculates that as much as 25–35% of their operating expenses are discretionary in nature.

On the other hand, by treating every decision as an intervention it is easy to overwhelm the forecast process with detail – in large enterprises there may be thousands of projects active at any one time. Management is unlikely to have the detailed knowledge to make considered judgments about such a large number of projects, few of which will have a significant impact on the performance trajectory of the business. As a result we recommend you apply the 80:20 rule. The incremental impact of the projects that do not 'move the dial' should be treated as part of 'momentum': business as usual.[18]

Wherever the line between momentum and intervention is drawn it is important to ensure that the assumptions that are made are consistent. If, for instance, interventions made in the past have had a 'one off' impact, then that impact will have to be stripped out of the historical record used for the statistical modeling of momentum (see Figure 4.6). If this is not done you would be double counting the impact of initiatives.[19]

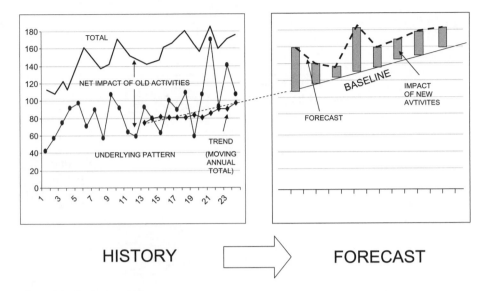

HISTORY ⟹ FORECAST

Figure 4.6 Combining models.
This example demonstrates the use of two different types of models to produce a combined 'momentum plus interventions' forecast. Here the impact which interventions made in the past has been excluded before extrapolating a trend statistically to produce a momentum forecast. This is supplemented by a judgmental forecast of the incremental impact of interventions to produce a combined forecast.

Problem: wearing blinders. Solution: capture interdependencies between entities and over time

The traditional approach to forecasting often involves dealing with different line items independently and can result in errors and inconsistencies in forecasting. Most interventions affect more than one line item in the income statement; so when one value changes the others should be changed as well. For example, a shortfall in profit might result in a decision to cut investment. This will have a delayed impact elsewhere (on volume or revenue) but this is frequently ignored. This is bad forecasting but it is also bad decision-making.

Another common mistake is to ignore substitution effects. An intervention will frequently generate a positive result in one part of the business but will have a negative impact on another. For example, a new product may gain market share from competitors but also from other parts of the business's own portfolio.

In addition, particularly when the forecast horizon stops at an accounting period end or the focus is purely on the period end position, lagged effects are often overlooked. Therefore, the positive profit impact of delaying a project is taken into

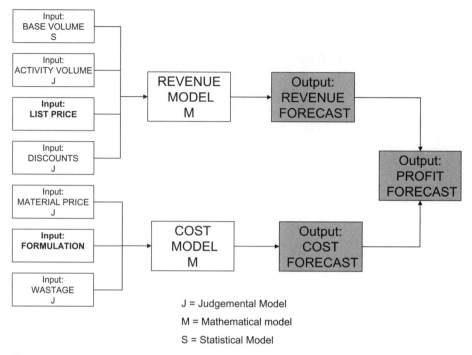

Figure 4.7 A forecasting system.
Showing how, in practice, judgmental, mathematical, and statistical models are used in combination.

account in the current period but not the negative impact on revenues or profit in future periods.

It is important, therefore, that forecasts take into account the full incremental time phased impact, on all line items and net of substitution effects.

We have described the type of models that you can use for forecasting and how to go about making choices as to which type to use and in what situations. Many forecasting authorities advocate one particular approach. In our view, for the reasons we have described, all but the most simple forecast processes will require all three kinds of models in combination (see Figure 4.7).

In particular, we believe the use of judgment is unavoidable. Judgment is the most straightforward approach to forecasting in many situations but also the only way to estimate the impact of novelty. It is also the most practical approach to apply to a transient situation where you do not have the time, resource or competence to use other techniques. In addition, even apparently straightforward mathematical models (for example those used to estimate product costs), are fed by assumptions that are themselves an output of a judgmental process (e.g. the estimate of the price of a raw material). Neither is statistical forecasting judgment free. The choice of extrapolation technique and the data used to feed it is ultimately a matter of judgment, as is the decision to recognize a discontinuity.

The fact that the process of business forecasting is steeped in human judgment is the reason why *managers cannot treat forecasting as a technical process best 'left to the experts'*. They have to be involved. It is also vitally important that the shortcomings of judgment, in particular the tendency to bias, are recognized and steps taken to deal with them. This makes proper measurement practices, the subject of the next chapter, and a key requirement for effective forecasting.

• • • • •

We hope that this chapter has helped dispel much of the mystique that surrounds forecast modeling, and that readers now have the confidence to participate in, or at least challenge, the process. If, in the past, the difficulty and importance of modeling has been exaggerated, the subject of the next chapter has been scandalously neglected. For most businesses, improving (or even instituting) measurement practices is the single most important thing that could be done to enhance forecasting quality. Furthermore, it is probably the quickest and easiest change to make. As with modeling, it is possible to blind the layman with science, but the basic principles are simple and easy to understand, as you must if you are to produce or interpret forecasts in a professional way. A little effort on this chapter will be amply rewarded. After the next chapter, there is only one more topic before you can claim to have mastered the basic forecasting skills, so 'hang on in there'.

• • • • •

SUMMARY

Any kind of forecast involves the use of models set within a process. A model is a simplified representation of the world; how we think that external events and our planned responses to them (the inputs into the process), will affect our business (the output). This model can be an explicit mathematical representation of reality, a statistical extrapolation from past events or it might be an implicit model 'in our head' – in which case we call it 'judgment'. Each kind of model has its particular strengths and weaknesses that need to be borne in mind when deciding which kind of model to use. In practice a forecast process will usually use all three types in combination. Often you will want to distinguish between the forecasting of trends (to which statistical and mathematical models are well suited) and discontinuities, perhaps arising from the result of management interventions. Exercising judgment is often the only way we can satisfactorily forecast discontinuities, particularly when they involve novelty. We therefore need to be on our guard for forecast bias that is the bane of judgmental forecasting, especially since those making the judgment might not be disinterested in the outcome of the forecast: in other words, forecasts will be susceptible to motivational bias.

KEY LEARNING POINTS

Types of forecasting model
- Statistical – extrapolation based on fitting trends to historical patterns.
- Mathematical – an explicit representation of relevant parts of the business.
- Judgmental – generated by individuals with relevant experience or knowledge.

Components of a forecast
- Momentum – underlying trends unlikely to be affected in the short term by decisions made in response to a forecast outcome.
- Interventions – the results of decisions made in response to a forecast outcome.

Weaknesses with forecast models which affect the choice of approach
- Systematic bias resulting from failure to react to evidence of bias (all types of model).
- Behavioral bias (judgmental forecasting only), either:
  - Cognitive – logical defects in reasoning
  - Social – the tendency to conform
  - Motivational – responding to perceived rewards or punishment for certain types of forecast outcome.
- Costs of building and maintaining models (mathematical and statistical).
- Costs of operating models (judgmental especially).
- Coping with novelty (mathematical and statistical).

NOTES

1 Climatologists modeling the effects of global warming fear that the gradual build up of carbon dioxide in the atmosphere will lead to a nonlinear driven discontinuity. There are many examples in the history of the earth; for example, ice ages do not come and go gradually – it tends to be (in geological terms) rather sudden. After the last ice age in Europe, the North Sea advanced at a rate of 100 meters every year, quickly drowning what had been fertile hunting grounds for our Neolithic ancestors.

2 The reason why we can learn catching so easily is that we have the ability to track moving objects hardwired into our DNA, probably because evolution has selected for organisms that are good at avoiding predators or catching prey.

3 Heuristics are not just a feature of the human brain. Commercial computer programs often use 'fast and frugal' heuristics to identify computer viruses.

4 It is now generally accepted that, while the natural world is made up of nonlinear systems, it is configured in such a way that the global system is relatively stable over geological time, and therefore conducive to life. This is the kernel of James Lovelock's Gaia hypothesis (Lovelock, 1979). Economic systems are also self-regulating to a degree, although as we have recently experienced, they can become highly unstable and unpredictable once certain thresholds are breached.

5 In fact there is good scientific evidence to suggest that many decisions might be made 'emotionally' – i.e. subconsciously – *first* and rationalized afterwards. We might *think* we have made a decision but in fact we have only justified one that our brain has made without consulting us (Dennett, 1991)

6 Gerd Gigerenzer is a powerful advocate of 'gut instinct' (see the book of the same name (2008)). Our stance is pragmatic. The use of judgment is unavoidable, so we should use it where it works and use other methods when it does not. Wherever judgmental techniques are used, we should take steps to minimize the risk of bias – most importantly through the application of rigorous measurement (see Chapter 5).

7 Non rational decision-making is a very lively area of academic enquiry, largely stimulated by the work of Kahneman and Tversky for which Kahneman received the Nobel Prize for economics in 2002 (Tversky having predeceased him). It has also spawned new sub-disciplines: 'Behavioral Finance' and 'Behavioral Economics'.

8 The correct answer is six.

9 Kennedy learned from the Bays of Pigs debacle. During the Cuban missile crisis, he took a number of steps to avoid making the same mistakes again. They included encouraging external experts to present to his advisors, encouraging them to discuss possible alternative courses of action with their teams, setting up subgroups and even removing himself from meetings altogether so as not to bias their deliberations.

10 There are other methods of structuring expert contributions advocated by forecasting authorities, but they all share the same weakness – they tend to be complex and slow and so are not suited to the forecasting of many variables at speed.

11 Adjusting a forecast might involve changing the output of a mathematical or statistical model, thereby injecting judgmental bias into processes that would otherwise not suffer from it. It is not a new phenomenon. Alfred Sloan wrote the following to his general managers in 1927: 'My attention has been called to a tendency which seems to be developing which I do not think is based on either sound accounting or sound reasoning. I am referring to the fact that some Divisions, after the forecasts have been developed by their Accounting Department … arbitrarily alter certain of their figures in order to have

a cushion ... (and this practice) is not sound accounting and serves to invalidate the whole process that has contributed so much to our welfare' (Axson, 2003). According to Hackett, forecast numbers are routinely adjusted in 72% of businesses (Hackett, 2008).

12 Econometric modeling is a form of sophisticated mathematical modeling. It involves searching for correlations between variables in the historic record. Another involves the use of Neural Networks.

13 It is standard practice to test mathematical and statistical models by 'back casting' – running the model using historic variables and assumptions to test whether the model successfully 'predicts' history – that is results that have already occurred.

14 For example, in our experience, activity based costing models can be very difficult to interpret.

15 It is, however, unwise to adopt any modeling technique without some form of statistical validation to establish that whichever technique you use is capable of coming up with 'good enough' results. Sometimes simple models *are* simplistic.

16 Examples of statistical techniques include simple moving averages, trends, exponential smoothing, decomposition and Box Jenkins analysis.

17 The Principles of Forecasting website contains a selection tree which gives detailed guidance on model choice. It also points users at relevant academic research, software and consultants. Often empirical evidence conflicts with commonly held beliefs about methodologies (Various, 2009).

18 This does not mean that they should be excluded from the 'funnel' – it might make sense to make sure that all discretionary activity is formally justified in some way. In addition, even if the impact of interventions is not modeled it might make sense to ensure that the cost is explicitly included in the forecast rather than assumed in a high level momentum forecast.

19 This might be the cause of the so-called 'hockey stick' effect common in long range planning.

Chapter 5

MASTERING MEASUREMENT – learning to love error

6 The best measure of a man's honesty isn't his income tax return. It's the zero adjust on his bathroom scale. 9 Arthur C. Clarke

6 You cannot measure a man by his failures. You must know what use he makes of them. 9 Orison Swett Marden

> *Why models will never produce a good forecast without help – the role played by measurement – what to measure – when to measure – why averages and other KPIs do not work – run charts – how to decide when there is a problem – and what kind of problem it is – the cause of problems – how to improve your forecast*

In the last chapter, we described how we used models to help us catch a ball. How we use models to create a picture of the future state of the world to inform our action. But, however good our model, it is never enough. What is missing?

Do this:

Draw a dot on a piece of paper like so (see Figure 5.1) (if you don't have a piece of paper handy you might want to use the the dot we have drawn for you!):

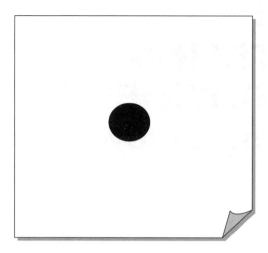

Figure 5.1 A dot on a piece of paper.

Put the piece of paper on a table in front of you. Now close your eyes and place your index finger on the dot.

How close did you get?

Usually when we do this, we find that we miss the dot, often by many inches. Why?

Obviously, the reason we failed is that we could not see what we were doing. An unremarkable observation you might think. But think again.

A continuous stream of feedback is crucial to the successful accomplishment of even the simplest task

What this demonstrates is that to successfully perform even the most simple, most trivial act, we need information about how we are doing, compared to our goal, in real time.[1] Knowing about the position of the dot a few seconds ago and how, in principle, to go about putting your finger on it is not enough; in other words *having a good model is not enough.*

In fact, when with eyes open we successfully put our finger on the dot, we are not so much putting our finger on the dot as we are avoiding *not* putting our finger on the dot. When we catch a ball we are really avoiding not catching the ball, albeit aided by a model that means that we run roughly in the right direction. *However good our model, it does not guarantee success. It simply helps reduce the chance of failure.*

More

How the past improves our understanding of the future

We are now dealing with two kinds of information about the world. Our model of ball catching, which is (without our knowledge) based on Newton's Law of Motion, provides us with information about the potential future state of the world. We call this *feedforward* information. In real life, even very good models (like Newton's Laws) will always be wrong; you can never allow for every source of interference. It therefore has to be given some assistance in the form of additional information. In the case of a catcher the information takes the form of knowledge about where the ball actually is – which is then compared to the estimate our model gave us. Based on this comparison we make compensating moves.

When we watch a catcher under a high ball we see this process in action. We do not see her move purposefully to one position, open her hands and wait motionless for the ball to arrive. Instead we witness a succession of moves and adjustments each of which represents a response to new information. The name given to this new information – about the actual position of the ball – is *feedback*. For any kind of forecast system to be reliable *feedback information is needed to correct for the inevitable inaccuracy of feedforward information*. Control system engineers call this kind of system 'error controlled'. The 'smart bombs' used in the Iraq War are only smart because they are good at correcting their mistakes!

Why go on about this? What this tells us is that *we stand very little chance of forecasting successfully unless we measure our performance continuously and correct our forecasts accordingly.* Compared to putting your finger on a dot or even catching a ball, business forecasting is astronomically more complicated. So, you might think, our measurement processes need to be correspondingly more sophisticated. Yet we find that *very few businesses routinely measure the quality of their forecast process with the rigor needed to guarantee acceptable forecasting performance.*

This is why, in our view, *the failure to 'close the feedback loop' is the single most important reason why business forecasting is so poor.*

Feedback corrects our models but it helps us to improve them. Without good
feedback information learning is not possible

One of the consequences of failing to measure forecasting is that we will fail to
perform tasks reliably; tasks like catching a ball or meeting business goals. There is
another, arguably more serious, consequence.

Consider again the role that feedback plays in helping us to reliably catch a ball.
First, feedback enables the catcher to identify the difference between the forecast
and actual position of the ball and so adjust her position in real time. She uses
feedback to help her avoid not catching the ball. But she is using the same feedback
for a second purpose: to improve her skill at catching in general. She is using feedback to improve the model that generated the forecast of the ball's position in the
first place. Consistent systematic errors (bias or variation) indicate inefficiencies in
the catching model which she improves by trial and error (that is practice). *The
process of improving a model in this way is termed 'learning' and the behavior associated
with the ability to learn successfully, 'adaptive'.* If we have no information about error
we are unable to learn, and organisms that fail to learn will ultimately perish.

 More

Two different types of learning
In fact the act of measurement helps creates the model in the first place. We have
no 'Laws of Motion' that we can use to build a 'raw model' that we can refine by
factoring in the effect of gravity, friction and so on. We start with nothing other
than a 'common sense' view of the world; a crude heuristic that we develop and
calibrate collecting and processing feedback. Over time we build a catching
model; often one that works better than the one built by a physicist with a computer! If you do not believe us, watch a toddler building its models of the world.

So, our catcher is continuously reforecasting based on feedback information
that she uses to adjust her model of the world. The better her feedforward model
(that is the more expert she is as a catcher), the lower the errors from the feedback
process and the less movement we will see as she waits for the ball to arrive.

In their 1978 book *Organizational learning: A theory of action perspective*
(Argyris and Schon, 1978), Chris Argyris and Douglas Schon called the first type

of learning – which involves correcting the model – single loop learning. The second – which involves improving the model – is termed 'double loop learning'. Sometimes these are referred to as 'first order' and 'second order' learning.

Peter Senge's book *The Fifth Discipline* (Senge, 1990) takes this concept to the next level: organizational learning. Our book helps to stimulate organizational learning of forecasting. The six principles of 'Mastering Forecasting' are a good point of departure, but the only way for your organization to become skilful is, using our 'model' as a starting point, to try something, observe the results and adjust or adapt accordingly.[2]

We need to build rigorous measurement into our forecasting processes

Part of the reason for the failure of businesses to measure forecast performance at all is confirmation bias: the tendency of human beings to avoid information that challenges our received theories of the world. One of our most treasured theories involves a misplaced sense of confidence in our own ability to predict the future. We therefore cannot assume that people will 'use their common sense' and measure their processes; we have to build rigorous measurement practices into our forecasting routines. That might sound easy but measuring forecast performance is not as straightforward as you might imagine.

To understand this, and what we need to do as a result, let us dive into a little more detail.

WHAT TO MEASURE

Most attempts to measure forecast performance are flawed

On the face of it the act of measurement sounds simple. Since our objective is to produce accurate (enough) forecasts, we just need to measure the difference between actual and forecast outcomes. Express that as a percentage and hey presto! You have the answer. A large error is bad and it signals the need to recalibrate or improve the forecast process. But if it is so straightforward, why do we assert that it is so rarely done well?

Let us go back to the example of our sailing boat (Figure 5.2).

As you will recall we made a plan but then got blown off course. Our navigator gives us a forecast: 'carry on like this and you will hit the rocks', and as a result we tack to port, miss the rocks and successfully arrive at our destination.

How do we measure his forecast performance?

Do we haul the navigator in front of us and berate him because his forecast ('we are going to hit the rocks') was wrong? Clearly not. On the other hand, do we

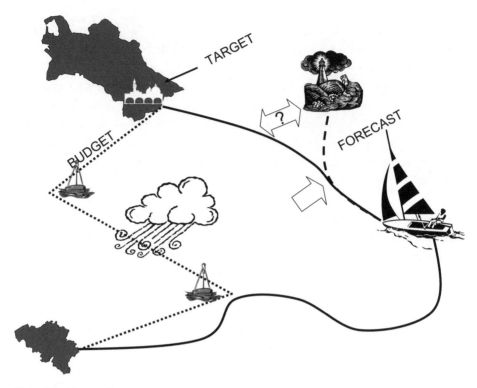

Figure 5.2 Measuring forecasts.

We can only measure forecast accuracy within the decision-making lead time. In this example, the fact that we have missed our forecast (which predicted a collision) is down to the decision we made to avoid the lighthouse, not the quality of the forecast. We should therefore measure the quality of the forecast before we started the maneuver (as indicated by the lower arrow), not after it was completed.

praise his skills as a navigator because we successfully arrived at the port? Not necessarily. And yet businesses commit this kind of error all the time. Errors are assumed to be evidence of poor forecasting, and success in 'delivering the numbers' is regarded as good forecasting.

We often fail to isolate measures of forecast quality from the impact of actions taken in response to the forecast

We can trace the source of the problem back to a failure to distinguish between the two types of forecasts we described in Chapter 2: the kind of forecasts we react to (weather forecast, short term sales forecasts) and the forecasts we use to make decisions that change the future. In the case of the former, the 'error' we measure is entirely due to the quality of the forecast. If a weather forecaster assures us that it is going to be hot and sunny and instead it pours with rain, it is clearly a failure of the meteorologist. He cannot claim that someone 'made it rain'. In the case of navigation or a business forecast however, since we set out to change the future, the 'error' may be due to the forecast *but it could also be due to the actions we took in response to the forecast.* Therefore, we missed the rocks because we took action to avoid them – we cannot blame the navigator. For the same reason the fact that we arrived at port may owe more to the skill and responsiveness of the helmsman and the crew than to the skill of the navigator. The forecast might have been really poor and the lives of the passengers saved by last minute evasive action. Since we cannot 'rewind the tape' of history we will never know. What implications does this have for measurement?

We can only confidently measure the quality of forecasts within decision-making lead times

This means that we can only reliably measure forecast error within decision-making lead times, that is, before any decisions we make in response to the forecast have had time to take effect. This will differ between businesses. In fast moving retailing businesses we might compare weekly forecasts and actuals. In a capital good business, we probably will not need to forecast sales at all in the short term because we *know* the outcome; we have the orders in hand. In this case, it might be more appropriate to look at errors over a three-month or longer horizon.

 More

Why measuring long run forecast accuracy is futile and what to do instead
You may be unconvinced by the approach we advocate here: measuring short run forecast error only. We are often challenged to find a way of measuring long term forecast quality. However, for the reasons outlined above, it is not possible to do this. Even if it were possible, it would be unnecessary and ineffective.

If you accept that you cannot forecast discontinuities (except perhaps those based on your own actions), then your forecast will be based on a trend. If this is the case short term error will be replicated in the longer term, just as when our watch loses time over the course of an hour we can assume that it will lose time over a week. Even if we could measure the quality of long term forecasts it would be too late to do anything about it. In the intervening time the forecast system or personnel may have changed, or patterns of bias flipped. We may also have made bad decisions based on poor forecasts.

While we cannot measure long term forecast quality, we can assess long term forecast *credibility*. Are there any breaks in the trend – if so can they be justified? Are there alternative ways of extrapolating past trends? What factors might lead to a discontinuity and how likely are they? All this and more will be covered in the next chapter: 'Mastering Risks'.

We often fail to compare 'like with like' when measuring forecast quality

Another common error in business is measuring the forecast error over inconsistent periods. For example, we often see businesses comparing the actual for Quarter 1 with forecasts made at the end of December, January and February. This approach is flawed since we are attempting to compare forecasts of three months, two months (plus one month actual) and one month (plus two months actual) respectively. Think of putting in golf. If you miss a 20-foot putt by four inches, is it better or worse than missing a five-foot putt by one inch? You should not attempt to compare the results from forecasts made using different time 'buckets' (as they are technically known). And there is no way we can compensate for the differences between them.

Neither can we compare a forecast for Quarter 4 made in January with a forecast for Quarter 4 made in June. Although we are using consistent time buckets the 'forecast lead times' (time lags between the forecast and the start of the period being forecast) differ. Since we have more information about the near term we should expect the forecast made closer in time to be more accurate.

So the general rule is to compare apples with apples. Measure forecast error within forecast lead times using consistent buckets and consistent forecast lead times.

WHEN TO MEASURE IT

How frequently should we measure forecasts? Here the simple rule is ... OFTEN!
Why?

The more often we forecast, the quicker we will be able to act to correct any problems with our process

The first, and most obvious, reason for frequent measurement is that any individual forecasts can be relied upon to be unreliable. There are many factors that can mess up forecasts and they change all the time. The environment can change, competitors may insist on acting unpredictably, our business might change or our people might start behaving differently. Any and all of these could happen at any moment and the sooner that you know about it the better chance you have of avoiding the rocks! You cannot afford to wait until year-end to find out that your navigation system has led you astray. You also cannot assume that the problem with forecasts over the last 12 months will be the same problem that causes grief over the next 12 months.

The second reason is a little more subtle.

We need to measure a process at least four times before we can be reasonably confident that a process is biased

The second reason why it is important to forecast frequently is that you need a certain amount of evidence before you can be confident that you have a problem. The only thing that we know for sure about any individual forecast is that it is almost always wrong. Recall the exercise in the Preface that had us trying to copy the letter 'a'. There is no process in the known universe that does not exhibit variation. Get suspicious if there is *no* error!

So clearly we should not 'correct' our forecast based on a single error. We need more than one. It turns out – for reasons that we will come to – that we need at least four. So if we measure the quality of our forecast process once a quarter then if we have a problem we will only have sufficient evidence to act after a year, which is likely to be far too late for most businesses.

But how, given the inevitability of error, *do* we measure forecasts?

HOW TO MEASURE IT

Since bias is a pattern of errors we need to use visual tools to help us spot it

We have described forecasting as a process, so a good way to help understand measurement is to use an analogy with another process. The example we will use is a manufacturing process: that involved in making baked beans – a culinary concept properly treated with contempt in most food loving nations but part of the staple diet in the UK.

The inputs into this process are cans, beans and tomato sauce. These pass through a packing line and from the other end we get cans of beans which should be, let us say, 100 grams in weight.

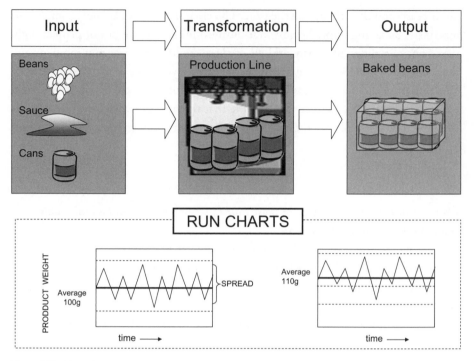

Figure 5.3 Measuring a process.
An example of how to use measurement to control the performance of a production process.

How do we know that this process is working as it should?

Earlier we established that a good forecast process should produce output that was unbiased with an acceptable level of variation. This also applies to our bean packing line. If our bean packing process is unbiased we would expect to see as many cans of beans above 100 g as there are below 100 g. In this process, an acceptable level of variation is defined by the appropriate government agency.

How do we measure the process to ensure that it conforms to these criteria? Bean manufacturers start by using graphs to plot weights in a time series (see Figure 5.3). These are known as 'run charts'.

If we react to random variation we make our process less reliable

A run chart shows a pattern of variation. If the variation is randomly spread around 100 g (and the average error is approximately zero) then there is no bias. So providing very few errors are outside the limits defined by the authorities, no action is needed. If there is bias in the process (perhaps the sauce is too viscous and so the machine is overfilling) then this will show itself as a series of successive errors above (or below) the target weight and the average error will be a large positive (or negative) number. However, how much evidence do we need before we can be confident that the process is biased, and our measurements are not simply the result of chance? And what happens if we get it wrong?

Take the second of the questions. There are two kinds of mistakes we can make. If we fail to spot bias then we have a poor quality process. We have cans of beans that are too heavy (we waste money) or too light (we face prosecution). If, however, we made the other kind of mistake and we react to random variation *as if* it were bias, we make things worse – by over correcting variation will increase, quality will deteriorate and it will be even more difficult to spot problems.[3] This is because we are correcting something that does not need correcting and in the process, we *inject a new source of error* into the system.

 More

A demonstration of how reacting to random errors makes things worse
An understanding of variation underpinned the philosophy and methods developed by W. Edwards Deming, the American quality guru who played a lead role in helping Japanese manufacturing become what it is today.

'Tampering', the tendency of management to interfere in a system unnecessarily, was one of Deming's deadly sins of management. One of Deming's acolytes, Lloyd Nelson, developed a simple exercise to help teach managers about tampering. You will find a good description of 'Nelson's funnel' in Neave (1990) and computer simulations on the Web.

So it is important that we react, but it is equally important that we don't overreact. This helps us to come up with an answer to the first question we posed.

Four successive errors of the same sign is a scientifically sound rule of thumb to help us distinguish between bias and random variation
In order to spot bias in a forecast process we must have scientifically based decision-making rules. Because of variation, no kind of measure can provide us with absolute certainty. We can only make judgments based on an understanding of probabilities. What rules should we use to help us spot real problems quickly but reduce the risk of a false diagnosis to an acceptable level?

While the principle is the same, the rules differ from those used to manage a packing line. A high speed packing line will provide hundreds of measurements every minute and the cost of failure is relatively small. By waiting for 100 measures before making a decision to adjust fill volumes, we might only have to wait a minute and scrap a small amount of low cost product. Our biggest risk is that we overreact and make the process worse. As a result, we set our decision-making rules such that we demand a lot of evidence before we take action.[4]

We are managing a forecast process, however, so the criterion we use is different. Since we might only have one measure a month if we waited for seven consecutive positive (or negative) errors before we declared that our process was biased we would have to wait over half a year. In the interim, we may have made potentially disastrous decisions based on unreliable forecasts. In addition, it is likely that over this period the process will itself have changed. Unlike a packing machine, forecast process is not mechanized so we cannot guarantee that it will be invariant over a period of time, and the inputs (forecast assumptions) are not subject to strict quality control procedures. As a result there is a high risk that by waiting so long we will end up trying to correct problems that no longer exist and miss ones that do.

As a rule therefore we recommend that you *use four consecutive errors of the same sign as evidence of bias*; less than four and there is a good chance that all you are seeing is the impact of randomness.

More

Why a run of four is a good indicator of bias

Why four? There is no magic here; the logic is straightforward. The chances of two consecutive positive or negative errors is 25% (50% multiplied by 50%), three in a row is 12.5% and four in a row 6.25%. If we ran a monthly forecast cycle and we chose three in a row we would run the risk of reacting when we shouldn't approximately twice a year (12 times 0.125). This feels too high; once a year feels like a better balance – hence the standard of four.

A consequence of adopting this as a standard is that a monthly forecast cycle using monthly buckets is essential for most businesses. A quarterly process would mean that we have to wait at least a year before we have sufficient evidence of a problem – way too late even assuming that the process hasn't changed in the interim (which it usually will have done).

Often people have a 'gut feeling' that they can spot a problem with less than four pieces of data, but this is a conceit of the human brain which is so good at spotting patterns that it often sees them where none exist, hence reports of people seeing the face of Elvis in a vegetable, or clouds in the shape of elephants. The impact of the tendency of even hyper rational business people to see patterns where none exist is the subject of Taleb Nassim's book *Fooled by Randomness* (Taleb, 2001).

A good way to start assessing the quality of a forecast process is to draw a run chart and to 'eyeball' it for signs of bias. Here are some examples (Figure 5.4). Can you spot which ones are biased?

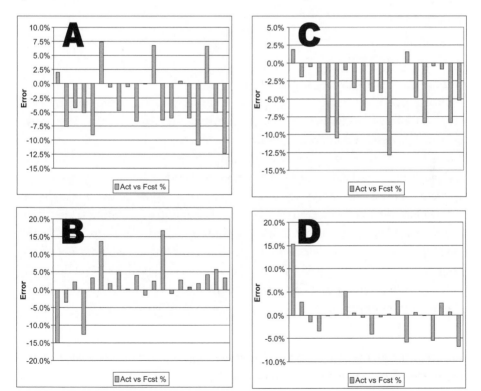

Figure 5.4   Four examples of forecast error run charts.
A and C come from processes which are clearly negatively biased, whereas B is positively biased, at least after the fourth period. See the panel below for an interpretation of D.

Run charts are an easy way of spotting very biased processes, and are a particularly effective way of dealing with motivational bias when someone is consciously providing misleading information. The graphical presentation makes it very difficult for someone engaging in politically motivated behavior to maintain their innocence and we very often find that bias 'disappears' without any additional action being taken (see Figure 5.5).

A run chart and the 'rule of 4' is a way of helping to eliminate processes for which there is no evidence of 'guilt' (but it is not foolproof – see the panel below). A run of four, however, is not proof of guilt (bias). If you are running on a monthly cycle you will still get a run of four from an 'innocent' process on average once a year, so it is important that you investigate further to see whether there is a plausible explanation for the apparent bias before taking action.

More

Interpreting run charts – advanced issues

Where processes are less obviously biased, run charts need to be interpreted with care; only very biased processes have completely unbroken sequences. Even with a biased process randomness might throw up an error with a different sign occasionally (and the system can be manipulated if the rules for spotting bias are employed too mechanistically). In addition, we need to be aware of suspicious patterns since it is common for a single run chart to provide us with evidence of two biased processes operating in parallel. For example in a business operating with quarterly targets it is not unusual to find something like a pattern of negative errors in the first two months (perhaps representing a failure to sell to expectations) being followed by a positive error in month three as the business tries to 'make up' for the first two months. There is some suspicion of this behavior in example D.

The conventional use of averages and arbitrary targets is a completely inadequate way of measuring and managing forecast quality

To some readers the approach we advocate may appear simplistic and imprecise, insufficiently scientific. Isn't there a simple Key Performance Indicator that you can use instead?

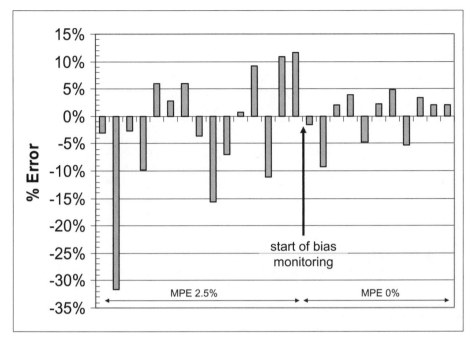

Figure 5.5 A damning publication.

An example showing how the simple act of publishing a run chart dramatically improved forecast quality in a business unit. Bias has been eliminated (the average net error falls from 2.5% to zero) but variation has reduced as well. A striking demonstration of the power of feedback.

There are forecast error metrics that can be used as KPIs but they are of questionable value for monitoring forecast quality and driving improvement. For example, MAPE (Mean Average Percentage Error), measures the average deviation from the forecast ignoring the sign so this is effectively a measure of variation. MPE (Mean Percentage Error) takes the sign into account and so measures bias. A perfectly unbiased process should have an average error of 0%. Often businesses will set targets for MAPE and MPE. This approach seems straightforward and simple. So why do we advise against it?

Consider this example:

	TARGET	ACTUAL
Average Net Error (MPE)	<1%	0.8%
Maximum Error (MAPE)	+/– 5%	<14%

The obvious conclusion to draw from this analysis is that this process is unbiased but that the level of variation is too high.

Now take a look at the run chart in Figure 5.6.

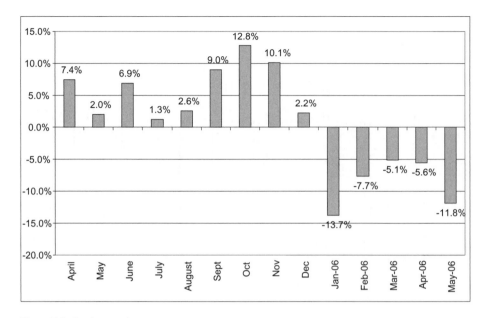

Figure 5.6 Another run chart.
This chart shows a change in the pattern of bias in a process which is not picked up by statistics based on averaging the results.

It is obvious even from a cursory glance that this process is highly biased. Up until December it is very positively biased; thereafter the bias was negative. As we have discussed, this feature is very common, particularly when we use judgmental forecasts infected by motivational bias. Patterns of bias often switch at accounting period ends, at the end of budgeting and target setting cycles or when key players move, and the conventional approach of using the MPE measure fails to capture this. In addition, any KPI based on an average is sensitive to sample size – even if a process is totally free from bias a smaller sample will usually result in a 'worse' score than a big sample due to 'the law of large numbers'.

What about the level of variation?

If this was a run chart describing the error for a monthly revenue forecast for a major multinational company operating in a stable market, we would quite correctly conclude that the company is appallingly bad at forecasting. If, on the other hand, it measured the daily performance of an ice cream stall on a beach in England in mid July we would probably reach the opposite conclusion. Given the vagaries of the weather and the buying patterns of individual consumers, if the stall was able to consistently forecast average sales of 100 ice creams to within 15 units, we should be impressed.

What this illustrates is that it is not possible to set arbitrary targets for variation. What constitutes an 'acceptable' level of variation is dependent on the inherent unpredictability of the variable in question and other factors such as the size of the business (this makes a forecast more likely to be undermined by small numbers of unpredictable or random events). Without the use of more sophisticated tools,[5] the only way to set guidelines for 'acceptable variation' is to refer to the decisions which are made based on the forecast. If an error of +/−5% does not compromise the quality of decision-making then, by definition, this level of variation is acceptable.

Key Concept

Aggregation and variability

The impact of aggregation on variability is called the 'portfolio effect' since it follows the same logic used to construct diversified share portfolios. With investment portfolios, if the risk (variation) of different shares is uncorrelated then it is possible to construct portfolios that enjoy the return of 'high risk' investments but without all of the risk. Some of the time, negative outcomes will be offset by positive outcomes. Thus the variation (as measured by the standard deviation) of the whole is smaller than the sum of the parts. The same principle is used in radio engineering for instance; 'noise' is fed back into a system to 'clean up' electronic signals.

The portfolio effect complicates the task of setting targets for variation since larger, more diversified businesses exhibit a lower level of variation than smaller ones. There are benefits to size, however, since *simply eradicating bias in lower level forecasts will result in more reliable 'high level' forecasts*. So our advice to CFOs of large companies worried about the quality of their guidance to investors is: forget about 'accuracy'. Eliminate bias and let the portfolio effect take care of the job of reducing variation.

To summarize: we cannot rely on conventional arithmetic measures of error to judge the quality of forecast processes in real time[6] because:

- of the existence of random variation – and particularly differences in the level of random variation between processes
- most forecast measurement will be based on relatively small sample sizes
- the 'state' of the process can change relatively quickly – either because the input assumptions (e.g. the market) or the process (perhaps because of motivation bias) are not stable.

Run charts are a simple tool that can be used to diagnose the existence of bias. They can be used in 'real time' to help spot problems as they arise. They should not be used mechanically; they need to be carefully interpreted if we are to avoid the twin dangers of overreaction and false complacency.

More

An advanced tool for measuring bias

A sophisticated approach to measuring and managing bias involves the use of Trigg's Tracking Signal (see Figure 5.7).

This uses the exponentially moving average of the ratio between MPE and MAPE to provide a real time measure of bias. Probability-based control limits can then be set. Only when the measure for a process exceeds these limits does action need to be taken. In this example the process 'goes critical' in March and April when the 98% confidence limit is exceeded. Because the level of confidence is so high this means that corrective action needs to be taken immediately. In October the 90% confidence limit is breached – this means that the forecast needs to be checked to determine whether this result is indicative of bias or simply 'bad luck'.

A technique like this is more sensitive than the 'run of 4' rule although the results are consistent. It also generates a 'score' which enables forecast processes to be compared.

So we are now using run charts to measure forecast quality. What do we do with this information?

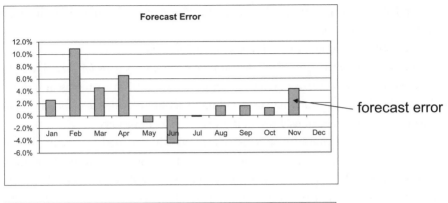

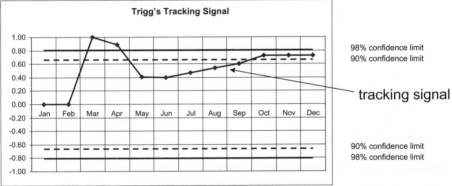

Figure 5.7 Trigg's Tracking Signal.

Improving forecast quality first involves eliminating bias and then, and only then, reducing variation

Measurement is never an end in itself – it should serve a purpose, in this case, to improve the forecast process. The way to improve the process is to eliminate the cause of problems: bias and (unacceptable levels of) variation.

There are three causes of bias:

1. There is a systematic flaw in the model in use. For example, a model might assume that all customers behave in the same way – but if different customer groups respond in different ways to environmental factors such as an economic downturn this may be manifest as a consistent pattern of error.

2. There is a systematic error in the assumptions used. For example, we might assume that our market will continue to grow at its long term rate of 5% but

if we fail to notice that this has fallen to 3% over the last few months, our forecast will show bias.

3. Behavioral bias has crept into forecasters' judgments.

There are two points to note. First, *there are no acceptable reasons for bias*. There is no excuse for failing to correct systematic errors in a model or in the assumptions used. Nor should you tolerate managers failing to act upon evidence of bias in their judgment or, worse, consciously providing distorted assumptions.

Second, the behavioral bias often associated with judgmental forecasting is not the only cause of bias. The existence of bias may be a sign that the mathematical and statistical models in use no longer predict outcomes well because there has been a significant shift in the behavior of the system.[7] In other words, it may be early evidence of a discontinuity.

 Key Concept

How tracking forecast bias helps improve business performance measurement

Measurements of forecast performance can be very powerful tools to help control the whole business. When you forecast, you create a performance expectation based on up-to-date plans and assumptions. It is therefore a far better comparator than a budget or historic trends. As a result, changes in the pattern of forecast errors can provide a sensitive early warning system for a business.

While the bias disease can be fatal to a forecast process, *once we have detected bias, it is relatively easy to treat.* We can usually easily adjust a model to eliminate a flaw, faulty assumptions can be corrected and biased behavior exposed and challenged.

Contrast this with an analysis of the causes of variation:

1. Unpredictability in the environment, as in the case of the fashion market or one which is sensitive to weather.

2. Structural factors, such as the inverted 'portfolio effect'. Smaller units are inherently more susceptible to variation than larger ones; they are more sensitive to

the unpredictable or random behavior of individual agents (such as customers or suppliers).

3. Weaknesses in the forecast model itself; the technique chosen may be simply not very good at prediction.

It is difficult, or perhaps even impossible, to do anything about environmental unpredictability or structural factors; they are a consequence of the context in which a forecaster is operating. While it is possible to improve the model (or set of models) used to generate a forecast this is unlikely to be a quick fix. It may take many months before lessons are learned and built into the model, staff retrained or new software commissioned. In addition, since it is very difficult to know in advance which of the three factors makes the biggest contribution to variation, it is not easy to work out whether the investment of time, effort and money in improving the model will be worthwhile.

As a result, *the best strategy for improving forecast quality is to first focus on eliminating bias*. When we have eliminated bias, and cleaned up our run charts, it will be much clearer what the true level of variation is. At this point you can decide whether this is acceptable. If not *only then consider investing time and money to reduce variation*.

 More

How to analyze variances properly
This chapter has focused on measurement rather than analysis, but does not mean that analysis is not possible or irrelevant. A good forecast process where assumptions are well documented makes it easier to understand error. Martin Jarvis explains: '[T]he difference between a good variance analysis[8] and a bad one is the way they tie back to assumptions. A poor analysis says, "this number has gone up and that one has gone down". A good one links back to assumptions; the drivers of change. The best ones link these together to create a story ... a credible hypothesis of what is happening to the business' (Jarvis, 2008).

In conclusion, measurement is critical to successful forecasting. Failing to measure and learn from forecast error is like trying to learn to catch blindfold. Through measurement – closing the feedback loop – you are able to make adjustments to calibrate your current forecast model (e.g. 'the ball is being held up by the wind so I need to get closer') or to improve it ('getting my body behind the ball works better'). It is also important to use measurement in the right way. 'The way we learn is by continuous feedback on how we have performed; "your bias was x% – just think why". We don't make judgments or punish people for bad performance. We encourage people to reflect and learn,' says Magolewski of the Unilever Polish business.

Yet few businesses do a good job of measuring forecasts. Sometimes this is because the wrong things are measured at the wrong time. Good measurement is based on the use of consistent forecast horizons and units of measure (so-called 'buckets'). In particular, it is important to use only short term forecast error (i.e. within decision-making lead times) in order to avoid confusing true forecast error with the results of response to the forecast.

Sometimes this is because they measure forecasts in the wrong way. In particular, most conventional ways of measurement confuse systematic error (bias) which is bad and can be easily avoided, with unsystematic error or variation, which is often difficult to avoid.

'Variation' may be an unfamiliar concept, but most business people will recognize the concept of risk. Despite this familiarity, conventional approaches to performance management in general and forecasting in particular often fail to deal with it properly. We will focus on this subject in the next chapter.

• • • • •

Risk is a topic people feel like they understand, but struggle with in practice. In the absence of practical guidance (and there is very little in this area) it is tempting to guess, throw the problem over the wall to the statisticians or ignore the problem and hope it goes away. It is rare to find forecasts accompanied by a systematic assessment of risk. In the next chapter we will lay out a simple and theoretically sound approach for dealing with risk and uncertainty. We will also demonstrate how understanding risk around a single point forecast changes the decisions that you otherwise might have made. Having conquered the last two chapters, this challenge should be well within your compass.

• • • • •

SUMMARY

Even the simplest forecast processes must be properly measured if a forecast is to be made reliable. Measurement is required to correct for defects in forecast models and to improve them so they are capable of making better projections in the future. However, forecast quality is usually not measured at all, and when it is measured it is often done badly. Measurement involves analyzing forecast error. We should use consistent units of measurement, over consistent lead times. Only short term errors should be used to avoid corrupting measures with the impact of actions taken in response to the forecast. Since bias cannot be detected with a single measurement, forecasts need to be measured frequently and analyzed using run charts. Average error statistics, however they are calculated, cannot be used since they do not take account of the sequence of errors. A run of four consecutive errors of the same sign is usually considered as evidence of the likelihood of a biased forecast. There are no good reasons for a forecast to be biased, and once detected it can be corrected relatively easily. As a result the elimination of bias, rather than the reduction of variation, should be the first priority.

KEY LEARNING POINTS
Qualities of a forecast
- Bias: systematic error that needs to be eliminated.
- Variation: unsystematic error which may be outside the control of the forecaster.

Causes of bias
- Failure in the process
- Failure to detect changes in the world
- Psychological.

Causes of variation
- Controllable: poor forecast process
- Uncontrollable:
  - Real world unpredictability
  - Structural factors (e.g. offsetting errors – the portfolio effect).

Rules for measurement
- Using consistent units of measure
  - Buckets (units of time)
  - Horizons (forecast period)
  - Forecast lead times (elapsed time from forecast to start of forecast horizon)
- Within decision-making lead times (i.e. before decisions made in response to forecast take effect).

How to improve forecasts

● Eliminate bias then

● Reduce variation (if unacceptably high and the result of a poor process).

Uses for bias measures

● Improve the forecast model

○ Adjust/calibrate (single loop learning)

○ Change it (double loop learning)

● Help spot discontinuities in business performance quickly.

NOTES

1 An experiment performed by French psychologists Fourneret and Keannerot (in Frith, 2007) demonstrates the importance of feedback to simple everyday operations of our body. Subjects were asked to trace a line on a computer screen using a mouse. The computer, however, deliberately biased the feedback – so that, for example, when the hand was moving in a straight line the screen showed it veering off to the right. The experiment demonstrated that subjects corrected for the false feedback by veering off to the left without realizing it. False visual feedback completely overwhelmed whatever sense subjects had about what their hand was actually doing!

2 Chris Frith, in his book 'Making up the Mind' (Frith 2007), provides an illustration of how the brain monitors the reliability of its mental models. The brain contains reward cells, so-called because food and drink cause them to secrete the neurotransmitter dopamine. Initially, a spike in secretion appears after feeding. Later it occurs after the signal that precedes feeding (as with Pavlov's dog) rather than on receipt of the food. This demonstrates that the animal has built a model that predicts the arrival of food. If, however, the food does not arrive after the signal, there is a drop in the production of dopamine, alerting the animal to the fact that its model has failed. What this means is that the animal is informed, *by exception*, that its mental model needs attending to. This is an approach that we should copy in designing our measurement practices.

3 We have encountered this problem before, in the context of our shower. There was a small change in the input temperature at the start of the sequence, but by clumsily tampering with the controls we introduced wild oscillations in the output temperature – we overreacted to an overreaction. As a result we failed to notice that the best strategy was to do nothing!

4 The criterion most commonly used in manufacturing – 3σ – is based on the work of Walter Shewhart (Shewhart, 1931). Three sigma is equivalent to seven successive errors of the same sign and means that there is a 3 in 1000 chance (or less) that the pattern of errors is the result of chance variation – i.e. bad luck.

5 The most sophisticated approach to measuring processes uses statistical process control charts, originally devised by Walter Shewhart in the 1920s and later developed and promoted by Deming and others. These use statistical techniques to set control limits; the limits define the natural variation of the process (common cause variation) and anything outside (special cause variation) represents something that needs investigation. Potentially we could use a technique like this to help us measure variation in our forecast process and to spot bias, though traditional SPC tools do not always work well outside of a production environment. For this reason we recommend using Trigg's Tracking Signal (see panel).

6 It is acceptable to use statistics such as MAPE and MPE in other circumstances. For example they can help select a statistical model to apply to a data series.

7 This is an example of double loop learning. By definition, statistical models work less well after a discontinuity since the past is no longer a guide to the future.

8 We are very strongly against the conventional budgeting variance analysis for two reasons. First, the budget is not a good comparator. Second, all of the variation from budget is assumed to be meaningful but much of it will be random noise and there is no way to tell the difference between the two.

Chapter 6

MASTERING RISKS: how the paranoid survive

❝Prophesy is a good line of business, but it is full of risks.❞ Mark Twain

❝It is easy to predict a future, impossible to predict the future.❞ David Donnelly.

> *Why single point forecasts, on their own, are not enough – the difference between risk and uncertainty – and the different strategies needed to manage them – how to assess risk – skewed distributions – the texture of risk – why risk doesn't add up – consequences and options – contingency plans, uncertainty and scenario planning – time compression: the real benefit of risk assessment*

There is only one thing we know for sure about a forecast. It is likely to be wrong!

Given what has happened in credit markets over the last two years this might not seem a surprising statement. However, as Lowell Bryan and Diana Farrell, writing in the *McKinsey Quarterly* (Bryan and Farrell, 2008) comment 'even in normal times, the range of outcomes most companies consider is too narrow'.

Debating 'what is the right number' is a waste of management time. Instead the focus should be on 'what is the range of possible outcomes'

In many businesses a lot of management time is pointlessly consumed by interminable and unproductive debates about 'the forecast'. Not only is this a waste of resource, it helps foster the false belief that it is possible to predict the future; that we have a destiny which, with the right tools, we can divine. The future is rich with possibility but the exclusive focus on a single number constricts management perception and focuses it on a small number of potential outcomes, perhaps those advocated by politically motivated parties. In effect, most businesses have 'tunnel vision': the inability to be able to perceive the world outside a narrow field of vision.

 More

How the animal kingdom deals with risk

Tunnel vision is a debilitating illness associated with a range of disorders ranging from glaucoma and strokes through to pituitary tumors but all forms are characterized by a loss of peripheral vision. Range forecasting provides peripheral vision to an organization, so in the interests of understanding how to do it well perhaps it is worth reflecting on how it works in animals.

Whereas the center of the retina is populated by two kinds of structures: rods and cones, the periphery contains only rods.[1] Rods cannot supply clear images or color but they are very effective at detecting movement, particularly in reduced lighting. This suggests that range forecasts needn't be precise or detailed; they need to be good at detecting outlines, shape and particularly changes in form.

Those who suffer from a lack of peripheral vision are very vulnerable to the unexpected; because their gaze is directed by their expectations they will, quite literally, see only what they are looking out for. So it is with organizations that only have single point forecasts. They may have their attention focused on the wrong things and when disaster strikes, people say 'how come nobody saw it coming? It was obvious!'

As Arie de Geus, formerly Chief Planner for Shell, remarks 'most managers spend far too much time on a relatively useless question: what will happen to us. A far more useful question is what will we do if such and such happens' (Geus, 1997). *The real issue is, therefore, not 'what is the right number?' but 'how far might it be wrong?' and more to the point: 'why?' and 'what can we do about it?'* What has happened over the past couple of years in the financial markets has amply demonstrated what happens if you fail to understand the range of possibilities.

But, how do we go about working out 'how far the forecast might be wrong'? It would be a pyrrhic victory to stop arguments about which was the right 'single point' forecast and instead waste time debating the 'right' level of risk for a forecast!

Before we can answer these questions, we need first to understand what we mean when we use the word 'risk'.

Risk is not the same as uncertainty ...

Earlier in this book, we drew a distinction between trends and discontinuities. Forecasting trends is relatively easy since the future is rather like the past; we just need to find a forecasting methodology that reliably captures those historical patterns and extrapolates them into the future. Like any kind of forecast, the forecast of a trend – even if the trend does not change – is likely to be wrong, but because the nature and level of variation – the risk – is not abnormal, we can often make a good attempt at estimating what it might be. In this book *we use the term risk to mean variation around a trend.*

 Key concept

Some important definitions
Risk is sometimes treated as though it were a separate subject – the province of expert 'risk managers' – whereas it is really an expression of a lack of confidence in our ability to forecast the future because 'more things can happen than will happen'.

Another reason for the confusion around the subject is that we are badly served by our language. Unlike the scientific community we play fast and loose with terms and as a result we fail to communicate and think clearly.

'Risk' is often taken to mean the same thing as 'uncertainty' and the opposite of 'opportunity'. As a result we often believe 'risk and opportunity' are 'negative and positive' manifestations of the same thing and fail to distinguish between different types of ignorance about the future.

In this book we use the work 'risk' to describe an outcome that can differ from an expectation in a way that we are able to estimate, probabilistically. It can be positive (upside) or negative (downside) in form.

Uncertainty, however, describes something that, because of its rarity, cannot be estimated probabilistically.[2]

'Opportunity' we will use to describe a potential to act to exploit an upside potential (risk or uncertainty). 'Mitigation' describes an action used to avoid downside potential.

On the other hand, it is very difficult to forecast discontinuities, significant changes in the pattern of behavior of a system. *Discontinuities are the source of uncertainty.* Sometimes the cause of a discontinuity may be the result of a management intervention, but an intervention of the scale that brings about a significant shift in a trend is often difficult to forecast accurately. Frequently, however, the discontinuity is brought about by an external factor, perhaps a change in the market, economy or the actions of a competitor. Even when we know something is going to happen – and we often do not – it is difficult to forecast the timing and the scale of the change. As a result, discontinuities are difficult to estimate; they are associated with a high degree of uncertainty.

... and therefore we need to adopt different strategies for managing them

Faced with risk and uncertainty we should adopt Baden Powell's motto for the Boy Scouts: 'be prepared'. However, this begs the question, 'prepared for what?' and 'how?'

By their nature, outcomes that we classify as 'risk' occur frequently; dealing with them should be a normal part of managing a business. We should be able to estimate, quantitatively, the likelihood of occurrence and their scale; which are likely to be highly probable and (relatively) low value. If we can do this we can then devise plans to deal with the risk – to mitigate the downside risk or exploit the upside risk. This may simply involve adjusting existing plans ('course correction') – perhaps by changing the timing of interventions. It may also mean building 'contingency plans' – creating a set of alternative interventions which can be deployed if and when required. Businesses may attempt to avoid risk altogether, but it could be a shortsighted policy. In limiting the downside potential by placing constraints on the freedom of managers to use their initiative, for example, we often forgo the upside potential as well.

More

How diversification helps manage risk

Indeed, one of the benefits that large companies with diversified portfolios have is that each individual unit can bear more risk than it could if it were independent. A large company has deeper pockets but also, providing the risks taken are not correlated, the risks will net off to a degree, resulting in an overall reduced risk. We exploit this phenomenon when we construct a diversified portfolio of shares to support our retirement plans.

However, managing 'uncertainty' is a more difficult proposition.

Uncertain events are by definition relatively infrequent and so are difficult to anticipate. The scale of the uncertainty is also difficult to estimate and, since such events are infrequent, they are likely to be larger in magnitude than those treated as risk. Managing uncertainty therefore demands a different strategy. A negative event could imperil the whole organization so, as far as possible, the goal should be to try to avoid the downside potential altogether, either by eliminating the source of the vulnerability or by some form of compensating measure (such as hedging, insurance or diversification). On the other hand, a positive event could transform the prospects for your company overnight, but just like winning the lottery, it is not probable, so it would not be wise to bet large sums on it. Instead, it might make sense to make a few small wagers just in case you get lucky.

More

Why rare events are more common than they 'should be'

Although 'uncertain' events are rare they may be a lot more frequent than we (and the CEO of Cisco and Alan Greenspan) think. Our perceptions of risk – indeed, most of the risk models used by financial institutions – are based on the assumption that risk follows a Gaussian (normal) distribution. In fact, there is an increasing amount of evidence that many real world phenomena (including the movement of stock prices) follow power law distributions. That means that if you plot them on a graph they have 'fatter tails' than a normal distribution would have; in other words there is a much higher likelihood of extreme events.

To illustrate what 'much higher likelihood' means in this context, assume that wealth was distributed according to a power law (which it actually is). If there were a 1 in 63 chance of someone having net worth of more than $1 million there would be a 1 in 1000 chance of net worth of more than $4 million. If wealth distribution were Gaussian, on the other hand, 1 in 63 would have net worth of $1m but only 1 in 886 000 000 000 000 000 would have over $4 million.

This example is taken from *The Black Swan*, a book by Nassim Nicholas Taleb, an iconoclastic former Wall Street trader (Taleb, 2008). It is a simplification, but it is not wrong. Indeed his work is based on the empirical work of Benoit Mandelbrot who some 40 years ago was the first to demonstrate that stock price (and commodity price) variations in the real world did not fit in with the predictions of the theory used by most economists (the 'Efficient Market Hypothesis'[3]) which is predicated on a Gaussian probability distribution. There have been many more extreme market events over the last 30 or so years than standard theory would predict.

The chart below (Figure 6.1) summarizes these two views of probability and the consequences for management.

However, because it is so difficult to anticipate uncertainty, it might not be possible to avoid it altogether. As a result it is extremely important to spot discontinuities quickly; to have a good 'early warning' system, so that you can take swift action to avoid tragedy or to court good fortune.

While it might not be possible to forecast uncertainty, the process of forecasting helps enormously because *in the act of considering possibilities, we enhance our awareness*, and the more aware we are, the sooner we will spot discontinuities. As Mark Beresford-Smith, Senior Economist at HSBC, said when reflecting on the recent turbulence in the financial markets '[N]o model can cope with current conditions, since any model will make assumptions about the way the world works that might be false, for example "the financial system is sound". All we can do is sound alarm bells based on what we see happening' (Sawers, 2008).

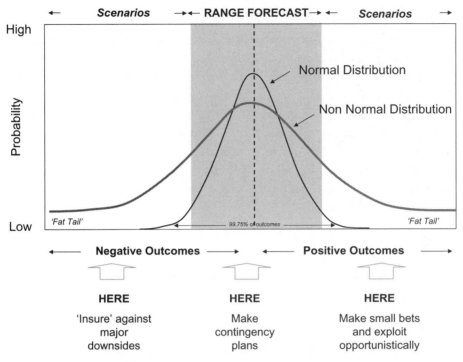

Figure 6.1 Two alternative views of risks and uncertainty and how to manage them.
Note that the curves represent different views of probability – they are not drawn to scale.

More

How considering risk and uncertainty improves your organization's 'eyesight'
If we have not contemplated the possibility of something happening we might actually fail to perceive it. Most of the data that we receive through our eyes we 'throw away' – we treat it as being irrelevant. The criterion we use to sift the wheat from the chaff is 'does it fit a valid model of the world that I already have?' If our model tells us 'this piece of information isn't relevant' we ignore it. As a result, if we are using the wrong model, we can fail to see 'the obvious'.

Most of us will have experienced this when we are in a crowded place that we have not been to before. We see a blur of faces, but we literally take no notice of most of them. Then, should a friend tap us on the shoulder, for a fraction of a second we do not recognize them. While we had *seen* them, we had not *perceived* them because *we had not expected to*. You cannot *perceive* something which you had not already *conceived* as being possible. Our perception is very selective, because the model we have of the world acts as an informational filter.

So it is with organizations. If we have not conceived of the possibility of danger – perhaps because we have delegated the task of risk management to mathematicians with clever models – we will not see the warning signals when they appear, so some of the criticisms of banks after the recent collapse may be misplaced. Perhaps they did not have a culture of risk taking; perhaps they were simply blind to the risk. That is why, in Andy Groves' (1997) words, 'only the paranoid survive'.

So far, we have dealt in generalities. Some of this might be new, but much of it will be very familiar and obvious. For sure, it is difficult to find many people who would disagree with the view that it is important to consider risk and uncertainty when forecasting. In our view the reason why this is so rarely done – and when it is done, it is done so poorly – is because some basic principles are not well understood. If the principles are not understood, technique will be poor. If technique is poor, results will disappoint. So let us now turn to the problem of application.

ASSESSING RISK: ESTIMATING A RANGE

We all have an intuitive grasp of how to make range estimates in our private life. For instance, we say 'I will be there in five to ten minutes' without thinking about the processes we have gone through in our heads to arrive at this estimate. However, there is little practical guidance about how to do this in a formal business setting, where a potentially large number of people need to have a consistent approach so we can combine their estimates to produce a range forecast for the organization as a whole. The shortage of guidance is perhaps one reason why most attempts at range forecasting that we come across are lamentable.

So how do we work out what the range should be?

It is not possible to measure forecast accuracy over the longer term;
instead we should be assessing forecast credibility

An obvious way might seem to involve measuring how far you have been wrong in the past and use this as a measure of risk. This works in the short term but we have already discussed why you cannot measure forecast accuracy over the long term. The further ahead we look the more we are measuring the results of actions we took *in response* to the previous forecast rather than the quality of the forecast itself. The other problem is that while the short term is very repetitive – you can compare the results of your forecast process this month with the results of next month's without too much concern – the longer term is not. Just because you were only 0.5% out in your long range forecast last year when markets were calm doesn't mean that you can assume the same level of reliability from the long term forecast this year when oil prices have increased by $50 a barrel, financial markets are turbulent and so on.

What is the answer? We think that this is another example of the kind of problem we deal with almost subconsciously in the context of our home life but struggle with at work. While the size of the numbers and the complexity is of a completely different order of magnitude the basic principles – the 'science' – is the same. So perhaps a good way of finding answers to our questions is to create a 'real life' domestic scenario. We can expose the basic principles and then work out how to apply them in a more complex work environment.

HOW TO ASSESS RISK
Donna's dilemma
Let us introduce Donna.

Donna sells property for a living. Two years ago, and a thousand miles away from her parental home, her life was in a big mess. Three years out of college and in the first job, she had money for the first time in her life but completely lost control of her finances. A couple of good years for sales and bonuses and a bachelor girl lifestyle had seen her credit card debts mount up and she found herself paying out more in interest than she was receiving in sales commission – which then plummeted when the housing market collapsed. However, belatedly, she discovered the joys of financial control. She found that if she was careful about forecasting her income and only bought a new car (her only real asset) when she was sure she could afford it, she could survive comfortably, pay off her debts and still drive around in a flashy sports car.

But she has just been brought down to earth with a shock. Four weeks ago her father died suddenly, and as an only child she now had to think what to do about her mother. She had suffered with arthritis for years, but with help from Donna's father had been able to cope. With Dad gone, no other family and only a small pension, who was going to provide the support she needed now? How long would it be before she became permanently wheelchair bound? Donna decided that her mother would have to come and live with her in Florida, which meant a change in accommodation for Donna and a whole new set of financial control problems.

However, she knew that the key was good forecasting; so she sat down and produced her forecast for the year. On the face of it, it looked pretty good – a surplus of $6000 to spend on a holiday for her mother, who hadn't had one for 10 years. Also she had just heard that her boss was leaving in six months' time and Donna had been tipped off that she was in the running for the job and the pay hike that went with it. However, she had a rather uncomfortable feeling. She had always had to deal with having a volatile income, depending on the state of the housing market and how many hours she put in, but she now had to deal with a set of new uncertainties.

She had spotted a good investment property on the other side of town. It was big for the two of them but it was a real 'one of a kind' bargain and could be converted to provide independent accommodation for her mother so she wouldn't cramp her style too much. The problem was that, even with the capital from the sale of her mother's old house, the mortgage was a lot more than her current rent and she was also worried about the state of the property. They hadn't had the inspection back yet, but it was an old house and if it needed a lot of work doing on it she would have to increase the size of the mortgage. There was also some talk that the current property prices had peaked on the back of cheap credit. An interest rate rise would not only increase her bills but might also lead to a slowdown in sales and a reduction in her sales commission and bonus.

Worse than that, her nice car was beginning to make some odd sounding noises and her mother already complained about having to squeeze into its small seats. If the car had another run of visits to the mechanics she could see that she would be forced to get a new car, which might have to be something that could be converted for use with wheelchairs, depending on her mother's health.

So Donna sat down and produced what her boss would have called a range forecast. A forecast with upsides and downsides attached – positive and negative risks that Donna reckoned would have about a 50% or greater chance of occurring. But, horror of horrors, she now discovered that not only could she not afford a holiday – it looked like she would have to stop eating, since the downside risk was seven times the cost of the break she had been planning. On the other hand, she might find herself with a spare $13 000. What was going on?

		Estimate	Upside	Downside
Monthly Salary		24000	1000	
Monthly Commission		12000	6000	-6000
Regular Income (pa)		**36000**	**7000**	**-6000**
Annual Bonus	Three months before year end	10000	5000	-5000
Total Income (pa)		**46000**	**12000**	**-11000**
Monthly Household Bills		-24000		
Monthly Rent		-1500		
Monthly Mortgage	Purchase in 3 months time	-13500	900	-3150
Car Repairs		0		-3600
Regular Expenditure (pa)		**-39000**	**900**	**-6750**
Replacement Car		0		-25000
Total Expenditure (pa)		**-39000**	**900**	**-31750**
Net Income		**7000**	**12900**	**-42750**

Figure 6.2 Donna's range forecast.

Here are her calculations (Figure 6.2).

Because of her bad experiences, Donna was determined not to go into debt on her credit card again. So she did what many companies do when they come up with an answer that doesn't make sense. She took a decision that she could not justify mathematically, but felt right. Rather than risking running up high interest credit card bills again, she took out an unsecured loan of $20000, went ahead with the holiday plans and hoped for the best.

The usual approach to managing risk in business is to create a contingency – a buffer – often based on no more than 'gut feel'

Many people involved in business forecasting will be familiar with this kind of situation, although the numbers will be a lot bigger! In these circumstances it is clear that arguing whether the 'right' single point number for forecast profit is $6m or $5.6m or even $5m misses the point. We know all these numbers could be wrong, perhaps in a big way. On the other hand, a cursory attempt at producing a range forecast shows numbers that are too huge, too embarrassing, to present to colleagues.

Often, businesses do something similar to Donna. Instead of taking out a loan, they hold back on committing $20m of advertising money (which *feels* like the right level of contingency) until things get clearer. By doing this, sales will take a hit, but not until next year, which is 'a bridge to cross when we come to it'. If things turn out better than we fear, we can release the contingency back into the income statement and get a little profit boost before Christmas. It will be pats on the back all round for 'beating profit expectations'.

And yet … although many of us have done this, we may have a gut feeling that this isn't right. A panic cut in advertising or taking out an arbitrarily sized, and probably unnecessary, loan may not be the appropriate reaction. So using the Donna case study let's try to work out why, and in so doing identify some general principles for handling risk in forecasting.

It is important to understand the timing of risk factors

Donna took out a loan to cover what she believed was her downside risk at year-end. In business we put investment plans on hold to make sure we could 'deliver' our numbers.

There is a cost to taking out an unnecessary $20 000 loan: interest, which on an unsecured loan will be high. There is also a cost to deferring $10m of advertising investment and it is called 'the opportunity cost of lost sales in the future'. However, because it is difficult to quantify and falls into another accounting year you can pretend it does not exist.

On the other hand, $20 000 or $20m might not be enough! Perhaps at mid year a combination of negative events might leave Donna with $5000 on her credit card at a rate that makes her eyes water.

The point here, as we all know from domestic planning, is that you have to look at the risk profile *over time not at a point of time.* You can go bankrupt at any time in the year – not just at year-end. Just as we would not expect our forecast to assume the same outcome every month, we should not assume that risk is evenly spread. The fact that risk profiles are variable in nature and time sensitive creates new opportunities for managing risk beyond those employed by Donna and our hypothetical company. Let us analyze these.

It isn't fair: risk profiles are often highly skewed

We have often observed a tendency for forecasters to assume that risk should be evenly distributed around the central point, and if it is not, they tend to assume that the central point as being 'wrong'. Often this is not the case; the distribution of risk may be *skewed* (Figure 6.3).

Donna has recognized this in analyzing the risk around her mortgage payments. The risk is skewed because the probability of payments being greater than what she has allowed for is higher than the probability of them being lower because 'credit has been too cheap'. Also she may have to spend money on repairs to the

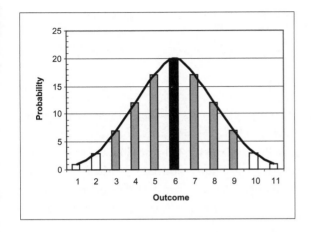

Normal Distribution

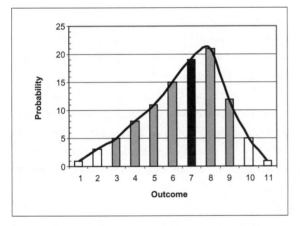

Skewed Distribution

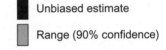

■ Unbiased estimate

▨ Range (90% confidence)

Figure 6.3 A skewed distribution.

house which could increase the mortgage. In addition, she recognizes that it is possible to have a risk against a forecast of zero as in the case of her car repairs. But is it right to assume that the risk around her commission income or her bonus is evenly spread for instance? Because of the mechanics of the situation, risk can often be skewed. Perhaps part of the bonus is attached to something that is 'easy' to achieve. Perhaps the fear about interest rates means that there is more downside than upside risk. In addition, rental contracts are often constructed so that revision is upwards only.[4] They will be the same or higher, therefore the risk profile is skewed.

More

Why risk is often skewed

In business, we often find that there are more ways for things to go wrong than right. For example, we often find skewed risk around 'activity' forecasts because, in any new endeavor, there are usually more ways to fail than there are to succeed! The level of skew around profit forecasts is often exacerbated by the fact that we often commit to investment (which usually has a high degree of certainty attached to it) before we know whether the investment will deliver the forecasted revenue (high risk).

How forecasts often fail to estimate skew correctly ...

While it is wrong to assume that risk will always be evenly distributed, a common feature of poor range forecasts is excessive skew, for example a profit forecast with no upside risk. This is simply not credible – it is wrong.

The reason for this is that, if a forecast is unbiased, there should be an equal chance of actual outcomes being on the low side and on the high side. It is possible for outcomes on the upside to have a lower average value, but if there is no upside risk, then the implication is that the average value of each of the upside outcomes is zero. Since this is not possible, either the upside risks have been ignored or the central forecast is too high.

... and how to get it right

As a rule of thumb, it is possible to have an unbiased forecast and a distribution of risk that is skewed 1/3:2/3. Any bigger skew should lead you to question either the risk assessment or the central forecast.

This is illustrated in Figure 6.3, where the central forecast is 7 and the range (at 90% confidence) is 3 on the downside and 9 on the upside. Note that the unbiased central forecast (the median) is not the same as the 'most likely' outcome (the mode). When a distribution is skewed the 'most likely' outcome will not exhibit a 50:50 distribution of potential results above and below. This is why you should never ask for 'most likely' forecasts; always ask for unbiased or '50:50' estimates.

You have to take the lumpy with the smooth: continuous risk can be expressed as a range – discrete risk should be expressed as scenarios

Another matter that can cause a lot of confusion is the 'texture' of risk.

Some risk is 'smooth'; we call this *continuous* risk. By this, we mean that the outcome (positive or negative) could assume (theoretically) any value. So for instance, next week the price of oil could be any dollar value for a barrel between, say, $50 and $100. The risk attached to the momentum forecast, for instance, is always continuous.

More

Assessing momentum and intervention risks

We would recommend that 'momentum risk' and 'intervention risk' be modeled separately.

There are two common mistakes to avoid:

1. A failure to recognize momentum risk. Because it is not associated with an easily identified or dramatic event it is easy to underestimate momentum risk (because of the availability heuristic). In many businesses, momentum risk can account for as much as 90% of the total risk.

2. A failure to recognize that intervention forecast risk carries a significantly higher percentage risk than momentum risk. For instance, according to Martin Jarvis '[F]orecasting of innovation often fails to recognize the inherent risk; perhaps assuming that it might be 5% more or less than the central forecast. Whereas in reality, true innovation may result in volumes half or five times what was expected' (Jarvis, 2008).

The other kind of risk is 'lumpy'. We will call this *discrete* risk. This arises whenever there are two (or a limited number of) possible outcomes – for example, in the case of an event that may or may not happen, or a new product that will either meet or beat expectations or be withdrawn. Therefore, in Donna's example, either her car will be replaced or it won't. It will not be partly replaced! In business, either we will get that new account or we will not. In reality things are often more complex because continuous risk is often attached to a discrete risk. So, in the event we get the new account (discrete risk) it could be worth anything between, say, $1m and $5m (continuous risk). Risks around interventions can often be 'lumpy' in this way.

Dealing with continuous risk is usually straightforward. We might estimate for example, that there is a less than 10% chance that the price of oil will drop below $60 and a less than 10% chance that it will rise above $120. The actual value will be any number between these values.[5] *Sensitivity analysis* is the name given to this approach: where we vary the assumptions made in the central forecast. Discrete risk is more difficult to handle. How do we do it?

An obvious way to deal with discrete risk is to calculate the weighted value; so if the probability of getting the new account is 50% and the most likely value was $3m then the central forecast would be $1.5m and the downside risk $1m ($1.5m less 50% x $1m) and the upside risk $1m (50% x $5m less $1.5m). If the discrete risk is small, this is probably a reasonable way to handle it. If it is significant, however, we would not recommend this approach. Either Donna's car will have a major breakdown or it will not. If the probability of a major breakdown is 50%, she cannot buy half a replacement car if it happens!

In these circumstances, the best approach is to perform a *'what if'* analysis. A 'what if' (or best/worst case) analysis involves making different assumptions to those made in the central forecast. You will therefore construct a series of forecasts using different assumptions about discrete risks: a *set* of alternative outcomes (perhaps best case, worst case with a few variations) rather than a *range* of outcomes.[6]

 More

How to improve judgmental estimates of risk

Whether you are using sensitivity or 'what if' analysis the assessment of risk is likely to rely on judgmental techniques, which means that they carry a significant risk of bias. There is also a lot of evidence to suggest that naïve judgment tends to underestimate risk. As with single point forecasting, you should ensure that the assumptions behind risk assessments are clearly and explicitly stated, but also use alternative approaches to help keep minds open to other possibilities.

It doesn't (always) add up: risks are often overstated because of the misuse of arithmetical procedures

Think about this. On your journey home from work there is a 10% chance of there being a snarl up at a busy junction, which will delay you by up to 15 minutes, and there is a 10% chance of there being road repairs somewhere along the journey that carries a penalty of 15 minutes. Does that mean that there is a 10% chance of being late by 30 minutes (i.e. 15 plus 15)?

The answer most people give is 'no'. They would probably guess that the risk was somewhere between 15 and 30 – perhaps 20 to 25 minutes. Why? Because we recognize that these risks are *independent* – that is they are not related to each other. A problem at the junction will not increase the likelihood of a problem with road repairs. What this means in practice is that you cannot simply add up the risk – if one thing happens then there is a good chance the other will not.

And yet in most of the range forecasts we see this is exactly what people do. They assume they can add up risks arithmetically and end up with huge numbers that are simply not credible, or which panic people into rash actions. This is the major reason why Donna's numbers look stupid. Intuitively she must have recognized this, because she ignored her own arithmetic when she decided to take out a loan.

On the other hand, the situation is different if two events are related. If being trapped in road repairs increased my chances of getting stuck in rush hour traffic later on then the risks are said to be *dependent* and you *can* 'add them up'. An increase in interest rates will increase Donna's mortgage and probably (with a lag) lead to a downturn in the housing market that will reduce her commission income.

 More

Aggregating risk

What is the right way to 'add up' the risk of independent or partly independent risk?

This can become a complicated subject – financial institutions employ scores of analysts who crunch calculations using techniques such as Monte Carlo simulation. There is no substitute for complex math when you can reliably estimate the risk attached to each component of your forecast and millions hang on every decimal point. But for most businesses the stakes are not so high and the initial assessment of each risk element is often very subjective. In these circumstances, it is probably acceptable to make a judgmental estimate of the effect of combining the risk in the same way that we do in our everyday life. The important thing is not to make the mistake of adding up risks arithmetically, unless you are sure that they are all dependent.

Consequences and options: risk is often overstated because compensating actions are ignored

Adding up risks that are independent of each other is one cause of overstated risk. Another common source of overstatement is the failure to distinguish between options and consequences. Let us illustrate this with a simple example.

Imagine you are a potato wholesaler. You buy potatoes from farmers and you sell them to shops. Quite correctly, you identify the price of potatoes as a risk and let us say that because of the very dry weather conditions, there is a significant chance that the price will go up by 20%. Since (as you will all know) margins in the potato business are wafer thin, the range forecast shows that you are staring into financial oblivion.

Clearly this is unlikely to be the case. Why? Because if the price of potatoes went up, then you would almost certainly put up your price to retailers to compensate for it. Since you have a fantastic forecasting process, which includes a range forecast, you will be aware of the possibility, so at the first sign of trouble you increase output prices. Your risk is therefore actually zero! At worst, the risk will be the time lag between the input prices going up and being able to raise the output price.

Often in business, we see people making the 'potato' mistake in constructing their range forecasts.[7] They fail to recognize that some events will automatically trigger action that will eliminate or offset the risk (or exploit the opportunity). As a result, the range is too wide and the forecast loses credibility.

 More

The importance of understanding how our own actions change risk

A more complex example is a new product launch. Say the forecast assumes sales of 1000 units producing a gross profit of $5m. The launch is supported by advertising of $4m leading to a forecast profit of $1m. This new product is completely novel and so you rightly recognize that there is a high level of risk attached to the volume forecast; volume may be as low as 50% of the central forecast. As a result you assume there is only downside risk; the lost gross profit – $2.5m (50% of $5m).Why might this be wrong?

The reason it is wrong is that probably you will have some idea whether the product will 'fly' early in its life – before you have committed all the advertising money, since with such a risky venture it will be very unwise to have committed everything up front. So, in the event that the product is withdrawn the advertising can be as well. So perhaps the real downside risk is much less than $2.5m.

The lesson here is that, when building range forecasts, we need to be aware of what actions may follow the crystallization of a risk. If the probability is very high that action A will follow outcome B – it is effectively a consequence (i.e. it is dependent) – then it is essential that the gross risk will be netted off with the compensating action in the range forecast. This is rather like an insurance policy. The real economic risk of a domestic house fire is not the $1m it will cost to replace the house and its contents – it is that part of the cost that is not covered by the insurance policy.

If, on the other hand, the causal link between A and B is not that great (i.e. it is independent) then the potential action is not a consequence but an *'option'*. In this case, there are two kinds of actions that can be taken; *'mitigating actions'* (to deal with downside risk) and *'exploitative actions'* (to take advantage of upside risks). Since these represent potential decisions that can be made *in response* to the forecasts, they should not be included in the range forecast. They should be separately documented and presented along with the range forecast. If the situation is complex we may need to present these as a set of linked actions that we call a *contingency plan*.

ASSESSING UNCERTAINTY USING SCENARIOS

So much for the process of assessing risk through range forecasting. In these uncertain times, it would be wise for Donna to consider the possibility of extreme outcomes – in other words, she should contemplate uncertainty. Perhaps she might lose her job. Perhaps she has a distant rich aunt who is ill. Will she pull through or might she perish? If so, is she going to be remembered in the will or did her aunt bequeath it all to the cats' home?

How does the process of assessing uncertainty differ from that of assessing risk?

Firstly, since risk is present and ever changing, assessing it is likely to be a routine activity. Uncertainty is associated with rare events, so we would not expect it to be part of the monthly or even quarterly process.

Second, while a large rare outcome might be associated with a single event (like a plane crashing into the computer center), it is much more likely that the kind of uncertainty we are interested in is a result of a series of related (i.e. dependent) events. In combination, these will take the business on a trajectory that is completely different to that on which we based the central forecast.

We only have to look at the recent credit crunch for an example of this phenomenon. Underpinning the catastrophe was the structural risk inherent in the 'sub-prime' market. However, the losses suffered by the banks and the financial system as a whole went way beyond the value of simple debtor default. Assets were structured and traded in such a way that it undermined confidence in the solvency of many kinds of banking institution. This led to lines of credit drying up which increased the chances of a bank collapse, which of course a number did. All this precipitated a rapid contraction in activity in the real economy that in turn increased the chance of high levels of mortgage default and so on.[8]

The full scale and consequence of this series of events are unlikely to have been anticipated by assessing risk around a 'business as usual' forecast of the kind that many organizations involved in this debacle probably produced. The difference between the actual outcome and the one they were forecasting was not quantitative, it was qualitative – it was of a completely different nature. Indeed, it is likely that if we were to rerun history things would work out completely differently. What would have happened if Lehman Brothers had not been allowed to go to the wall, or if any of the other institutions had not been rescued? We will never know.

Consequently assessing uncertainty requires a completely different approach to that used for assessing risk.

The approach we recommend is *Scenario Planning*. This involves the creation of a limited number of credible, but different, alternative 'futures' based on *very different assumptions* about the world: the political, economic, social and technological and, increasingly, environmental context. The aim is not to predict the future in any precise sense but to identify how the organization might be vulnerable to a significant and sudden change in external milieus and what new opportunities such a shift might throw up. 'Companies must now take a more flexible approach to planning,' say Bryan and Farrell. 'Each of them should develop several coherent, multipronged strategic-action plans, not just one ... These plans can't be academic

Stable
political/economic
environment

NEW WORLD ORDER	MORE OF THE SAME
• Strong interventionist transnational government	• 'Laissez faire' government
• Global framework in place to control CO_2 emissions	• Stable customer base, compete on service/range
• High regulatory and inspection burden on manufacturers/ retailers	• Consolidation/rationalization of supplier base, focus on economy of scale and other efficiency saving
• Rise of 'responsible consumerism' – move away from global brands	• Price inflation slightly below (predictable) cost inflation
• High cost and price inflation	• Large scale innovations supported by large marketing budgets and international brands
FRAGMENTED WORLD	**DOG EATS DOG**
• Competition between economic power blocs for scarce commodities	• Collapse of euro zone, volatile currencies
• Different carbon control waste/recycling regulations adopted in different regimes	• Rise of protectionism – trade barriers
	• Rise of hard discounters and unbranded label manufacturers
• Volatile energy prices/exchange rates	• Narrowing of product ranges
• Emergence of new retailing power blocks and supplier networks	• Price deflation and high level of promotional discounting
• Erosion of consumer brand loyalty	

Environmental crisis (left) Environmental issues contained (right)

Unstable political/economic
environment

Figure 6.4 Possible scenarios for a European manufacturer of fast moving consumer goods.

exercises; executives must be ready to pursue any of them – quickly – as the future unfolds' (Bryan and Farrell, 2008) (see Figure 6.4).

So, for instance, Donna might choose to take on a bigger mortgage than she needs (at a low interest rate because it is secured against a valuable asset) to cover the possibility that all of the downside risks materialize. If she comes into some money, she can use that to pay off some of the loan. At the same time, she might dust off her resume, ring up some old contacts, just in case, and take out payment protection insurance on her mortgage.

 More

More about Scenario Planning
Scenario Planning is a technique imported into business from the military where it is often used in conjunction with 'war gaming' (i.e. simulation techniques).

The aim is to help train people to interpret and act in unfamiliar, unpredictable and dynamic environments.

Shell, under the leadership of the Head of Corporate Planning, Pierre Wack, first brought Scenario Planning into the mainstream business consciousness nearly forty years ago.

According to Wack, a Scenario Plan is not about creating 'an accurate picture of the future, but better decisions about the future'. 'Together scenarios comprise a tool for ordering one's perceptions,' says Peter Schwartz, another ex Shell planner and author of the most well known book on the topic, *The Art of the Long View* (Schwartz, 1998).[9] The goal is to 'make strategic decisions that are plausible for all possible futures', not to bet on a prediction about a particular future. A good analogue for scenario planning is the flight simulators used to train pilots.

In the early 1970s Shell's planners created two separate scenarios. One that assumed that oil prices would remain stable – the default assumption of the company's forecast. The other assumed an oil crisis sparked off by a more assertive OPEC. The Yom Kippur war of October 1973 did in fact trigger a crisis, and the scenario work of Wack and his colleagues is credited with helping Shell prepare for the trauma.

What scenarios do is to help prepare us to deal with discontinuities, structural breaks in the time series where the forecast models based on prior experience prove to be false. In effect, they help speed up the process of 'double loop learning'.

The primary purpose of assessing risk and uncertainty is to raise organizational awareness and to stimulate contingency planning

This last discussion brings us to the nub of the issue tackled in this chapter. While it is important to understand the level of risk attached to forecasts for the purposes of communication to stakeholders and so on, in our view range forecasting is not fundamentally about producing a 'correct' set of estimates. Nor is it about reducing the amount of management time spent debating what is the 'right' single point forecast (although this is also undoubtedly a benefit).

Any journey into the future is a voyage of discovery, and no sane explorer sets out into the unknown without being prepared for eventualities. Experience from previous expeditions is helpful but it may not be enough. An appreciation of risk helps us steer the business away from negative situations and more quickly exploit positive situations. An appreciation of uncertainty helps us avoid catastrophe and create options that we could exploit should events conspire with us. The *primary reason for incorporating considerations of risk and uncertainty in forecasting is to explore the territory of the future, in a risk free way (in our heads) and to stimulate a debate about what courses of action may be appropriate in the future.* 'In range forecasting it is important to understand the drivers,' says Artur Magolewski, 'but the main value of the debate is the debate itself.' As the bankers who employed 'rocket scientists' to crunch the risk calculations on their behalf have found out to their cost, managing risks is more than mere math. You cannot contract out understanding and judgment.

In summary, 'being prepared' in this way provides three advantages:

1. We take steps to avoid potential catastrophes altogether
2. We become sensitized to what might happen and as a result, we identify positive (opportunities) and negative events earlier than we otherwise would. The US Marines call this process 'developing situational awareness'.
3. We think through in advance exactly 'what would we do if' – we build a plan that is contingent on a set of circumstances. In effect we cut out the 'ideas' and 'feasibility' and 'planning' stage of our decision-making life cycle.

The last two of these things have the same effect – they reduce decision making lead times so making us more flexible and responsive and, a result, more likely to 'win'. 'The future will belong to companies whose senior executives remain calm, assess their options and nurture the flexibility, awareness, and resiliency needed to deal with whatever the world throws at them,' conclude Bryan and Farrell.

Example

Range forecasting at Unilever Poland and AMEX

A major risk factor for Unilever Foods in Poland is the exchange rate. Most raw materials are denominated in euros or dollars rather than zlotys. The financial controller therefore maintains a close watch on currency fluctuations and other risk factors such as the price of oils used to make margarine, and every quarter agrees in advance with the country management what will be done in the event of any of these risks materializing. 'Range forecasts help us have an open dialogue,' says Richard Sciver. 'The old system of single point forecasting closed down discussions about options. Now we are thinking all the time "what if this happens? What about this?"' (Morlidge, 2005).

The former AMEX CFO, Gary Crittenden, sees having a flexible business model as one of the key attributes of a 'best in class' company. 'It gives us the ability to maintain stability in the face of external turbulence, because we have a "play book" we can use to compensate for our level of billings being 5% higher or lower than we anticipated, for example,' says Jamie Croake. 'We call these our "flexibility plans" and we look at them every month. They are particularly helpful in helping to for manage our performance over the very short term' (Croake, 2008).

Back to Donna: the solution

By this time you are probably getting worried about Donna. She has clearly not understood what range forecasting is all about and is about to …

Fear not! She has been listening and has taken our advice. This is what she came up with (Figure 6.5).

As you can see, Donna has phased her risk analysis over four quarters, and separated the two big discrete risks (a big repair bill – not requiring a new car – and a car replacement) into alternative scenarios. The risk of both of these two scenarios is independent of the other downside risks, so she has discounted them, because she recognizes that by adding them arithmetically she will overstate the risk. However, most of her other risks (upside and downside), with the exception of the salary uplift, are dependent, since they are all tied to interest rates and the state of the property market. As a result she decided she was right to add them together.

What Donna discovered is that, excluding the cost of the holiday, it was likely that her bank account would be in credit until Quarter 3. Indeed, if things turned out well she may avoid going into the red at all. As a result, she decided to raise an unsecured loan for the cost of the holiday ($6000) now (with a view to paying it off in Quarter 4) and wait and see how things developed in Quarter 1. She hopes that the market holds up and any short term cash flow problem can be covered by a bank overdraft, but if business does fall off, or she finds her car needs repairing, at the end of March she has the option of increasing her mortgage by a modest amount (say $8000) to provide her with a cash buffer to cover the period of

	Q1	Q2	Q3	Q4	TOTAL
Base Case					
Salary	6000	6000	6000	6000	24000
Commission	3000	3000	3000	3000	12000
Annual Bonus				10000	10000
Bills	-6000	-6000	-6000	-6000	-24000
Rent	-1500				-1500
Mortgage		-4500	-4500	-4500	-13500
Cash Flow	**1500**	**-1500**	**-1500**	**8500**	**7000**
Bank Balance	**1500**	**0**	**-1500**	**7000**	**7000**
Best Case (continuous risk only)					
Salary			500	500	1000
Commission	1500	1500	1500	1500	6000
Bonus				5000	5000
Mortgage		300	300	300	900
Discounted			-100	-100	-200
Best Case Cash Flow	**3000**	**300**	**200**	**15200**	**18700**
Best Case Bank Balance	**3000**	**3300**	**3500**	**18700**	**18700**
Worst Case (continuous risk only)					
Commission	-1500	-1500	-1500	-1500	-6000
Bonus				-500	-500
Mortgage		-1050	-1050	-1050	-3150
Worst Case Cash Flow	**0**	**-4050**	**-4050**	**5450**	**-2650**
Worst Case Bank Balance	**0**	**-4050**	**-8100**	**-2650**	**-2650**
Worst Case (discrete risks)					
Repairs	-3600	-3600	-3600	-3600	
less discount	500	1000	1000	1250	
OR					
Car	-25000	-25000	-25000	-25000	
less discount	500	1000	1000	1250	
Worst Case Bank Balance (*discounted by 30%)					
Repair Scenario	**-3100**	**-6650**	**-10700**	**-5000**	
New Car Scenario	**-24500**	**-28050**	**-32100**	**-26400**	

Figure 6.5 Donna's solution.

uncertainty. In all but the very worst case (a new car) she is borrowing less than she was originally contemplating, and at a much lower rate because the loan is secured against an asset. In the event of needing a new car the loan would be secured against the vehicle.

• • • • •

We have now reached the end of the first leg of the journey. At times the path has been steep, and at first sight some of the obstacles challenging, but the view from the top is impressive. Having got this far you now have as good a grasp of the basics of the craft of forecasting as many forecasting professionals! This knowledge (which is summarized in Appendix 1) will help you diagnose problems with your existing processes, help you design better ones and become a more discriminating and better informed consumer of forecasts.

The next section takes the principles we have described over the last five chapters and shows how to apply them in practice. You have a choice. If you are involved in designing or implementing a new process or running an existing one you might decide to tackle the next section in the same spirit as the last. If, however, forecasting is not at the heart of your role, you might choose to skim read it, picking on those elements that seem pertinent or intriguing. In either case the subject matter is no more demanding than that encountered in the last section.

• • • • •

SUMMARY

Most forecasts are expressed as a 'single point' but since we know that the forecast outcome will almost certainly be 'wrong' to some degree it is a waste of time and effort to engage in extensive debate about what the number should be. Instead we should try to understand the assumptions upon which the forecast is based in order to expose why and how far the forecast might be wrong so that we can work out what we would do in the eventuality. It is helpful to distinguish between the forecast risk that is predictable to a degree (because it is largely the result of factors inherent in the business or its environment), and uncertainty which is less predictable and often larger in impact. We should build plans to help us quickly adapt to risk. We should try to insure ourselves against uncertainty and generally raise awareness so we can react more quickly. Assessing risk is often done poorly, because forecasters fail to understand how to manipulate probabilities properly. This can easily be remedied. Scenario Planning should be used to assess uncertainty. It is important that the likely scale and nature of risks are understood, but not for their own sake. Our objective is to improve situational awareness and so speed up response.

KEY LEARNING POINTS

Definitions

- Risk – any deviation from a central forecast (positive or negative) where the probability of occurrence can be estimated with a degree of confidence.
- Uncertainty – any possible deviation from a central forecast (positive or negative) where the probability of occurrence cannot be estimated with a degree of confidence.
- Central forecast – the 'single point' forecast.
- Range forecast – the estimated range of possible outcomes (risk) around the central forecast at a defined level of probability. The outcome of sensitivity and 'what if' analyses.
- Sensitivity analysis – creating a range of possible outcomes by varying the assumptions made about continuous risk.

- 'What if' analysis – alternative possible outcomes resulting from the use of different assumptions about discrete risks.
- Scenario Planning – an approach to assessing with uncertainty. It involves the creation of alternative scenarios by making completely different *sets of assumptions* about political, economic, social, technological or environmental factors.
- Skewed – where risk is not uniformly distributed around the central forecast.

Types of risk

- Underlying – risk around a momentum forecast. The level of risk may be estimated based on historic patterns of variation around a trend.
- Event – risk attached to an intervention. The level and nature of risk is likely to be unique to that particular intervention.
- Continuous – 'smooth' risk which can assume any value along a scale.
- Discrete – 'lumpy' risk that tends to assume one value or another (often one value may be 'zero').

Calculation of risk

- Dependent risks (highly correlated): these can be added arithmetically.
- Independent risks (not highly correlated): these need to be combined statistically (or estimated judgmentally).

Responses to risk

- Mitigating actions – actions which may be used to offset the effect of possible negative risk (unfavorable circumstances).
- Exploitative actions – actions which may be used to exploit positive risk (favorable circumstances).
- Contingency plans – complex sets of mitigating or exploitative actions.

NOTES

1 'Normal vision is, in fact only two to three degrees around the dead center of the eye. Our perception of the world as a canvas laid out before our eyes is a trick of the brain which stitches together patches of signals provided by our eyes' continuous scanning of the environment. This is another illustration of the inadequacy of an exclusive focus on a single narrow view of the world.

2 In 1921 Frank Knight, a University of Chicago economist, was the first to make the distinction between risk and uncertainty (Knight, 1921).

3 There is an increasing body of scientific literature on this subject, and the significance of power laws and network effects is beginning to be recognized by business. For an

example of this, refer to a recent interview given by Eric Schmidt, CEO of Google (Manyika 2008).

4 This is an example of a 'ratchet effect', which is a common feature of business, that produces a skew in forecast risk.

5 This is clearly a highly judgmental process; indeed assessing risk and uncertainly nearly always is. 'Range Forecasting always has a scientific element, but there is an emotional element which is just as important,' says Artur Magolewski of Unilever Poland. As with judgmental modeling of a single point forecast, it is important that we explicitly and clearly document our assumptions. Indeed, anything that is significant enough to qualify as an assumption for the purposes of constructing a central forecast should appear in our forecast of risk. After all, if there isn't a chance of material variation there is little point in documenting an assumption.

6 This approach should not be confused with so-called, 'Scenario Planning'. This is a technique commonly used to deal with uncertainty rather than risk, of the sort encountered in strategic planning. It involves creating alternative 'stories' of potential futures rather than varying assumptions contained in a single forecast.

7 A common variant of this mistake is to include in 'upside risk' an action that you might take in response to a risk e.g. deferring discretionary expenditure. It should either be netted off against the negative risk (if it is a consequence) or presented as a mitigating option.

8 Such effects are usually excluded from the quantitative risk models used by bankers because they complicate the math. The Bank of England's director for financial stability recently blamed the lack of consideration given to such 'network externalities' and the use of short time series to drive the risk models for their failure. 'With the benefit of hindsight, those models were both very precise and very wrong' (Cohen, 2009).

9 Schwartz's book is very practical, and is recommended reading for anyone with a serious interest in the technique.

Section 3
'PRAXIS'

The purpose of this section is to deal with some of the issues involved with implementing and running a forecast process.

Section 2 will have equipped you with the knowledge to design a simple forecast process.

This section discusses some common process and implementation issues organized around three themes. This will provide guidance about:

- running a routine forecast process;
- how to structure forecasting in large or complex organizations, where a number of processes run in parallel;
- how to decide who should be responsible for forecasting in your organization.

By the end of this section, you will be equipped to design and run a forecast process.

This section is aimed at practitioners, whether they are responsible for running the process or involved in another capacity.

❝There is nothing as useful as a good theory.❞
Kurt Lewin 1890–1947

In the last section, we used straightforward logic supported by practical examples to expose the first five 'principles of forecasting':

1. Mastery of Purpose
2. Mastery of Time
3. Mastery of Models
4. Mastery of Measurement
5. Mastery of Risk.

These basic principles of forecasting have a general level of applicability wherever forecasting is carried out. In the language of science, they are *invariant* because they are based on robust logic, supplemented by an understanding of the working of systems gleaned from a number of disciplines. We recognize these principles as valid because, without realizing it, we use them all the time in our everyday life.

Business people are practical people, however; most are not inclined to theory. In this sense, they are more like engineers than physicists. While engineers need to have a good grasp of physics (nobody would like to cross a bridge built by an engineer who did not) there is a lot more to good engineering than good physics. One of the things that engineers need that physicists do not is context. Newton's Laws are invariant but there are many ways to build a bridge depending on the terrain, what you want it to carry, how much money you have and so on.

That is the problem we tackle in this next section which deals with the last element of forecast mastery: Mastery of Process. In this section our challenge is how to help practitioners apply these conceptual principles in real life without making sweeping assumptions about the nature of the business, its objectives, the challenges it faces, the type of person who we are trying to help and the particular circumstances he or she might be facing.

What we have done is distill some learnings from the experience of ourselves and others which will serve as a map to help guide you as you seek to apply the principles we outlined in the last section. We cannot hope to cover every situation that you might face, nor can we do justice to every topic that we touch upon, but what we offer will point you in the right direction, help you ask the right sort of questions and avoid the quicksands that lie in wait for the ignorant or unwary.

This section is organized around three practical questions:

1. How do I go about building a routine forecast process that is effective and efficient?
2. How do I integrate this routine process with other routine processes – particularly other forecast related processes?
3. Who should have the responsibility for forecasting?

Having read Section 2 you will now have mastered forecasting in principle. The challenge we address in the first of the three themes is that posed by Arie de Geus in the preface: how do we develop the capacity to act intelligently collectively in practice? This is a problem of organization, and since forecasting is a routine rather than an ad hoc activity this involves understanding what it takes to build an effective process; one that helps ensure that we apply the five principles consistently well and on a large scale. Process management is an underrated skill in western management, particularly outside the shop floor where competitive pressures have forced western managers to adopt many of the practices of Japanese manufacturers. In order to reliably achieve good results from a process involving the coordinated collective efforts of many people it is important for everyone involved, in whatever capacity, to appreciate the basic simple principles of effective process management.

Chapter 7

MASTERING PROCESS: the mother of good fortune

THEME #1 RECIPE FOR SUCCESS: TIPS AND TRAPS

> ❝A good forecaster is not smarter than everyone else; he merely has his ignorance better organized.❞ Anonymous

> ❝We think in generalities, but we live in detail.❞
> Alfred North Whitehead

How to design a forecast process – how it fits with the management process – how to design out bias – why standardization is key to process improvement – the critical role of behavior – bad behavior – the balance between principles and pragmatism

---

There is no one 'right way' of forecasting. Every business will have unique features that mean that a 'cookie cutter' approach to design will not work. However, forecasting is a process, and when it comes to running a process, there are many lessons that we can learn from companies that excel at process management that we can adopt, adapt and apply to forecasting.

In our experience, too few businesses take the task of designing and running administrative processes seriously. Management is often not involved in the detail; lower level staff are often left to 'sort out' the design, individual tasks are not properly defined, and too little attention is paid to the interdependencies between related processes. Clearly, process rigor and discipline are important for large scale manufacturers of say, cars, but is it appropriate to apply the same approach to small scale administrative processes? We believe it is. The first lesson to be learnt is: design a process that makes sense.

RULE NUMBER 1 – GOING WITH THE FLOW: ORGANIZE YOUR PROCESS IN A LOGICAL SEQUENCE

Put simply, a process is made up of three things; an input, an output and a set of routines (tasks) that transform the inputs into outputs. The first lesson in 'process technique' is to order these tasks logically, in the correct sequence and at the right time. This might sound obvious and banal but it is sobering to discover how many companies do not organize the process steps in a logical order.

Often you find businesses trying to force steps of the forecasting process into a pre-existing pattern of meetings. This means that things are discussed and agreed out of sequence, often without the relevant information at hand and without sufficient time between meetings to complete the work required.

In the chart (Figure 7.1) you can see a logical order: collect the actuals, use these (and innovation plans) to build a volume forecast, check that there is a capacity to supply, value the results of this exercise, then review the output and so on. Each step in this process is itself a process and so will have its own predefined inputs and outputs, which need to be defined and agreed. Between steps there will also be 'offline' processing that should be defined with adequate time allowed for completion.

The large 'M' in the boxes donates major cross-functional meetings. The whole management process should be organized around the necessary steps in the forecasting and decision-making process and not accounting deadlines. Also note that the forecasting process is closely integrated with other management processes: innovation, capacity planning and resource allocation. Finally, the process loops back on itself creating a natural flow. The speed of this cycle sets the metabolic rate for the business; where information is metabolized into action.[1]

We recommend that you start with a blank sheet of paper and map out the 'ideal' process, based on the needs of the business rather than anyone's idea about what is practical. It is helpful to set a tight deadline – one that seems unreasonable

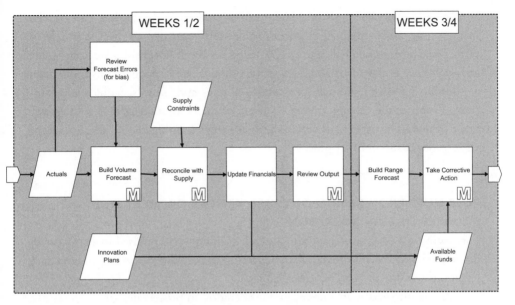

Figure 7.1 An example of a flow chart for a monthly forecast process. *'M' denotes meetings.*

 **More**

How to reduce the burden of more frequent forecasting

To some, particularly those who have been brought up with traditional budgeting whereby you rebudget only when required, the prospect of running a monthly (or more frequent) forecast routine might be horrifying; a recipe for bureaucracy. We dispute this. First, constant repetition speeds up learning and improvement (see Rule number 3 below). Second, one of our top tips is to *focus only on what has changed since the last cycle*. 'Look at the change in the forecast assumptions rather than the absolute numbers,' says Martin Jarvis. 'A disciplined process maintains an organization's focus on what is changing, thereby preventing it slipping into tackling the 'crisis du jour' when it becomes impossible to ignore. It is easier to repeat the process frequently concentrating on change than it is to do it from the bottom up every time' (Jarvis, 2008).

at first – and then challenge the design team to work to it. Forecasting is an exercise in managing time; imposing a unreasonable restriction like this forces people to think creatively and to challenge received wisdom about how things are done. Only after you have designed an idealized process should you introduce constraints such as meeting patterns, externally imposed deadlines and other scheduled interventions. If you cannot change these, be aware of the compromises that you have to make in designing your final process and take steps to mitigate the risks associated with having a sub optimal process.

RULE NUMBER 2 – DESIGN OUT BIAS: REMOVE OR TREAT THE SOURCES OF BIAS 'INFECTION'

Forecasting is a process of exercising judgment: judgment exercised in a structured, disciplined and co-coordinated way. However, as we have discussed, judgment is notoriously prone to systematic error: bias.

Minimizing bias is an important consideration in process design.

In the process we have mapped out, measurement is a mandatory step; it is not optional. Measurement is a vital countermeasure, but it might not be enough to wipe out the bias virus, so you need to consider other steps that might help stop the process becoming infected in the first place. The practical steps that you can take to reduce the risk of bias include:

1. Ensure that forecast assumptions are properly documented and widely shared. The discussions that take place about the forecast should be discussions about the validity of assumptions (inputs into the process), not whether the forecast (output) is correct or 'acceptable'.

2. Try to exclude all reference to targets in forecast discussions. A major cause of bias is the desire to demonstrate that a target will be hit. A forecast is an expression of the likely possible outcome; comparison with target – the desired outcome – is a step that should take place *after* the forecast is produced, not as part of the forecast production process itself. Often targets are expressed only in financial terms, so we recommend that you delay the 'dollarization' step for as long as possible. For example, in the process diagram above, we can see that the process of constructing the financial forecast (often referred to as 'cash up') takes place after the volume forecast has been agreed. As a result consideration of 'are we on target' does not 'infect' the volume discussion.

3. Ban adjustments to the forecast.[2] Bias is often introduced when forecasts are adjusted after they have been produced. While most people know that it is

'wrong' to adjust numbers that have been produced in good faith it is often difficult to resist the temptation to do so, particularly if pressured by someone more senior. One tip here is to legitimize dissenting views by using the Range Forecast to register potential alternative outcomes.

 More

If you have to adjust forecasts make sure you keep a record
If eliminating adjustments to forecasts altogether is a 'step too far' for your business we insist that you set up a process for recording adjustments. It may be appropriate to use the Range Forecast to do this since, by definition, an unsupported adjustment to a carefully considered forecast introduces a new risk. By making adjustments transparent this helps the user of the forecast interpret it, but it also discourages political manipulation and makes it possible to analyze whether the process of adjustment actually improves the forecast as those that do it are inclined to believe. In our experience, adjustments worsen bias as often as they reduce it. In these circumstances, adjustment simply increases variation.

4. Be thoughtful about how you allocate roles and responsibilities, ensuring that 'checks and balances' are built into the system. This will be discussed in detail in Theme #3 'Roles and Responsibilities'.

RULE NUMBER 3 – WHEN YOU HAVE DESIGNED YOUR PROCESS, STICK TO IT AND CONTINUOUSLY IMPROVE BY LEARNING FROM EXPERIENCE
Having designed a 'good' process, what next?

A good source of insight and inspiration about process management is Toyota, the Japanese car manufacturer. Toyota's whole business is founded on process excellence. The Toyota Manufacturing System (TMS)[3] – a philosophy, approach and set of practices – has rightly come to be regarded with awe across the business world. Who hasn't heard of Quality Management, Kaizen and Kanban? More to the point it clearly works. At the end of 2008 Toyota displaced General Motors as the world's largest car maker, having been most profitable for many years with its cars consistently recognized as amongst the highest quality.

Toyota's success has made it one of the most studied businesses of the last 20 years. One author, Jeffrey Liker, sets out 14 principles that underpin the excellence of Toyota in his book *The Toyota Way*. All 14 principles are worthy of study but we would like to highlight one that is particularly relevant for processes like forecasting. Principle number six states: 'Standardized tasks are the foundation for continuous improvement and employee empowerment'. What does this mean and why is it important for us?

As we have designed a process that 'makes sense' it is obviously important to take steps to ensure that what has been designed is what is done – in the same way, everywhere and for each forecast cycle. The main reason for standardizing is not – as it first might appear – to force employees into compliance. It is because success – doing things more effectively and efficiently – relies on harnessing the ideas and creativity of employees to improve and learn, and *it is only possible to improve a process that is standardized*.

 More

Why discipline isn't the same as conformity

To those have been brought up in traditional western management practices this way of thinking about standardization might sound odd. We are used to thinking about 'standardization' applied in the tradition of Frederick Taylor, the most famous advocate of 'scientific management'. In his philosophy, which still infects the thinking of many western managers, standardization is a way of reducing cost by specifying and enforcing the 'best way' of performing any task, thereby eliminating the scope for variation of processes. Taylor was actively seeking to discourage employees from exercising their initiative. Perhaps this is a reason why many people resist attempts to impose discipline and structure on administrative processes; they fear that it will be used to impose conformity and to stifle thinking.

Figure 7.2 Improving a process.
In order to improve a process – like a golf swing – it is important that it is consistent.

To illustrate this take an example of a good process from the world of sport. The way to become a great golfer is by first spending hours over days, months, and years at the driving range, 'grooving' (standardizing) your swing based on an appreciation of 'good technique' – head down, left arm straight and so on. Second, you need to seek help to diagnose and correct faults – you ask the golf pro to have a look at your swing (see Figure 7.2). If you start with too many bad habits, do not practice, or if you do practice but swing in a different way every time you hit the ball, then there is little chance that you will bring your handicap down.

Let us apply this lesson to the task of building a good forecasting process. First, define the process to the best of your ability and follow the defined process in a disciplined fashion through every forecast cycle. Second, when something works, or when something fails, understand why and change the standard practice to incorporate the necessary changes to practice. Toyota has mastered this process on an industrial scale. Every employee is encouraged to make suggestions for improvement, and a high proportion of these are implemented (an estimated 20 million over the last 40 years – equivalent to one per employee per week). In summary you need to organize yourself for learning. There is no way that you can do the clever and creative things, in art, sport, or in business, without mastering the basic techniques of the discipline. How to mix paint, represent perspective, catch a ball, or produce a reliable forecast.

RULE NUMBER 4 – MORE ABOUT DISCIPLINE: MANAGERS SHOULD BE MADE TO FIT THE PROCESS, NOT THE OTHER WAY AROUND

Running a good forecasting process demands discipline, which includes issuing pre-reading produced in a standardized format, distributed at a defined time so many days before each key meeting, consistent agenda and meeting structures adhered to rigidly, and so on. This might feel onerous but we find that once the templates and routines have been set up, and tasks 'grooved' through repetition, like any habit it soon becomes 'second nature' and soon things just 'happen' without the need for petty bureaucracy. In addition, if business critical information is produced in a disciplined and routine fashion then one real killer of efficiency can be almost eliminated – ad hoc short notice information requests.

One of the biggest challenges is changing ingrained behavior, particularly that of senior people. Leadership has to be intimately involved in the process, indeed leaders have to be seen to be leading – it should be perceived as *their* process. Too often processes are organized around the schedules of the top brass and their poorly specified short notice information requests, issued without any regard to the impact on the rest of the organization, are often treated as a privilege of rank. Ultimately, the process we have described must become *the way* that the business is run rather than an administrative process that fits in with the boss. Under this kind of regime, the schedule is fixed perhaps a year in advance and stays fixed. Meetings should not be cancelled, rearranged, or the agenda changed, except under exceptional circumstances.

RULE NUMBER 5 – ALIGN BEHAVIORS: ELIMINATE THE BAD PATTERNS OF BEHAVIOR WHICH CAN DESTROY THE BEST DESIGNED PROCESS

Very often, the difference between success and failure lies in the spirit in which the process is run. We have already discussed how badly designed processes, or the inappropriate use of forecast information, can infect a forecast process with bias. The need to minimize and manage motivation bias is important but this is only one facet of the critical role that behavior and culture play in forecasting. The 'mistake number one' for many companies, according to Fritz Roemer, 'is to underestimate the degree of cultural change required' (Roemer, 2008)[4].

A bad process intelligently and sympathetically applied can be more effective than a good process infected by bad behaviors. How people talk, communicate, and interact is as much part of the forecast process as any of the tasks we plotted on our process map.

More

Why you can't separate process and behavior

To illustrate the interdependency of process and behavior let us take the example of the process of 'law enforcement'. There is scarcely a better defined social process; laws are drafted with painstaking care, extensively debated by law makers and carefully interpreted by judges and juries, often in the context of centuries of precedent. Law enforcement officers are rigorously trained, bound by procedures and their conduct subject to independent scrutiny. Despite this, as anyone who has been part of the process of law enforcement knows, the whole experience of being subjected to the law enforcement process is conditioned by the manner in which the process is carried out – specifically the behavior of those enforcing the law. Are you treated as a potential criminal or are you listened to sympathetically? Is your behavior interpreted in a strict procedural fashion or is consideration given to context or previous 'good behavior'. The experience of the law enforcement process and the effect this has on your future actions is, in fact, at least as much a product of the interaction between yourself and the other human beings in the process as it is the dictates of the law or police procedures.

What are 'bad behaviors'? Any action or communication which constrains
or distorts the expression of honest judgment and opinion

Our objective in producing a forecast is to create a faithful picture of what could happen in the future, along with a good understanding of other 'possible futures'. To do this well we need to enlist the knowledge, experience and expertise of everyone who can contribute. Anything that constrains or distorts the process of honest exchange of information and opinions is, therefore, 'bad'.

Here are some examples of what we mean:

A good forecast is 'honest'; it contains no 'wishful thinking'. If there is a chance that your ship is going to hit the rocks you need to be told that – however unwelcome the news might be. Indeed, it is almost a mark of a good forecast that it *does not* come back to the target (at least without corrective action being taken). How managers react to 'unwelcome news' has a big impact on forecast quality. Comments like 'This forecast is unacceptable', 'You are being negative; you are not a team player', 'I don't want to signal that to x' are incompatible with quality forecasting.

The key feature of a good forecast is the absence of bias. Any behavior which results in errors of one sign (i.e. persistent under- or overestimating) being 'rewarded' or 'punished' will drive bias into forecasts. 'Reward' and 'punishment' need not take the form of money. In one division of a large multinational company we know, for example, only those who had fallen short of forecast (but not those whose results were consistently over) were asked to justify themselves to senior management. This sent a clear signal that bias was acceptable providing it was the right sort of bias. Arbitrary adjustment of forecasts, as well as undermining efforts to improve the process, also will encourage 'gaming' behavior, resulting in higher levels of variation as well as bias.

 Example

Leadership behavior at AMEX
Jamie Croake points to the behavior of business leaders as a key reason for the success of AMEX's transformation (Croake, 2008). 'You need strong sponsorship from your leaders; it can't be just one person. They are important as advocates but they also need to demonstrate that they are comfortable with looking forward and with change to forecasts.'

Good forecasting relies on the open and honest exchange of information and opinions; no one person or group has unique access to the 'truth'. Indeed, there is no 'truth' in forecasting; there are only better or worse judgments. A forecasting process therefore should be a collaborative cross-functional endeavor. We have encountered organizations where forecasting is treated as a battle between groups to prove 'who is right'. In these cases, information is closely guarded rather than shared, analyses are skewed to support a particular point of view and alternative perspectives are dismissed out of hand. In other words the forecast process has become a 'political process', a power struggle for control over forecast information. Forecasting should be treated as a 'social process', where information is shared, diversity recognized as a source of strength and where logic and knowledge, not the protection of interest groups, are the criteria for decision-making (see Figure 7.3).

How an organization reacts to variation and change are other cultural traits that also have a big impact on the quality of forecasting. No process in the known uni-

POLITICAL PROCESS	SOCIAL PROCESS
•Based on individuals or factions	•Based on the team
•Motivated by access to: •Money •Influence •Status etc	•Motivated by the collective good
•Mode: competitive	•Mode: collaborative
•Characterized by exercise of power; applying or withholding •Co-operation •Information	•Characterized by organization of knowledge and rational debate
•Organized through negotiated agreements between individuals or faction	•Organized through procedures, maintained by collective discipline

Figure 7.3 Two different sorts of behavioral process.
Which best describes the way in which your organization's culture works?

verse is immune from variation, and forecasting is particularly prone to it because it involves (albeit informed) speculation about an unknown future. Reactions like 'why did you screw up', 'I want explanations for all the variance' or 'why is your error larger than x's?' will breed 'gaming' behavior, dishonesty and the manipulation of numbers. The business environment is never static. If your organization treats change as evidence of bad forecasting then information will be suppressed and suppression leads to surprises. Indeed, *if forecasts do not change between iterations then there is something wrong.* Either you are forecasting far too frequently or, more likely, the numbers are being 'massaged' in order to avoid unwelcome challenges like 'why has the forecast changed – do you know what you are doing?'

 Key Concept

Why it is dangerous to incentivize people for forecasting accurately
Often, the 'solution' advocated is to 'incentivize accurate forecasting'. This is positive to the extent that attaching money to forecast quality strongly signals that 'this is important'.

On the other hand, as we have already argued, we do not want 'accurate' forecasts; we want reliable forecasts, which are not necessarily the same thing. Forecast error is to be expected, and providing it is unbiased and contained at a reasonable level, it is perfectly acceptable. Paying people to produce accurate forecasts can, and does, drive gaming behavior. Incentivizing forecast accuracy can convert the forecast into a target and managers will soon learn ways in which they can meet this particular target without doing what you really want them to do – improve the quality of their forecasts.

In fact, *you should distrust your forecasts that never display error* since the only way this can be consistently achieved is by manipulating outcomes to make a forecast come true.[5] One of the first things we look for is to see if a company's results display a characteristic peaking pattern around accounting period ends. If so, this is prima facie evidence that results are being managed back to a number – and very often this is a forecast number.

The 'golden rule': 'hard on facts, soft on people'

Good forecasting demands that we face up to the way the world is, not the way we would like it to be. Unless we have evidence to the contrary, we should assume that those producing and contributing to the process are honest, competent and share common goals. The default position should be that any 'failure' is not the result of any personal shortcomings – it is an indication that the process is defective or that an individual's capability needs to be enhanced. On the other hand, if an individual demonstrates that they are *not* honest, competent or that they are self-interested they need to be removed from the process before they infect it.

There is a second 'golden rule', which will resonate with any parent. To influence the behavior of others, *the power of action outweighs the power of words* by a factor of 10 – at least. That is not to say that written 'rules' or 'ways of working' are not important. Making it explicit what behaviors you want can be invaluable, but they need to be followed through – if bad behavior is not 'called' when it happens the effect can be negative. You have just added 'hypocrisy' or 'weakness' to the list of bad behaviors that are tolerated in your organization!

Key Concept

How good forecasting practice is built on respect and trust

It is difficult to overemphasize the importance of treating employees contributing to forecasts with care and respect. Managers make decisions based on two sources of information: information about the past and information about the future. If systems are well designed, information about the past is widely available and is factual in nature. Of course, it is possible for information to be suppressed or 'spun' in the process of communication but in the end, facts are facts.

On the other hand, *the only information we have about the future is based on what people choose to share with us*. Managers are totally dependent on the skill and integrity of those people in their organization. These people carry in their heads the knowledge about the business, the market and 'what is going on' needed to make any form of reliable estimate about the future. If they believe that they will be punished for being honest or praised for telling people what they want to hear; if the values of an organization do not include respect for the truth and for people in general, then it is very unlikely that your organization will produce good forecasts.

If you want to hear what you want to hear, do not expect good forecasts. If you want good forecasts don't expect to hear what you want to hear.

RULE NUMBER 6 – BALANCE PRINCIPLES AND PRAGMATISM: ADOPT A 'GOOD ENOUGH' APPROACH

Throughout this book, we have advocated a principle-based approach to forecasting – the principle that the purpose of forecasting is to help make decisions, and that this should determine the design of the process. Forecast horizons should be driven by decision-making lead times and the frequency of update by the rate of change in the environment. And so on.

While success in forecasting is built on a good grasp of such theory, it is important that you implement these ideas in a pragmatic fashion. If you become obsessive about exactly how long your forecast horizon should be, or what the perfect model is for forecasting overheads and so on you will have missed the point. 'What I see a lot of are people over designing processes and then failing to run them,' says

Martin Jarvis. 'Make sure that you can live with it not just in an ideal month, but in more difficult times and through holiday periods. Better to forecast a few big things properly than many things poorly' (Jarvis, 2008).

The purpose of setting out forecasting practice in the way we have is to help people design and operate forecasting processes that do the job they are supposed to do well. Processes which are *useful* or *'fit for purpose'*. If as a result of reading this book, you spend more time debating how processes should be designed than you do working out what they are telling you and what you should do about it, we will have failed in our mission. We also should not wait for 'the perfect software solution' before we act – sometimes the right thing to do is just get on with it.

In addition, while the principles we have set out are robust you need to apply them in a way that works for your business. We say: try stuff out, if it works, do some more; if it does not, scrap it and move on.

Pragmatism also teaches us that, while we may strive for a working life that is well ordered and calm, there will be times of crisis. When they were being chased by a tiger our ancestors needed a shot of adrenalin that boosted their heart rate, sent food to muscles and shut down processes that were not essential to short term survival. In these circumstances, poise and elegance are less important than saving your bacon. There will also be times in business when getting a result is more important than how it is accomplished. Sometimes the elegant forecasting process you have designed will need to be short circuited and cherished practices and disciplines set to one side. The trick is to do this only when necessary and 'get back to normal' as soon as possible afterwards. Unfortunately too many businesses are run by adrenalin junkies where the ability to cope in a crisis is treated as a badge of honor, so things never get back to normal.

We believe that the best businesses are those where exceptional results are achieved without exceptional effort. In these organizations people can sleep eight hours a night, go home on time and spend their weekends with their family. There is nothing clever about chaos. However, eliminating chaos requires knowledge, intelligence and diligence. Hopefully, we have contributed to at least one of these.

• • • • •

Over the last few pages we have tackled a simple problem of organizations: how should we arrange the activities and shape the behaviors of a large and diverse group of people so as to consistently achieve a defined objective – in this case reliable forecasts. For those in simple, single unit, organizations what you have just learned might be enough. But if you work in very large or diverse businesses there is another big organizational challenge – how to coordinate the potentially independent forecasting processes of many different groups, which may serve a wide range of different purposes. The next section deals with this topic, and is necessarily more complex than the last. It may be irrelevant for some readers, in which case they may wish to skim read or skip it. It is required reading for almost everyone in a large organization, however, not least because it addresses a fundamental question that they face in different forms almost every day: when and in what ways is it OK to be different?

• • • • •

SUMMARY

Good forecasting practice is based on a set of principles that can be successfully applied in many different ways, in different business contexts. While there is no single 'recipe' to be followed there are lessons to be learned from those businesses who can claim process excellence. The keys to success include: defining processes in an explicit logical fashion, recognizing interdependencies with related processes, following these standardized processes in a consistent and disciplined manner but in such a way that learnings are exposed and incorporating these in the standardized approach. Also, take steps to design out the sources of bias. Well defined processes are not enough, however; appropriate behavior is just as important. The ultimate test of a good process is 'does it work?' and 'is it useful?'

KEY LEARNING POINTS

Process design

1. Organize the process around a logical flow of information.
2. Design out bias.
3. Standardize and operate in a disciplined way to learn and improve.
4. Managers should fit the process.
5. Eliminate unhealthy patterns of behavior.
6. Balance principle and pragmatism.

How to design out bias

- Fact-based – make assumptions explicit.
- Hide 'anchors' such as targets.
- Eliminate or restrict forecast 'adjustments'.

Healthy forecasting behaviors

- Model good behavior, expose and deal with bad behavior
- Data driven
- Openness
- Trust
- Acceptance of variation, uncertainty, and change.

THEME #2 COORDINATION IN A COMPLEX SYSTEM: HOW DIFFERENT CAN WE BE?

❝A schedule defends from chaos and whim. It is a net for catching days. It is scaffolding on which a worker can stand and labor with both hands at sections of time.❞ Annie Dillard

---

Why do forecasts need to be aligned? – bias, variation and one set of numbers – close and loose coupling – decoupling forecasts – alignment: design choices

---

Tight alignment can lead to bureaucratic logjams. Insufficient alignment breeds chaos

The observant reader, including those struggling to apply these concepts within large organizations, will have noticed that there is one element of the mnemonic TARAC introduced in Chapter 2 that we didn't explicitly tackle in Section 2: the criterion of *alignment*.

It seems obvious that forecast processes should be 'aligned'; that there shouldn't be dozens of different groups of people in a business working on 'their own forecasts' coming up with conflicting and contradictory answers. How would you like to be on a sailboat where every crew member had a different view on which direction you were heading? Yet this is the situation that we often come across. In many organizations lots of decisions are being made by lots of people, and there is a tendency for them to produce lots of different forecasts to support their own decision-making process or to resist having decisions they don't like being imposed upon them. Our record for the number of different forecasts in a business is eight (one for every function plus a few spare ones produced by functional dissidents!). This is clearly a recipe for chaos.

However, once you get about the task of trying to eliminate these 'surplus' forecasts a host of knotty practical problems present themselves. For example, how can you provide a single forecast that meets the needs of every stakeholder? How do we reconcile the needs of operations for detailed weekly Stock Keeping Unit (SKU) level forecasts with the needs of finance that might only be interested in product group level of detail? How do you align the needs of local salespeople managing a fast moving campaign with those of the corporate center who need to forecast for 'the Street' only every quarter?

The obvious solution is to create a process that accommodates the lowest common denominator, that is at the lowest level of detail demanded by any of the stakeholders, and updated at the frequency of the most time sensitive. The desire to accommodate all the diverse needs of an organization and maintain alignment at all times carries a risk that the entire process becomes bureaucratic and slow; like a convoy where everyone is forced to travel at the speed of the slowest.

A counter argument (following the principles we have established) is that, since different decisions *are* being taken – decisions to do with scheduling production, reallocating resources and communicating with shareholders – it is appropriate to have different forecast processes.

This problem will be familiar to many people who have been responsible for implementing forecast processes in a sizeable or complex organization. How do we resolve this paradox?

The answer is that 'alignment' does not require that every element of every forecast everywhere in the organization must be in perfect agreement at all times. While total alignment is not necessary, we need to make conscious, well informed decisions about why and how different processes, or similar processes in different business units, can be allowed to differ.

Some forecast elements can be allowed to vary, but one should never be out of alignment: the criteria for good forecasting – unbiased and with acceptable variation.

Without exception, any forecast process should be designed to produce unbiased forecasts ...

While it may be possible to compromise on the degree of alignment, we cannot compromise on our definition of the criterion for a reliable forecast: no bias and an acceptable level of variation. The criterion of zero bias *must* hold for any kind of forecast anywhere in the organization without exception. End of debate.

Why be so dogmatic? The reason is that you can only use a forecast with confidence safely if you are clear what it purports to represent. How can you rely on a number to make a decision if you do not know whether it reflects a neutral, optimistic or pessimistic view of the future? This is particularly important in a complex environment where there are a number of forecast processes, perhaps where the output of one process becomes an input into another. For example, assume you are responsible for a profit forecast and have just been provided with sales forecasts as an input into your own process. If you did not know what criterion was used by your supplier you might start adjusting them, perhaps taking 5% off the growth rate because you suspect they are too optimistic. What is the recipient of your forecast meant to do? Perhaps they may adjust your forecasts, just to be safe? What about the next person in the chain?

This might sound far fetched but we know of one case where, in the absence of clear definitions and a policy that restricted 'judgmental adjustments' or made them visible, low level forecasts were adjusted by at least four levels of the management hierarchy before they were communicated to the market. A profit warning and market downgrade soon followed.

There is no point in defining 'a good forecast' in any way other than 'unbiased'. If you encourage or accept any other definition you inject uncertainty and doubt into the process and effectively condone large scale tampering with forecasts which only serves to confuse and heighten doubt and uncertainty.

... but what constitutes 'acceptable variation' may vary

While it is clear that any kind of forecast, and that means every kind of stakeholder, should strive to produce forecasts that are 'unbiased', it is perfectly legitimate for different stakeholders to have different views about what constitutes 'acceptable variation'. They will also have different approaches to managing the risk associated with variation.

Therefore, for example, inventory stock planners deal with variation in forecasts by building safety stock, probably with different levels of cover depending on the product. If the product is a low value item which is easily substituted, then stock cover might be low. If, on the other hand, they are planning for a major new product launch, where any failure to meet demand would be fatal to the product's chances of success, stock planners may want to build very high levels of safety stock to compensate for the unusually high level of risk and the high cost of failure.

If the level of downside risk in the financial forecast is exceptionally high, a CFO responsible for dealing with analysts may choose to stress the downside risks in a forecast. He does so to lower expectations since there is a higher cost attached to failing to meet them than there is a reward for beating them.[6]

Both these are examples of a reasonable approach to take to risk – unavoidable variation.[7] It is unnecessary and wrong, however, for anyone involved in forecasting to deliberately distort the forecast in anticipation of what someone else, in this case the CFO, might do with that information. Once you go down that road the process can become corrupt with poor decision-making (and potentially disastrous relationships with the investment community) being the inevitable consequence.

To summarize: *there is no reason, 'in principle,' why there need be more than one set of (forecast) numbers.*

Key Concept

Beware of targets in forecast clothing: the risk of false purposes

In your organization are forecasts used to set targets – for sales people for example? How often have you been told to 'deliver the forecast'?

This kind of practice undermines the practice of good forecasting, and the forecast for the whole organization is only as good as the weakest link in the chain. Why?

A forecast is a statement of 'where we think we will be' given current assumptions about the world, and a target describes 'where we want to be'. Both the practices outlined above – the use of forecasts for target setting or the expression of a desire that a forecast be achieved as a goal to be achieved – lead to the distinction between the two becoming blurred.

Proctor and Gamble fell into this trap in 1999–2000. As part of 'Organization 2005' CEO Durk Jager introduced the concept of 'stretch goal forecasting'. 'This unsettled product managers, prompting them to estimate demand that was not there and this led to severe inventory build ups that the group is still working off' reported the *Financial Times* in June 2000. The result? Three profit warnings in a quarter, a drop of 50% in the stock price and Mr Jager out of a job (Bogler and Michaels, 2000).

The lesson is that *if you do anything that encourages people to manage back to a forecast you change your forecast into a target.* And once you convert it into a target it stops being a useful forecast.[8]

While in principle all forecasts should agree, in practice, however, the alignment need not be exact and at all times. The reason for tolerating this situation lies in our starting premise: that forecasts are there to help managers make decisions.

Understanding the degree and nature of interdependence is the key to designing a forecasting architecture for large and complex organizations

A good way to understand this apparent paradox is with another analogy. Imagine that you are the commander of a division of tanks. As well as the tanks themselves, you will have support units responsible for the supply of food, ammunition and fuel to the front line fighting units. In these circumstances, you need a good forecast of where the tanks are going to be and you will need to share it with other relevant parts of the organization. If there isn't tight alignment (close coupling) then the tank advance will come to a grinding halt, or at worst your forces will be annihilated because they have run out of fuel or ammunition.

On the other hand, you may be the commander of a unit of Special Forces; perhaps made up of a dozen or so small teams of soldiers operating behind enemy lines. Typically, Special Forces are extremely self-sufficient; they are highly trained, can live off the land, and travel on foot carrying most of the weapons they need. As a result it may not be necessary for the units to provide a forecast at all – the whole raison d'être behind Special Forces is to be flexible and secretive. Perhaps the only kind of coordination needed is to enable a food drop and the ability for the units to request 'backup' in the form of air strikes etc. in order to help them achieve an objective.

How might we apply these two different views of coordination to the work of organizations?

Where 'coupling' is close there needs to be 'one set of numbers'. Alignment may be unnecessary for weakly coupled operations

The key to understanding this apparent dilemma is the notion of interdependency. Dependency exists where planned action taken in one part of a system has an impact (i.e. may influence decisions made) in another part of the system.

 More

Some good sense on alignment from the US military

We have already mentioned that modern military philosophy is based (influenced by the thinking of John Boyd) on the principle of maneuverability, so it is not surprising that a lot of thought has been given to the nature of planning in military affairs – specifically how to manage the trade-off between coordination and flexibility.

We can do no better than to quote directly from the US Marines planning manual (the best treatise on the subject we have read) which offers some very practical advice for commanders and managers alike.

'Whether a plan should have tight or loose coupling depends on a variety of factors, most important of which is the nature of the action being planned. Some plans or actions require tight coupling. When the integration and allocation of scarce resources, including time are the overriding concern, plans generally require tight coupling ... carrier flight deck operations require tight coupling. Other plans, such as for a main attack by one battalion and supporting attack by adjacent battalions, may not require close coupling ... in situations with high levels of friction, chance, unpredictability and interaction between independent wills, loose coupling is more appropriate.

'For most tactical or operational situations ... we should strive to design loose, modular plans. Compared to tightly coupled, integrated plans, modular plans are generally simpler to execute and control, are easier to modify, better endure the effects of friction and disruption, and provide greater latitude in execution.

'A plan can provide for necessary coordination in three ways. The simplest and loosest way is to direct two elements to coordinate locally. Another way is to provide the mechanism for coordination – such as a control measure – but let the elements involved effect the coordination as necessary. A third way is to provide the mechanism and to regulate its use ... Situation permitting the first is the most preferable. Plans should not attempt to couple actions which do not need to be coupled' (Unknown, 1997).

In the case of the tank division there is a high degree of interdependency between the various units. If the fuel supply unit does not have an accurate and up-to-date forecast of where the tanks are likely to be x days ahead (where x represents the lead time in the fuel supply chain!) then the tanks will grind to a halt. On the other hand the Special Forces Division deliberately makes its individual fighting units as independent as possible to be fast and flexible. The interdependencies are therefore small (by comparison with the tank division) and so the coordination needs are small. As a result, a periodic or 'on demand' process of alignment may suffice (perhaps replenishment drops made on a weekly cycle or conditional on certain criteria). Any attempt to force them into tight alignment is unnecessary and would lead to a loss of responsiveness.

Now consider a business example. A manufacturing company needs a sales forecast to plan production. They will also need to produce a financial forecast to allocate resources. If different parts of the organization used different forecasts, the result would be incoherent decision-making and a lack (or surplus) of stock. For example, resources might be allocated to projects for which no production is planned which could then result in a failure to supply – thereby invalidating an assumption on which the financial forecast was based. This is like a captain making a decision to change course in our sailing boat only to find that the crew are all below decks having lunch! In this case – an example of high interdependency (or 'close coupling' to use a systems term) – we should aim to have a single forecast updated on a frequent basis.

On the other hand, a good factory manager in the same company might routinely forecast his own manufacturing costs to ensure that he is delivering the savings from new investment in plant. He may do so whether or not the corporate center requires him to, and we would not necessarily expect him to formally share the results with anyone else, *unless the outcome materially affected the information upon which decisions were made elsewhere in the company.*

 Example

Working without formal forecasting at Svenska Handelsbanken
In Svenska Handelsbanken – the blue riband 'Beyond Budgeting' case – there is no formal forecasting process at all in the retail bank, but branch managers are encouraged to forecast informally. This might strike you as perverse, the height of irresponsibility. The reason why it works is that decision-making authority is delegated to individual branch managers who, because they are 'close to the ground' are able to anticipate and respond to local events very quickly. The center does not need forecasts for decision-making purposes, since they are all made locally! The center periodically produces high level forecasts for cash manage-

ment or investor relation purposes, but since they are not used to influence decision-making in the retail bank these forecasts do not need to be detailed or tightly coupled with branch forecasts.

Here, therefore, is the answer to the conundrum. Where there is 'close coupling' between parts of the organization, because interdependencies are high, it is important that forecasts be tightly aligned. There should not be conflicting or competing 'views of the future'. Where interdependencies are few, and units are loosely coupled however, differences can be tolerated. In these circumstances, it is likely that some parts of the forecasting process will be informal in nature.

More

The argument for multiple forecasts
We believe multiple forecasts (two or more 'sets of numbers') are generally a bad thing – but the academic literature makes a strong case for using multiple forecasting methodologies in parallel. No one forecasting technique is better than any other in all situations, and it has been demonstrated that combining forecasts often improves the quality (accuracy) of forecasts. For practical purposes, however, we would not recommend that businesses routinely produce forecasts using different techniques, particularly if judgmental techniques have been used (which are notoriously prone to bias). This is costly and cumbersome to manage on a routine basis and it is also likely to reduce the understanding of and commitment to the forecast within the organization.

The solution: align forecasts only as and when necessary:
consider different horizons, timing, and frequencies
This demonstrates that, whether and how to align forecasts is not an issue of principle about whether it is right to have 'one set of numbers'. It is a decision based on purely practical considerations – how the decisions made in one part of the

business relate to those made in another. Since organizations come about only because there is a need for people to cooperate, the issue faced by a designer is usually 'how and in what circumstances should forecasts be aligned' rather than *whether* they need to be aligned. The designer should exercise discretion. Their aim should be to decouple as much as possible, in order to keep costs and bureaucracy down and to promote organizational flexibility and resilience.

Here are some of the choices open to an architect in deciding how to 'couple' different parts of the forecast system:

1. Direction. It may be that the degree and nature of alignment across an organization, in a horizontal direction – say between functions – will differ from the degree and nature of alignment on the vertical plane – say between a business unit and the division of which it is part.

2. Level of detail. Because different types of decisions tend to be made in different parts of organizations it is unlikely that they will require the same level of detail. To 'pass on' superfluous detail (i.e. irrelevant to the decisions to be made) is unnecessary; unnecessary data is noise and noise only serves to complicate and confuse.

3. Frequency. Some parts of an organization will be faced with a dynamic environment and both the need and ability to make short term corrections. In this case they may need forecasts to be updated very frequently. Other parts may have a longer decision-making cycle.

4. Horizons. There is no requirement for all parts of an organization to be working with the same forecast horizon. For example, a production scheduling forecast horizon may stop three months out, whereas the forecast horizon for product development may effectively start at three months and look a further five quarters out.

5. Source. It is not necessary for forecasts to have a single source. In the example cited above, the production forecast may be the source of information for the near term horizon of the development forecast, but the longer term forecast horizon could be generated by product development and fed back into production – not to inform scheduling decisions but in order to help manage production capacity.

6. Timing. It is not necessary to have forecasts aligned at *exactly* the same moment of time. A forecast is an input into decision-making and, particularly in the case of vertical alignment, a receiver of forecasts may want to see a forecast *after* course correction changes to plans have been taken into account (see below).

Example

Restructuring the forecast process at Tomkins PLC

Over recent years Tomkins, a UK-based engineering conglomerate, has organized its entire performance management process around rolling forecasts. Whereas in the past forecasts were produced every six months, they are now produced every month and are used to drive a quarterly business review process and real time capital expenditure allocation. One of the most important moves they made was to decouple the month-end reporting process and the forecast which is now produced mid-month. 'There is now as much energy put into preparing the forecast as closing the books,' reports Dan Disser, CFO of global operations. This change has also helped to position the forecast at the center of the management process since business leaders now have the time to seriously consider their options before the forecast is reported to the center. Hitherto the demands of the timetable meant that forecasting was a hurried numbers driven exercise owned by Finance (Hope, 2005).

7. Routine or by exception. The process of alignment does not have to be 'hard wired' into the design; it may be triggered by circumstances. So for example, it may be that the factory manager we encountered earlier be required to submit only one forecast once a year, unless his 'informal' forecast signals a deviation of more than $k. Exception-based forecasting can also be triggered 'from above', for example in response to an 'event' which impacts a number of units.

Many years of experience have taught Martin Jarvis that intelligent differentiation is the hallmark of a good forecasting process.

In my experience a good forecast has varied levels of detail. The process should be improved through iteration; by trial and error, people should have worked out what information is needed and what isn't. Bad forecasts on the other hand often have a huge amount of detail at the wrong level. I've gone away from saying that you might like to use different levels of detail in different horizons to saying you have to. It is easier to deal with the ambiguities at the boundaries between different forecast processes because they don't quite line up than the complexity that comes with doing everything at the same level of detail across all horizons – something which we in Supply Chain are often guilty of. (Jarvis, 2008)

In making choices about how our forecasts should be 'wired up' we are designing an organizational nervous system. A system which allows the corporate body as a whole to respond appropriately to anticipated future scenarios without having the whole organism work at the pace of the slowest process or the detail of the most demanding subunit. The human nervous system itself makes extensive use of what we might call 'conditional coupling' – only passing on signals to the next level in the hierarchy when certain thresholds have been breached. That we have come to the same conclusions as nature without the benefit of several billion years of Research and Development is a sign that we are on the right track.

A final word of warning. It is easy to be seduced by the intellectual challenge of crafting our corporate nervous system. We must always bear in mind that simplicity is the hallmark of good design in nature; it is another trait that we should seek to emulate. If our 'solution' is more complex than the problem we are attempting to solve then we should screw up our beautiful designs and start again.

• • • • •

For many readers the issues we have just explored may seem arcane. The next and final topic we tackle under the banner of 'Mastering Process' is one that is easy to understand and relate to, and which some believe lies at the heart of their problems with forecasting: 'who should be responsible?' It is not possible to provide a definitive answer to this question, but we do offer a number of practical suggestions that will help organizations make intelligent choices.

• • • • •

SUMMARY

A dilemma faced by virtually all but the smallest businesses is how to build forecast processes that support alignment and coordinated action across the enterprise without creating an unwieldy bureaucratic nightmare. The trick is, first to determine the extent to which forecasts need to be aligned – do they need to be close coupled, loose coupled or can they be decoupled? Then, depending on the objective, align different forecasts at different frequencies, timing and levels of detail, across different horizons and using different rules as determined by the purposes for which the forecast information is to be used. While aligned forecasts may tolerate different levels of variation, we should never tolerate bias.

KEY LEARNING POINTS

1. Be clear about the purposes for which forecasts are used in different parts of the business.
2. Establish the degree and nature of interdependence (coupling) between the interventions of the different parts.
3. Establish the information needs for the purpose in terms of:
   (a) Direction of information flow
   (b) Detail
   (c) Frequency
   (d) Horizon
   (e) Source of information
   (f) Timing
   (g) Trigger – routine, by exception.
4. Where there is close coupling, build processes to transfer consistent forecast information that meets the minimum needs of the receiving unit.
5. Where coupling is loose transfer forecast information by exception according to predefined criteria.

THEME #3 'WHOSE JOB IS IT ANYWAY?' ROLES AND RESPONSIBILITIES

> **❝ Organization ... is a process by which the people are free to choose the man who will get the blame. ❞** Adapted from Laurence J. Peter

---

Is there a silver bullet? – three criteria for allocating roles – dividing responsibilities – checks and balances – a forecasting responsibility matrix

---

A common misconception: that poor forecasting can be improved by changing 'who gets the job'

One of the most common questions we are asked is: 'who should be given the job of forecasting?'

It is not an unreasonable question. All too often we are confronted with situations where forecasting has been run as an 'ad hoc' activity. Where what started out as a simple request by, say, the Sales Director – 'how much are we going to sell this quarter' – has over time been transformed into someone's job, perhaps a job for the poor unfortunate who happened to be in post when the request became a regular quarterly event instead of 'every so often'. Often it is the guy with a load of experience that the business wants to keep but doesn't know what to do with.

Often, in these circumstances everything is fine as long as the numbers are being hit. But as soon as things start to get a little tricky, the spotlight is turned on the guy in the corner with the spreadsheet, who just can't win. Forecast bad news and he gets beaten up. Forecast good news – 'we will hit the target' – and if that doesn't happen, he gets beaten up. It is clear to management that this guy isn't up to the job. We need to make some changes, and, as happens depressingly often in business, the change that managers make is to the organization chart.

Here are some variations on this theme:

1. 'Our problem is that forecasts are political. Jo works for Sales so of course she is going to
   (a) talk up the numbers to protect her boss or
   (b) sandbag the numbers to negotiate lower targets.'
   'What we need to do is give the job to the Finance guys. They don't have an axe to grind. We can rely on them to be honest.'

2. 'The basic problem is that Jo is really out of touch. Five years ago she knew what was going on and so did a good job. Now the business has changed; all her old contacts have gone and she doesn't realize that things don't work in the way they used to. What we need to do is to ask the people who really know what's going on to produce the forecast – the guys in the field who talk to customers every day. They were in diapers when Jo was helping to build the company, but they are the future and we have to accept change whether we like it or not.'

3. 'Forecasting is a science. Jo thinks regression analysis is something that happens when you go to the shrink. You can't expect someone like that to have a clue about the job. What we need to do is to create a new department and put everyone who is involved in forecasting in there. Let's get professional and employ some PhDs.'

You can make a case for each of these points of view and we often find organizations embroiled in a religious war based on competing dogmatic views on 'the right person to be given the job', or flip flopping between different 'solutions' depending on prevailing fashion, the view of the boss or out of sheer frustration.

What is the 'right' answer?'

Simply changing the organization chart is not a silver bullet for your forecasting problems (or most other things for that matter)

Problems that businesses have with forecasting are a consequence of a failure to understand the 'science' of forecasting and to organize the process and align behaviors appropriately. The problem is rarely a single individual or where she sits in the organization chart, so changing them or the person they report to is unlikely to provide anything more than temporary relief and a self-righteous sense that 'action has been taken'.

But there is a 'but'. While changing people is not *the* solution, how you deploy them in the forecasting process certainly plays a role, and there are some clear principles that should guide your thinking. We will discuss these under three main headings.

Deciding who should be responsible for producing the forecast involves striking a balance between independence, knowledge, and expertise

The essence of the scenario we presented above was 'who should be made responsible for producing the numbers?'

What lay behind each of the points of view were considerations of:

(a)   Independence: free from bias

Since all forecasting in business involves judgment, to a greater or lesser degree, it is critical that you protect those responsible for producing the forecast from sources of bias. This means that they should personally have nothing to gain from forecasting any particular outcome. Their sole motivation should be that the forecast is 'accurate' (free from bias with acceptable levels of variation). You should also protect them from the organizational pressure that those that DO have a stake in a particular outcome might apply to them.

(b)   Domain knowledge

Business is complex and fast moving. What has happened in the past (as represented by data on past performance) has limited use as a basis for forecasting. Every business (including your own) is trying all the time to 'do something different' and customers, consumers and economies are fickle beings that cannot be relied upon to replicate past behavior. Any attempt to build a forecast without an understanding of 'what is happening on the street' and the potential consequences for your business is likely to fail.

(c)   Technical expertise

Intuition and 'common sense' (i.e. crude heuristics) are unreliable, particularly when analyzing complex data sets. The key competence forecasters need to have, other than basic numeracy, is some understanding of statistical principles, just as some knowledge of engineering is needed to fix a car.

All three of these factors – freedom from bias, domain knowledge and technical expertise – have to be taken into account in making decisions about assigning responsibilities in the forecast process. In any forecast process, NONE of them will be irrelevant. The challenge is to strike the right balance.

The challenge is to strike the right balance, for the forecasting task at hand, and take steps to address the potential risk of 'bias' or the lack of appropriate knowledge or expertise resulting from the choices you make

In a perfect world, the individual producing a forecast would be organizationally independent. But in these circumstances how do we make sure that he or she has the requisite access to domain knowledge? One way to achieve this is to require the individual with the domain knowledge to provide assumptions but, to guard against the likelihood of bias,[9] to give the (independent) forecaster the right to treat this as one source of information to be taken into account in making their judgment, rather than an input that cannot be challenged. So a sales person might say 'we are running the promotion next week and the uplift will be x%'. The forecaster will then make a decision whether to accept this assumption at face value or not, ideally based on the past performance of similar promotions or the reliability of the individual's previous estimates. In this case, the supplier of information is still accountable for producing unbiased forecasts and the forecaster for the choices he/she has made. Both sets of judgments should be measured, so that the supplier reduces the bias in their input and the forecaster will need to make few interventions to eliminate any residual bias and damp down variation.

 More

How forecasters can compensate for a lack of domain knowledge
Another technique forecasters can use to compensate for their lack of domain knowledge, without contracting the 'bias disease' from those that do have it, is to combine estimates from a number of sources. There is good academic support for this approach. A prediction market (as described earlier) is one kind of mechanism that can be used, but like most techniques suggested in the literature it is probably impractical for routine, high volume, forecasting tasks.

Rather than trying to allocate responsibility for forecasting to a single person or group of people it may make sense to exploit the skills of potential contributors by segmenting the process. In doing so you design interdependence into the process, promote collaboration and build in checks and balances. For example, the momentum forecast might be statistically generated, in which case it would make sense to give this responsibility to someone with technical expertise. The forecasting of 'interventions' relies on business judgment, supported by market research and analysis of historical patterns. Therefore, it might be a task given to someone with appropriate domain knowledge. The two parties have to collaborate to produce a forecast and doing so can help to moderate their individual biases.

Segmentation across time horizons could also help to allocate responsibilities. For example, a business could take the view that forecasting the short term horizon is best performed by technical analysis of historic patterns whereas the longer term is much more an exercise in understanding deep trends and patterns and the likely impact of novel events. In this case, long term forecasting requires someone with experience and understanding whereas, in the short term, technical expertise may be more important. The need to make sure that short and long term views form a continuum also helps foster a spirit of dialogue, collaboration and constructive challenge of assumptions.

Whatever organizational designs you make there are many options. It is important that you underpin your forecast process with rigorous measurement of its quality and that you *follow it through*. With this discipline in place the organization is much less dependent on finding a perfect match of people to roles since any bias or weaknesses in modeling will be exposed and learning accelerated.

Ownership of the forecast: forecasting is unavoidably a complex interdisciplinary process

Even if it were possible to isolate everyone with responsibility for 'producing' the forecast in one department, it would not be a good organizational solution. First, as 'Jo' experienced earlier, when 'bad things' happen, the 'blame' is often transferred to the people who produced the forecast. If management does not like these numbers and doesn't want to believe them, it is a short step to deciding that it is the forecast that is at fault. If the forecast is 'theirs' rather than 'ours' – that is if there is no management ownership or involvement – then finding a scapegoat is too easy a way out. Moreover, when the forecasters are attacked it is natural for them to become insular and defensive. Before long we find other parts of the business producing their own forecasts, in competition with the discredited 'official' estimates. When this happens – because there is no consensus about the future – decision-making can become no more than a process of negotiation.

The second reason why setting up a separate forecasting department is not a good idea is this: forecasting is not a discrete, technical exercise; it is a BUSINESS process. It should be 'owned' by everyone – and in particular by the leaders of the business. There should be collective responsibility for the forecast outcomes. The forecast process should be treated as part of the way that the business is run – the engine of decision-making – rather than an exercise in producing a 'prediction' of the future.

More

Organization without organization charts: how to run forecasting as a complex cross-functional process

As forecasting is a complex interdisciplinary process there is a risk that the lack of clarity about who 'owns' the forecast will lead to confusion and a loss of discipline and rigor. The organization chart is not the only mechanism we can use to help define responsibilities, however.

In project management, another interdisciplinary process, it is common to use a tool known as a RACI diagram to allocate responsibilities. The letters stand for:

R – responsibility for carrying out a task

A – accountability for the performance of a task (only one person per task)

C – someone who has knowledge or capability who is consulted, i.e. with whom there is two-way communication

I – someone who needs to be informed, i.e. with whom there is one-way communication.

In practical terms, 'A' means being accountable for forecast reliability. If it isn't measured you cannot be held accountable. 'R' is responsible for process performance (e.g. meeting deadlines – as measured by 'on time in full'). 'C' means that you will be involved in meetings and those that are in the 'I' category should be copied with information.

We recommend you use this tool to help design your forecast process; applied seriously it helps get over the 'which function' debate which can easily derail attempts at reform. You might apply it to each forecast step and to the process as a whole, for example:

R – Demand Planners (volume), Management Accountants (financials)

A – CEO

C – Sales Managers (volume), costs center managers (financials)

I – The innovation project management forum.

By exposing the exact nature of roles in this way it is easy to design a process which – like a good constitution – has an appropriate arrangement of checks and balances.

• • • • •

You are now equipped with an understanding of what it takes to design an effective forecasting process and how to run it effectively. But, as anyone who has attempted to implement any kind of change into an organization can attest, implementation is rarely a simple or straightforward affair. Unfortunately, 'being right' and having a compelling business case is usually not enough. Attempts to bludgeon the organization into change by applying overpowering logic or hierarchical power rarely succeed. The next section addresses the topic of change. Some elements of this are common to any change process but there are a number of aspects which are peculiar to changing a performance management practice such as forecasting. To address this topic we need to shift levels; we will no longer be dealing with the forecast process itself but instead addressing the context in which it sits, in particular the cultural milieu and the wider range of performance management processes in which it is embedded. This makes the next section of particular relevance to those with a broader range of organizational responsibilities, but the subject matter is not demanding and so should interest most readers.

• • • • •

SUMMARY

There can be no simple and neat 'organizational solution' for forecasting because it is, by its nature, a complex multifunctional process. There are, however, some principles that can be used to guide organizational design. They include the need to involve those with an intimate understanding of the business (since judgment underpins all business forecasting), while at the same time taking a range of measures to mitigate the risk of introducing bias into the process that usually accompany individuals having a stake in the business. Particularly given the multifunctional quality of forecasting, it is important to be very specific about the exact nature of the role played by each contributor to the process.

KEY LEARNING POINTS

Criteria for effective organizational design
- Maximize domain knowledge
- Minimize the risk of bias
- Provide access to appropriate technical expertise.

Types of roles played in the forecast process which need to be defined as part of the design (RACI)

R – those **responsible** for carrying out a task

A – that person **accountable** for the performance of a task (only one for any task)

C – anyone who has knowledge or capability who is **consulted**, i.e. with whom there is two-way communication

I – someone who needs to be **informed**, i.e. with whom there is one-way communication.

NOTES

1 'Sales and Operations Planning' (S&OP) may take the form of a process like this, indeed there are many points of agreement between what we advocate in this section and good S&OP practice.

2 It is acceptable to adjust a forecast if an assumption is incorrect, e.g. an intervention has been cancelled. It is also acceptable to adjust the model used to produce forecasts to eliminate bias for example. What we counsel against is adjusting the forecast output without good cause, i.e. based on unsubstantiated 'judgment'.

3 The TMS has its roots in the teaching of W. Edwards Deming whom we first mentioned in the context of measurement of variation. What Deming preached was that sources of variation be relentlessly eliminated as this led to poor quality and other forms of waste (time, cost, inventory and so on). In order to identify variation one has to have stable processes and to have stable processes you need standardization and process discipline.

4 Mistake number two is to 'overestimate the impact of technology change'.

5 An extreme example of this is provided by Girolama Cordono, the sixteenth century astronomer, who predicted his death to the hour. He committed suicide rather than ruin his own reputation!

6 Persistent communication of biased forecasts to the market – a lower number than your internal forecast tells you can be achieved – is, however, self-defeating since analysts will learn to adjust their own guidance accordingly and your shares might be written down when you start telling the truth!

7 We should not forget that there is a cost associated with variation. In the examples we have quoted it will be the cost of holding higher stocks or bearing a risk premium in your share price. If the cost is too high then the variation might be deemed to be unacceptable and steps must be taken to improve forecast quality – either by improving the forecast models used or by enhancing your ability to anticipate and compensate for sources of risk (see Chapter 6).

8 Targeting has a habit of infecting other parts of the performance management process. For instance Charles Goodhart, an economic advisor to the Bank of England, coined the aphorism which bears his name: 'once a measure becomes a target it ceases to be a good measure'.

9 We are not condoning the existence of bias. We are simply recognizing the likelihood in practice, despite best intentions.

Section 4

TRANSFORMATION

In this section we will address the issue of how to introduce significant changes in a forecasting process. This will involve exploring the cultural and process context in which it sits.

In particular we will:

- outline a simple model to help us understand the process of organizational change in general;
- describe the specific issues likely to be faced when introducing forecasting into an organization, particularly one using a traditional budgeting process;
- suggest ways in which budgeting processes can be modified so that they do not compromise the effectiveness of forecasting;
- examine the option of abandoning traditional budgeting altogether. Should you decide to do this we recommend that you consider using the Beyond Budgeting model since this provides a way of managing a business that is more in tune with the needs of twenty-first century business, as well as providing a framework for more effective forecasting.

This section is aimed at those managers and leaders that appreciate that the successful implementation of change on such a scale requires a sound understanding of the performance management system as a whole and serious consideration of a range of options. It will also be of interest to the serious student of management.

By the end of this section, you will have a holistic understanding of the issues involved in a change of this nature and a good grasp of some of the choices open to you.

Chapter 8

IMPLEMENTATION:
beginnings and endings

❝There is nothing more difficult to take in hand, more perilous to conduct or more uncertain in its success than to take the lead in the introduction of a new order of things.**❞** Niccolo Machiavelli

> *The process of change – getting started – the Change Equation – why you need push and pull – where to start – where not to start*

There is no 'right way' to introduce change but there is a consistent set of principles that underpin all successful change

Implementing any kind of change is difficult – only about 30% of change programs succeed, a figure which hasn't changed over the last decade (Aiken and Keller, 2009). It is therefore no surprise that, of the questions we are asked (whether in the context of forecasting or Beyond Budgeting generally), one of the most common is: 'what is the best way to implement?' It is tempting to give a formulaic answer like, 'first enroll the CEO and then …' but this is too simplistic. The truth is that *introducing any form of change requires more than a good solution and powerful advocacy* – you have to do battle with the status quo. A significant part of the change manager's job is to deal with the forces of resistance: all those things which get in the way of change.[1] These are likely to be different depending on where you are in the organization, where you start from, the nature of the organization in which you work and the timing of your effort. In every battle, the context will be different. Getting the support of the CEO may or may not be possible. It may not even be necessary. As a leader of change, you should try to choose the terrain to suit your purposes, but in the end, you have to play the hand you are dealt.

However, bringing about effective change is not a lottery. There are strategies that increase your chances of success, and tactics and techniques that help you break through barriers. Change management is a huge subject in its own right, and we cannot do it justice in a few pages, but here are some ideas we use that you might find helpful in your campaign.

Change process (such as growth) goes through three stages

In nature the process of change typically follows a distinctive 'S' shaped pattern like the one below in Figure 8.1. This curve is ubiquitous and could represent anything over any timescale: the sales of a new product, the adoption of a technology, the growth of an animal population or the acceptance of a new idea (Modis, 1992).[2]

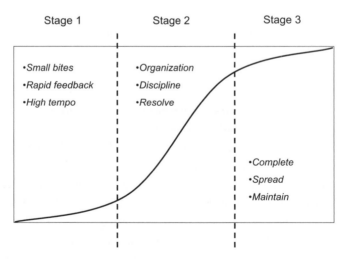

Figure 8.1 The change curve.

An 'S' shaped curve of the sort typically associated with the introduction of change – of any sort.

More

What other uses of the 'S' curve have to teach us about spreading an idea

The 'S' shape curve is also used to help forecasting innovations such as the adoption of a new product or technology. The models used by forecasters in businesses (such as the Bass Diffusion Equation) are very similar to those used by epidemiologists to model the spread of a disease (the SIR model). Our premise is that change management involves the promotion of an innovation in social technology – in our case an innovation in the way we manage the future. The progress of a change process is analogous to that of an epidemic, the 'success' of which is determined by the amount of people susceptible (the S of the SIR model) to change/infection and the relative rate of conversion/infection (I) relative to the rate of relapse/recovery (R). So bringing about successful change involves doing the opposite of what health authorities have done to try and stop the spread of Swine Flu (H1N1): increasing the infectiousness of the idea and the opportunities for onward transmission and reducing the rate of 'recovery' after infection.

In the first stage, the situation is stable: it is dominated by patterns of behavior which help maintain the status quo; the forces of resistance (stability). In this stage the aim is to get some movement. Kurt Lewin, the father of Organizational Development (and an early systems scientist) called this process 'unfreezing'.

The second stage is the 'growth' or 'transformation' stage. Here the aim is to create and then maintain momentum. This is done by making changes that promote more change, perhaps either by generating positive sentiment or by enabling or facilitating related activities. This stage is often associated with confusion amongst those subject to change, and this should be managed.

The third and final stage is when the changes that you have brought about in the second stage are made 'business as normal'. The job here is one of consolidation; you need to create a new set of stabilizers (or forces of resistance) to make sure that the change that has been brought about does not morph into something else or revert back to the old way of working.[3] This is sometimes called 'refreezing'.

The most difficult part of any change process is 'getting started'. The Change Equation helps us understand how

Often the most difficult part of the change process is the first stage – starting out. Management folklore has it that 'you need a burning platform' or 'it needs to be driven by the CEO'. Neither of these viewpoints is wrong, but they do not paint the full picture. For instance, W.L. Gore has a well earned reputation for innovation, but they have an aversion to top down driven change. 'On the one hand you've made a quick decision … but then you have got all kinds of resistance,' says CEO, Terri Kelley (Stern and Marsh, 2008).

We find the model popularized by Beckhard and Harris (Beckhard and Harris, 1987) to be a useful tool to help think through what needs to be done to get a change process started. We call it the Change Equation.

$$D \times V \times S > R^{4}$$

Taking each of the terms in turn:

D stands for DISSATISFACTION.

The concept of a 'burning platform' – an emergency that puts the organization in peril – is clearly a source of dissatisfaction with the current situation, but we do not have to rely on a life threatening crisis to mobilize change. This is fortunate, since forecasting (or the lack of it) is not often seen as a 'burning platform'. Perhaps the problems are not visible, or not often seen as important. Even when the unsatisfactory nature of the status quo is recognized, people have often learned to live with it, perhaps believing that there is 'no alternative' or things 'will always be this way'. So one of the most important, and relatively easy, steps in mobilizing an organization for change is exposing and magnifying unhappiness with the way things are now. As William Bridges, author of *Managing Transitions* (Bridges, 1991) says a change leader should 'sell problems, not solutions'.

V stands for VISION.

Vision means the existence of a picture of the future that inspires people to action. Getting this right is a matter of balance. If a vision is made too concrete and detailed it is unlikely to be inspiring. If it insufficiently clear and tangible people are unlikely to commit to it, or at the very least will not have a clear sense of what needs to be done to bring it about.

Creating a vision with the right level of stretch is also important. If a vision is too far fetched, gaining commitment will be difficult since it will be difficult to engender belief. If it is too much like current reality it will be difficult to mobilize enthusiasm; there is no challenge. Clearly the more explicit the leader's commitment to the vision the more currency the vision will have in the organization, but the power of personal commitment, wherever it comes from, is underrated. Sometimes the quality of the vision and the authentic passion of the individual promoting it are more important than their job title. An important point to remember is that organizations do not change; only people do. This means that the vision must resonate with what those being asked to change care about, and these are probably not the same things that motivate the CEO (Aiken and Keller, 2009).

S stands for FIRST STEPS.

If the vision has the right amount of stretch, one that is challenging but not impossible, it is unlikely that you will be able to completely specify the change program at the start. Even if it were possible, issuing a set of instructions would disenfranchise those you need to enroll in the process. People will only commit to what they help create. Our advice is design to 50% and let others, and the lessons you learn from getting into action, look after the other half.

R stands for RESISTANCE.

Resistance can take many forms. It might represent an individual who sets out to block or undermine efforts to bring about change. More likely, however, resistance comes in the form of FUD: Fear (e.g. 'I'm not sure that I can do this'), Uncertainty (e.g. 'how will this affect me?') and Doubt (e.g. 'will this work?').

To bring about change we have to work on all the sources of change and resistance at the same time

What this model tells us is that, in order to bring about change it is necessary for the value of the terms on the left hand side of the equation to be greater than the forces of resistance on the right. It is not simply a matter of having a 'burning platform' or a 'compelling vision'. The model says that you need a value for *each* of the terms on the left. If 'V' is zero, no one will follow you since they do not know where they are going. If there is no 'D' then there is no energy for change; people are satisfied with the status quo. If 'S' is zero there will be energy and a sense of purpose but nothing will happen because no one knows what to do next; and in such circumstances the energy and commitment will soon be lost.

There is another subtlety in the equation. In a physical system such as a stationary car, increasing the pressure for change (pushing it) will overcome the forces of resistance (inertia). Organizations are biological systems, however, and they behave differently. Any parent knows that simply increasing pressure on a child often increases resistance rather than overwhelming it.

To illustrate this point try the following experiment.

Ask your partner or a friend to stand in the middle of a room. Place a ball to the side. Both objects – the ball and your partner – are in a stable state. They are in some form of equilibrium. Then tell both the ball and your partner that you do not want them to move.

Push the ball. Unsurprisingly it moves. This is because it was in static equilibrium. It was stationary only because there was insufficient force acting upon it.

Now try pushing your partner. Depending on how hard you push, they will most likely sway a little but then return to the upright position. This is because a person standing upright is in *dynamic equilibrium*.[5] It is the opposition of forces that holds the body in balance and stops it falling over. When a force is applied, sets of muscles around the lower back act to restore balance. Apply enough force and other, bigger, muscles will be brought to bear to increase the resistance.

So it is with organizations. Some organizations are described as 'chaotic' but in reality, they are not. Organizational life may be confusing but organizational forms are usually very stable. Organizations can sustain themselves despite being subjected to all manner of disruptive and destructive forces. The reason that they are so resilient is that members of the organization adapt their behavior to keep things going in the same form – not necessarily because the status quo is desirable but because *they have not agreed to (or have concerns about) an alternative.* Therefore, it is possible for members of an organization to agree that the current state of affairs is undesirable but, perhaps at a subconscious level, to resist change.

A consequence for the change manager is that it is important to weaken the forces of resistance *before* you apply pressure to change. In the example above, you might ask your partner to stand on one leg. In an organization, before committing too aggressively to action, you might reduce resistance by addressing sources of uncertainty or fear, by education and training. Another tactic is to avoid resistance altogether by focusing change work in the area where it is weakest – a common approach in military affairs.

Where to start the change process

When you *do* commit to action, however, what should the first steps be? The answer depends on where you start from.

Do you start with strong backing from the leadership of the organization or is this change driven from the 'bottom up'? Is there a forecasting process in place already or not? If there is, what are the problems with it? Where does the dissatisfaction lie? What else is going on in the organization that might be complementary to, or in conflict with what you want to achieve? Who are your natural allies? Where are the forces of resistance? What resources do you have at your disposal? Is yours a small organization or are you attempting to bring change to a large multinational business? Are your sources of support expecting a short campaign or are they committed to a longer 'journey of change'? All these factors differ from organization to organization, from place to place and from time to time.

There is no right answer to the question 'where should I start?' Indeed it is likely that there will be a range of plausible strategies you could employ. As a general rule, however we would recommend that you start addressing a major source of dissatisfaction. It will take less effort to mobilize the energy needed to bring change about and you are more likely to achieve 'quick wins' and so create momentum.

If, for example, the major source of dissatisfaction is the inaccuracy of forecasts, introducing bias measurement might be a good place to start. This will require the organization to buy into 'zero bias' as a definition of good forecasting and encourage more frequent forecasting/smaller forecast buckets. Since it is not possible or sensible to run 'budget type' processes on a monthly basis, this might shift the focus onto process efficiency, perhaps involving rationalizing information needs and so on. Improving modeling capabilities could be a good next step.

Another possibility is that a lack of flexibility is perceived as *the* problem. If so, the first step might involve increasing the frequency at which the business reallocates resources.[6] In turn, this might stimulate the need to forecast more frequently since the business will need to know 'what we can afford to commit'. This may require separating the incremental impact of 'interventions' from 'business as usual' perhaps leading to the development of momentum models to enable forecasts to be produced more regularly. And so on.

Example

The change process at AMEX

Every case is unique – it is dangerous to generalize based on the experience of one company. We can, however, use a case to illustrate some general points. In this spirit we will examine the change process in AMEX (Croake, 2008).

The process was kicked off by the CFO, Gary Crittenden, a man who clearly falls into the bracket of a visionary, someone who is driven by a sense of how things could or should be. He was also prepared to take personal risks, one of the marks of a good leader. Early in 2002, he communicated his vision: a finance function that would spend more time looking forward, engaging with the business, helping them do a better job rather than just crunching numbers. It helped that Crittenden had charisma and commanded the loyalty and respect of his teams, but for people like Jamie Croake pain associated with the previous process was a powerful motivator. The deep sense of frustration that their effort and sacrifices failed to produce anything of value also played an important role.

So there were the germs of a vision and some dissatisfaction in the corporate team but 9/11 accelerated the process. It also gave them confidence that it was possible to change (the 'back of the envelope' exercise they had to perform after the tragedy was effectively a small scale pilot) and an idea about the right place to start. Driver-based models clearly addressed a source of some pain by helping speed up and standardize the existing slow and fragmented process. In addition, the 'accidental' pilot project provided by their post 9/11 experience also helped deal with a potential source of resistance – the fear of loss of control was shown to be groundless.

The next step in their journey is crucial, as much for what they did not do as for what they did. Despite having strong leadership support, they did not 'mandate' change. The corporate team led the change, but they partnered with representatives from individual business units, and took an entire year to define and map the process they wanted to eliminate. Clearly, this was important from a logistical point of view, and some of their research (for instance into the amount of time that was spent crunching numbers – 83% – rather than doing value added work) helped convince the business units intellectually of the need for change. The major source of resistance, however, was always likely to be emotional – the resistance to head office dictates. In this context the role of the business unit representative was key, particularly because one of them always accompanied Jamie's team on business unit visits. 'It made a huge difference having someone from a business unit sitting by me and telling people "I am one of you and I believe that it is the right thing to do for our part of the business". It really helped get people on board,' says Jamie.

The time they took through 2002 prepared the ground for the transformation and also played a critical role in diffusing any resistance to change. Eliminating resistance does not need to be confrontational. It is also worth noting that the first practical step taken by AMEX on their journey was the decision to drop the word 'budget' and to stop asking for cost center information. It sent a very powerful signal that 'the center is serious' and also encouraged business units to think seriously about how they could benefit from the change themselves.

Because of this preparatory work, the implementation of the new system in 2003 went smoothly. So well in fact that when the team presented it to Crittenden in October 2003 his response was, 'Are we now flexible enough to do this every quarter with a rolling horizon?'

Although this might appear to be an obvious easy next step, the move to a five-quarter rolling horizon triggered skepticism and resistance in the business. 'It represented a big culture change and there was a lot of debate about what value this would bring. A lot of people thought that this was just a finance thing,' says Croake. It took a further year of detailed work on the process and a couple of run throughs with the new rolling process, demonstrating the benefits and removing any lingering suspicion that 'this was not for real', before business units stopped presenting financial year plans at their quarterly reviews.

What the AMEX experience demonstrates is that implementing large scale change rarely takes the form of a single, decisive set piece battle. While clear goals, senior management vision and support are critical, it is important to take time to allay fears and enrol people in the design process. The change process will unfold, evolve and loop round again and again. Often it is only seeing the results that will persuade people to let go of old ways of doing things. 'I don't think we have reached our point of arrival,' says Jamie Croake. 'I don't think we ever will. There are always things that you can improve.'

In our experience, there are certain 'first steps' that often result in failure because they carry implementation risks that are not obvious at first sight. This is usually because the wider consequences of what might appear to be a simple change in technique have not been thought through. In other words, a source of resistance has not been identified and, like a submerged iceberg, it can hole a change initiative below the waterline when everything seems to be set fair. In particular, forecasting change projects often flounder because the interdependencies between forecasting and budgeting have not been identified and properly dealt with. Indeed, traditional budgeting practices and the mindset that accompanies them is the biggest single source of the problems that derail forecasting change projects. We address this topic in the next chapter.

• • • • •

If you have a traditional budgeting system, at some point you will have to tackle the issue of whether and how forecasting and budgeting coexist, wherever you start the change journey. This is the subject of the next chapter. The motives of readers might differ at this point. You might find that budgeting practices frustrate your attempts to implement improved forecasting practices, in which case your interest might be to understand where the 'road blocks' lie and what can be done to avoid them. Perhaps you have an excellent forecasting system and you are wondering why you need to budget at all, in which case you will need to understand what the potential consequences of such a move might be, and what other steps you might need to take.

Whatever your motive it is important to fully appreciate 'the nature of the beast' that you are dealing with, which necessarily involves the exploration of some theoretical issues. The chapter will, however, conclude with practical recommendations.

• • • • •

SUMMARY

There is no one 'right way' to bring about change but there are some general principles you can use to guide the process of implementing change to forecasting processes. Successful change requires us to pass through three phases: getting started, getting momentum and institutionalizing the change. The Change Equation is particularly useful in the initial stage. It tells us that we have to work simultaneously on the arguments for change and the forces of resistance. While there is no standard 'recipe' it makes sense to start the process in a way that addresses the main sources of dissatisfaction with current practice.

KEY LEARNING POINTS

The three phases of change

- Starting up
- Getting momentum
- Institutionalizing change.

The Change Equation

$$V \times D \times S > R$$

V = vision for the future

D = sense of dissatisfaction with the present

S = knowledge of the first steps

R = sources of resistance.

What the Change Equation tells us

- You have to work simultaneously on the left (forces for change) and right hand side of the equation (forces resisting change).
- You need to address all three elements of the forces for change simultaneously.

NOTES

1 We are not suggesting that resistance to change is necessarily a bad thing or that those representing the status quo are 'bad' people. If organizations were not resistant to change they would not survive; they would not be cohesive and coordinated, nor would they be resilient in the face of adversity. Resistance plays a role like that of our immune system – usually it fights pathogens but occasionally it can turn against the body or reject life saving organ transplants. In fact, rather than try to defeat the forces of resistance we should be encouraging them to declare neutrality or to defect to us!

2 The curve shows the cumulative position over time. If we were to plot the incremental change we would come up with something which looks bell shaped; a device which has been used to describe the characteristics of those adopting an innovation at different stages in the process: pioneers, early adopters, early majority and so on. See Geoffrey Moore (2002) for an interesting take on the use of this model in marketing disruptive innovation.

3 If you want to learn more about managing an effective change process we recommend the work of John Kotter (Kotter, 1996). Kotter's eight characteristics of successful change can be easily mapped against this three-stage model. Bridges (1991) uses a similar structure to ours and is particularly strong on the social and psychological aspects of change.

4 One way of looking at this equation is to imagine that the left hand side determines how infectious the idea will be; the right hand side determines the strength of the 'immune system'. This idea is explored further in Chapter 9.

5 Technically this is called orthostasis; a form of 'dynamic equilibrium'. Another word for the ability of a system to maintain stability in a dynamic environment is homeostasis, a term coined by Walter Cannon in 1929 to describe the apparently miraculous ability of the body to maintain multiple variables (temperature, sugar, carbon dioxide etc.) within a narrow range under sometimes extreme perturbation from the environment. One of the most remarkable features of homeostatic processes in the body is that *there is no central controlling mechanism* – it is entirely an outcome of the way in which the system has been configured by evolutionary pressures.

6 This might sound difficult, but it need not be. For example, American Express first encouraged business units to allocate resources flexibly within business units. Next they asked business units to eliminate the weakest 10% of their projects to create a pool of resource for reallocation to the best unfunded projects from across the business. In this way confidence and trust, in the process and each other, were gradually built up.

Chapter 9

BEYOND FORECASTING: the biggest barrier

❢ Habit is stronger than reason. ❣ George Santayana

> *The five roles played by budgeting – the three characteristics of budgeting – how its strength is also its weakness – how budgeting undermines good forecasting practice – the need to introduce more flexibility, visibility and honesty – how to disable the budgeting immune systems – why eliminating budgets (on its own) is not the answer*

In the preface to this book, we referred to the difficulty of introducing forecasting into a control system based on budgeting. Fitting a forecasting turbocharger onto a budgeting engine does not work and it is usually the quality of the forecasting process that suffers. Also while we personally recommend considering alternatives to budgeting, we said it is possible to retain budgets, providing that you take measures to prevent the budgeting culture from undermining the forecast process. It is now time to address this issue.

A working definition of budgeting
Before we dive into the detail we need to clarify some terms. Unnecessary argument and rancor is generated when the protagonists in a debate do not have the same concept in mind when they talk of 'budgets' and 'budgeting'.

'The beginning of wisdom is to call things by their right names.'

Chinese Proverb

Charles Horngren's *Cost Accounting: A Managerial Emphasis* was first published in 1962 and the book has been a constant feature in the education of managers in the US ever since then. In the latest edition (the 13th) Horngren defines a budget as '(a) the quantitative expression of a proposed plan of action by management for a specified period and (b) an aid to coordinate what needs to be done to implement that plan' (Horngren *et al.*, 2008). In another authoritative text, Anthony and Govindarajam (Anthony and Govindarajam, 1995) set out the steps involved in the process of budgeting:

- estimation of the profit potential of a unit;
- stated in financial terms;
- generally covering the period of a year;
- representing a management commitment (to delivering the objectives expressed in the budget);
- subject to review and approval by an authority higher than the budgetee;
- which, once reviewed, can only be changed under specified conditions and periodically is compared to actual financial performance for analysis and explanation.

Budgeting has five key roles and three characteristics

From this we can see that budgeting has five key roles:

1. It sets TARGETS which are supported by a
2. PLAN: a set of actions which are forecast to reach the target. This is funded by
3. expense and investment BUDGETS which serve to
4. COORDINATE the actions of the entire organization.
5. Control is exercised through variance analysis. This involves MEASURING deviations from targets and budgets with the aim of bringing affairs 'back on track'.

A potential sixth component of budgeting is that of REWARDS. Incentive schemes are often anchored on budgets and budgeted targets.

In addition, traditional budgets have three defining characteristics. They are:

1. FIXED, covering the period of:
2. the FINANCIAL YEAR and arrived at by a process of:
3. ANNUAL NEGOTIATION.

One of the greatest strengths of budgeting is that it is a coherent
system for managing performance, but this quality also
makes it resistant to change

Budgeting is a comprehensive system for managing the financial resources of an organization but it has a profound impact on many other aspects of business since money (or its absence) acts to constrain and direct activities. Budgeting's great strength as a management tool is that it is a coherent system of control, making it robust and easy to understand.

This quality of coherence, which makes budgeting so resilient, is also a weakness. Because each of the elements of budgeting supports each of the others, because (to use the technical term) it is a 'tightly coupled' system, it is difficult to make changes to management practices in response to the business environment. A fundamental change in the way in which one part of the system operates, for example forecasting across a rolling horizon, introduces an inconsistency. A manager either has to eliminate the inconsistency, perhaps by moving all elements of the system to a rolling horizon or ignoring the forecast beyond the financial year-end, or, in order to live with the incoherence, convert budgeting into a 'loosely coupled' system.

This is the approach advocated by Bjarte Bogsnes of StatoilHydro. He argues that one of the major problems with budgeting is that it tries to do many different jobs with the same tool. For instance a good target needs to be stretching but a good forecast should be realistic. 'Forcing a target and a forecast into one number is guaranteed to result in either a bad target or a bad forecast' (Bogsnes, 2009). Also, if a manager believes that a forecast will be used to allocate resources you are unlikely to get an honest one. Bogsnes' conclusion is clear: 'separate, then improve. Going straight for the second part is bound to fail.'

If the problem was purely procedural perhaps this would not be of great concern. But budgeting is not just a logical system; it coexists with a cultural system: a set of budgeting behaviors. Among other things, the budgeting culture defines 'what success looks like' (hitting targets), 'good practice' (everything being reconciled) and legitimizes the gaming behavior that takes place around target setting ('how to win'). And it is the failure to recognize and address these patterns of behavior which often frustrates and undermines performance management change initiatives. 'We should not blame the managers,' Bogsnes argues. 'Their response is both natural and predictable; we should blame the process which puts people in difficult positions'.

Rejection of change is responsible for the symptoms of 'forecasting failure'

Michael Watkins, the author and consultant, makes a comparison between organizational culture and the immune system in the human body. The role of the immune system is to protect the body from infection, in other words to preserve the coherence of the 'self'. 'Organizational culture and political networks when they are working well prevent "bad thinking" and "bad people" from entering and doing damage to the organization.'[1] However, immune systems can go wrong. They can fail to distinguish 'good things' from 'bad things'. This leads to autoimmune disease (which involves mistaking parts of the host's body for that of an invader) and rejection of beneficial introductions, such as healthy organ transplants. The 'Seven Deadly Symptoms' we identified in Chapter 2 are all symptoms of 'organ rejection' by the budgeting immune system. The thought patterns and behaviors associated with budgeting are incompatible with those needed for effective forecasting and because they are deeply embedded in the psyche of the organization it is the resident behaviors that tend to win out. This is why we cannot just 'bolt' rolling forecasts and 'dynamic resource allocation' onto a traditional budgeting system and expect them to work perfectly.

So, what do you do if you want to keep your budgeting systems and introduce forecasting practices like those we advocate in this book? The answer is that you have to understand where the potential conflicts lie and take steps to disable the budgeting 'immune system' before introducing change. Let us now analyze what these steps might be, and what can be done to reconcile the potentially competing demands of the two different ways of working.

To introduce effective forecasting we first need to make budgeting practice more flexible

The first pressure point is the fixed nature of budgets. Effective forecasting requires that we recognize change and adapt plans accordingly. There is little scope for such adaptation however, if budgets cannot be changed. This means that you have to make resource allocation a continuous (rather than annual) process, but in a traditional budgeting process this is problematic. Once budgets are set they tend to be treated as an entitlement, so managers will resist attempts to redeploy resources elsewhere. As a result, making changes can be a fraught and time consuming affair.

An option might be to set aside an unallocated 'contingency fund' that can be used to fund new initiatives as and when the need arises. But, in this case, how are targets to be set? In a traditional system, a target is supported by the allocation of an appropriate amount of resources. If resources are not allocated at the same time as targets are set how confident can we be that the targets are reasonable? How can managers be held accountable?

An answer might be to adjust targets when resources are reallocated, but this can easily become an administrative nightmare. Another alternative is to introduce some 'give' into the targets, perhaps by setting targets as a range rather than a single point or by prioritizing some over others. Since competitors are likely to be facing a similar set of challenges another option is to use relative targets based on peer group performance.

Often it is the incentive scheme that is based on the targets that is the source of the problem rather than the target per se. Changing performance targets may be unsettling and disorientating but if this also impacts the basis on which people are remunerated the level of discomfort and difficulty is magnified. So you might consider basing rewards on relative performance, assessed after the event.

Second, we need to improve visibility beyond the financial year-end

The second source of conflict arises from the fact that budgets are anchored on the financial year-end, whereas we recommend that you introduce rolling forecasts driven by decision-making lead times. If the resource allocation process stops at year-end we cannot populate part of the forecast horizon with plans. As a result the forecast will be misleading (because of premature 'forecast decay'). On the other hand, intervention planning (and resource allocation) conducted in the absence of financial guidelines (because targets have not been set for the 'out year') can also be misleading because they may not be affordable. Thus, in order to create a meaningful rolling forecast in the absence of budget-based targets, you will need to create a target framework for the period beyond the financial year-end.

Third, the culture of target negotiation needs to be weakened

The third, and potentially most difficult, problem is associated with the annual negotiation of budgets. This process often starts with an attempt to forecast based on the assumption of a certain level of resource, but, because this forecast is used to help set targets it is likely to be heavily corrupted by motivational bias. One side of the negotiation table wants to talk forecasts of revenue and profit down and investment and cost budgets up; the other side is seeking to do the opposite. Jack Welch describes this process as 'the bane of corporate America' (Welch and Byrne, 2001). As a result, forecasts for the 'out year', made before targets are finalized, can be very biased. They are also often ignored, at least until they come into play as part of the following year's cycle.

It is possible to take some 'process-based' counter measures. Medium term targets (i.e. covering a period greater than a year), especially if they are aspirational or relative in nature, can help mitigate the risk of forecasts being biased by target negotiation. Decoupling rewards from the target can also help. But in order to create a forecast process that is effective it may be necessary to shift the entire performance management culture away from one where the measure of success is the achievement of a quantitative target based on a zero sum-based negotiation process.

Finally, budgets should no longer be used as the basis of performance measurement
The final pressure point is the need to maintain the coherence of the budgeting system itself. This is manifest in an insistence that targets be the same as forecasts, the use of variance analysis as the primary mechanism for analyzing, and judging performance,[2] and the use of budgets as a mechanism for coordinating activity across the organization.

Example

An example of corporate schizophrenia about budgeting
Sometimes attempts to maintain the coherence of the management system distort managerial behavior to the point that logic and common sense are abandoned.

We are reminded of an occasion in a management meeting involving senior managers of several ice cream businesses. One Finance Director, who had been accused of poor forecasting, stood up and excitedly pointed out of the window. It was May but it was still freezing and pouring with rain. How could he be held accountable for a forecast for the next quarter when he couldn't forecast the next week? In the debate that followed there was general agreement that ice cream businesses should focus on reacting quickly to changes in the weather rather than attempting to forecast them.

The next item on the agenda was transfer pricing, a classic coordinating mechanism. The same director who had been so reluctant to commit himself to a high level forecast for the following quarter agreed to supply a forecast for the whole of the following year at the lowest level of detail so that transfer prices could be calculated for the budget. The managers at the meeting failed to recognize the absurdity of the request and the inconsistency of their decision-making.

These issues should be tackled head on.

1. There is no necessity for targets to agree exactly with forecasts, although old habits can die hard.

2. Any number of approaches other than budgeting can be used to coordinate activities. Forecasts themselves are often used for this purpose (Section 3, Chapter 7, Theme 2 'Coordination in a Complex System'). Another option is to use internal market mechanisms.

3. We strongly advocate dispensing with variance analysis altogether. This can be done at a stroke with no adverse consequences since it contributes little to understanding performance. A comparison between actuality and what is often no more than a poor guess (the budget) is unlikely to provide meaningful insight. In addition, the mentality fostered by variance analysis runs counter to that we need to develop in order to forecast effectively. Traditional budget-based variance analysis purports to explain every error, whereas good forecasting recognizes the existence of random variation (which cannot be explained) and distinguishes it from bias (which can). In addition, variance analysis treats any departure from a plan as deviant rather than inevitable and potentially useful.

It might be tempting to simply 'throw the budgets out', but this is not the answer on its own

So, if you want to retain your budgeting system but introduce an effective forecasting system, there are a range of issues to take into account, probably involving making changes that you might not have anticipated when you started the journey. Given the scale and nature of these changes, it may be tempting to say 'to hell with it, let's just throw out the budgets and use a forecast instead'. But simply discarding budgets can be dangerous, because budgets fulfill at least one purpose that forecasts do not: that of setting constraints and providing direction (i.e. budgets and targets). Without directional guidance and boundaries that define what can and cannot be done, there could be chaos. So we cannot simply eliminate budgets; we need to put something else in their place. Ideally, something that is as coherent as the budgeting model but which promotes a more external focus, which is flexible, more able to deal with change and does not promote the unhealthy patterns of behavior we have come to associate with traditional approaches.

• • • • •

In the next chapter we describe one (and we believe the best) alternative to traditional budgeting: the so-called 'Beyond Budgeting' model. This has been developed over the last 10 years by the Beyond Budgeting Round Table, a cross-industry research collaborative originally based in the UK but which now has thriving communities in many parts of the world including the USA. If you have no interest in this, or stomach for the change involved, you may wish to stop reading here. Based on what you have learned so far you will be able to design, implement and run an adequate forecasting process which will deliver the benefits promised in Chapter 1. If your ambition is bigger, if you are interested in transforming the performance or indeed the whole performance management culture of your organization, or if you are just plain curious, we hope you will find the next chapter inspiring.

• • • • •

SUMMARY

Traditional budgeting is an exercise in 'fixing' targets and budgets for a financial year. Deviations from budget within the year are normally regarded as 'bad' and traditional practice requires these 'gaps' to be eliminated. Forecasting is an exercise in exposing gaps to help management respond appropriately. It also requires that we have visibility over the full decision-making horizon. Traditional budgeting can, therefore, undermine good forecasting practice, so changes need to be made in order to exploit the power of effective forecasting. These involve the introduction of more flexibility and a longer time horizon into resource allocation and other supporting processes that are also 'fixed' and 'time bound'. Variance analysis should be abandoned since it promotes intolerance of change and uncertainty. Equally important are the changes required in mentality and behavior particularly around targets and target setting.

DEFINITIONS

Budgets

(a) The quantitative expression of a proposed plan of action by management for a specified period and (b) an aid to coordinate what needs to be done to implement that plan.

Budgeting

Involving:

- estimation of the profit potential of a unit
- stated in financial terms
- generally covering the period of a year
- representing a management commitment (to delivering the objectives expressed in the budget)

- subject to review and approval by an authority higher than the budgetee
- which, once reviewed, can only be changed under specified conditions and periodically is compared to actual financial performance for analysis and explanation.

KEY LEARNING POINTS
The five roles of budgeting
- Setting targets
- Planning
- Resource allocation
- Coordination
- Performance measurement.

The three characteristics of conventional budgeting
- Fixed
- Set within a financial year
- Subject to a process of annual negotiation.

Four changes that should be made to traditional budgeting practice
- More flexibility – supporting changes within the financial year
- Greater visibility – beyond the financial year-end (core and supporting processes)
- Dilution of target negotiation practices
- Elimination of variance analysis.

NOTES
1 This is a continuation of a theme that first appeared in Chapter 7. See references to the 'Change Equation'.
2 We are not advocating that you do not attempt to understand the difference between 'what you expected' and 'what actually happened'. Our point is that a budget is not a good expression of expectation.

Chapter 10

BEYOND BUDGETING:
a new management model?

Budgets; an unnecessary evil Jan Wallander

The budget is the bane of corporate America. It never should have existed. Jack Welch

> *The origins of 'Beyond Budgeting' – the 20 questionable assumptions upon which budgeting is built – the origins of budgeting – why traditional budgeting is not appropriate for the age in which we live – the six Beyond Budgeting Process Principles – the six Beyond Budgeting Organizational Principles*

We are nearing the end of our journey. Let us take a few moments to recap.

We started off by observing that forecasting is fast becoming one of the 'hottest topics' in management practice. The world is becoming more turbulent and to survive we need to become better at anticipating and responding to change. Our existing processes are 'broken' – they are incapable of providing us with the degree of foresight and flexibility we need.

We have argued that one reason that we have failed to solve this problem was that we do not have the right conceptual toolkit. We then set out the principles needed to manage the future well:

1. Mastery of purpose
2. Mastery of time
3. Mastery of models
4. Mastery of measurement
5. Mastery of risk.

Finally, we explored a number of practical issues that businesses are likely to face putting this knowledge into practice.

We have been upfront about our background – the Beyond Budgeting community – but the underlying assumption for most of this book thus far is that by applying these principles you will get better results from your forecasting 'engine'. In the last chapter, however, we raised some caveats. We suggested that the prevailing management model, which has conventional budgeting at its heart, carries a lot of unhelpful baggage. As a result, in order to forecast effectively you need to significantly modify traditional budgeting practices and the mindset associated with them if you are to avoid the disappointments suffered by many who have tried to improve forecasting processes without considering the wider context.

The big question: if you abandon budgets what do you put in their place?

We cannot, however, simply eliminate budgets. A simple forecast process does not provide the full range of functionality required to manage the performance of an organization. If not budgeting then what should we use instead? We argue that the answer is the 'Beyond Budgeting Model'. What is 'Beyond Budgeting'?

The movement started in the late 1990s as a cross-industry collaborative research project, and over the last 10 years has developed a distinctive philosophy and set of practices which, provide an alternative to traditional budgeting. We have also come to recognize that other strands of management thought offer valuable complementary perspectives on the challenges that organizations face in managing their affairs. While we do not see ourselves as in competition with other management gurus who promote models of 'Twenty-first Century Management', we do believe that the BB model makes a unique contribution in the search for an alternative way of doing business. It addresses head-on one of the foundation stones of classical management philosophy – the budgeting system. It also merits attention because, without compromising its distinctive philosophical stance, it goes beyond rhetoric by providing practitioners with tools to help them manage in a different way. In this respect, it has much in common with the 'Lean' movement. As many have found, it is not possible to emulate Toyota by implementing elements of the 'Lean Toolkit' without embracing the philosophical and cultural underpinnings of their approach.

Second, while there are 12 principles to which we all subscribe (more on these later) there is no 'religious orthodoxy' within the Beyond Budgeting movement. There is a lively debate within the community about 'what it is' and 'how to go about it' which, although it can sometimes be confusing for new members of the community, is a sign of intellectual health and growth.

The conventional management model is based on a set of questionable assumptions about organizations, their environment, and the people that work in them

Before we describe the 12 principles of Beyond Budgeting let us first examine what we are setting out to replace. To identify our target better, we need to clearly distinguish it from its background. Let us consider the classical model, and the assumption upon which it is founded, and ask ourselves whether they still hold true in the early years of the twenty-first century.

20 KEY ASSUMPTIONS OF THE CLASSICAL MANAGEMENT MODEL

1. The world in general is predictable to a great degree.
2. Specifically the actions of suppliers, customers and competitors can be anticipated with a reasonable degree of confidence.
3. As a result it is possible to set credible fixed targets and objectives 'in advance'.
4. We know enough about our own plans for the future to be able to specify, in advance, the optimal set of interventions for our business and attribute a cost and benefit to them.
5. The most senior people in the business are best placed to make a judgment about what constitutes a 'good target' or the optimal 'set of plans'.
6. Senior people are motivated purely by the welfare of shareholders when setting, agreeing and overseeing the execution of the fixed plan.
7. It is therefore possible and appropriate to construct a set of fixed plans for the business in advance. If this set of plans is delivered the business will be successful.
8. The external world (investors etc.), shares our definition of success, that is: 'delivering the fixed plan'.
9. Success therefore requires that deviations from this fixed plan be measured and steps taken to eliminate such 'errors'.

10. Any measures taken to correct deviations will not require a significant change in the quantity or disposition of resources (as provided for in the financial plan).

11. The chances of success will be improved by allocating portions of the fixed plan to managers who are held accountable for meeting their quota.

12. The greater the precision and level of detail to which we 'hold people accountable', the greater the chances of success.

13. Since success comes through the actions of many managers successfully 'hitting their numbers' it is not necessary for any manager to have any information other than that required to discharge their own responsibilities.

14. If managers do not adhere to fixed plans agreed in advance, the organization will descend into chaos since there would be no means to coordinate the activities of management.

15. People are inherently lazy and untrustworthy, so financial incentives are necessary in order to motivate them to hit targets.

16. People will respond to financial incentives by modifying their performance rather than trying to manipulate the reward system and the information upon which it is based.

17. Twelve months is the most appropriate unit of time for the consideration of targets and plans.

18. Any changes required within a year will be relatively minor; they will not necessitate a significant change in targets or money allocated to interventions 'in advance'.

19. Strategy will not change within a year.

20. 'Operational activity' within a year will not be of a scale or nature that invalidates the assumptions on which the fixed plans were built.

We have stopped at 20 – no doubt you could come up with more. Even as it stands, we think the conclusion is clear. *Virtually all the assumptions on which the classical model is built – that is the beliefs we implicitly accept when we choose to manage our organizations in this way – are at best highly questionable, at worst plain wrong.*

The conventional management model is a product of an era when management faced a completely different set of challenges to those they face today

The budgeting system is systemically flawed, but in a previous era its weaknesses were not germane, given the scale and nature of the challenges faced by the pioneers of professional management. When James O. McKinsey (founder of the eponymous consulting firm) published the first book on budgeting in 1922 (McKinsey, 1922), large divisionalized companies, run by professional managers rather than owner entrepreneurs, were only just beginning to emerge. In the circumstances, it is perhaps not surprising that the early pioneers of management theory stole an idea from the only other large organization that had experience of managing resources on a large scale – the government. The major problem that McKinsey, Sloan and others were grappling with was this: in the absence of any form of business education, modern communications, and with only the most primitive adding machines – how do you maintain control of enterprises that are too large to be run by proprietarial direction. The classical management model, and the rigorous way it was implemented in companies like General Motors, was a spectacular breakthrough in management theory and practice. But times have moved on, and what was state of the art in 1930 has now become a serious handicap. And it is easy to see why.

We need a management model based on natural principles to replace the
mechanistic one we have inherited
The pioneers were children of their age. The practice they invented reflected what was going on around them; mechanization, standardization, the production line. The classical model represents an attempt to *manage an organization like a machine*. But organizations are not machines. We cannot isolate an organization from its environment. We cannot succeed by specifying and tightly controlling inputs into our business, or by mechanically fixing processes to perform tasks repetitively. Moreover we cannot treat people as mere ciphers, as cogs in a machine. It is dehumanizing and demotivating to treat people in this way and it strips them of those qualities which organizations need most to help them meet today's challenges: the ability to think and act creatively in response to an unpredictable and turbulent world. The budgeting model is simply too constraining, too static and based on too simplistic assumptions about cause and effect.

Our world has moved on since McKinsey and Sloan. Not only is it more turbulent, but we understand more about how complex systems work. Our mental models have changed – we are more inclined to think of organizations in biological rather than engineering terms. We also have powerful new technologies, undreamt of 100 years ago, but which, sadly, we too often use to help perform twentieth century tasks more quickly. Doesn't it make sense to use twenty-first century knowledge and technology to solve problems in a twenty-first century way?

What we need to help us run our organizations is *an organic model*, to replace the mechanistic model we have inherited. One that recognizes that our organizations are part of nature. One that is flexible – *adaptive* – not fixed. And one that helps us focus on today's major challenge: how to best react to changes in the external environment of the firm, rather than yesterday's problem: policing the internal environment. Finally, the way we run our businesses should be aligned with human nature not against it. It should cherish and exploit the unique capabilities of human beings rather than manage them like inanimate components in a machine or Skinner's experimental pigeons.[1]

We believe that the Beyond Budgeting model is a strong candidate for such a twenty-first century organizational model. Its great strength is that it is holistic; recognizing the complementary role of process and organizational structure and culture. But it has also been proven to work in practice. The Beyond Budgeting principles were distilled from scores of case studies of businesses with a proven track record of success. The Beyond Budgeting model also provides a platform for the practice of forecasting advocated in this book.

This is not the place to delve into the detail of the model, or to explore the experiences of the organizations that provided the inspiration for it. Deeper study is required to do the model justice. We point you in the direction of Hope and Fraser's book *Beyond Budgeting: How Managers can Break Free from the Annual Performance Trap* (Hope and Fraser, 2003) and *Implementing Beyond Budgeting* (Bogsnes, 2009) where Bjarte Bogsnes presents the arguments for change based on his personal experiences in two pioneering companies. We wholeheartedly recommend both books. We will content ourselves with a simple, personal interpretation of the 12 'Beyond Budgeting' (BB) principles, which we hope will give the reader a good sense of what BB entails.

The 12 principles comprise six 'Process Principles' and six 'Organizational Principles'.

THERE ARE SIX PROCESS PRINCIPLES IN THE BEYOND BUDGETING MODEL

1. Target setting: 'from ceiling to threshold'

In a conventional performance management system, targets are expressed as annual, fixed, absolute numbers (e.g. '$20m'). Such targets are usually arrived at through a process of negotiation. Once targets are struck, it is the role of management to deliver a performance in line with the targets. Because there is no obligation to go beyond the 'quota', targets expressed in this way set a ceiling on performance. Also since there is no way of knowing in advance whether the competitive or economic climate will be hostile or benign, any fixed target set in advance will usually either be too stretching or too slack.

In order to create an adaptive system – one capable of responding creatively to what is going on in the real world – a target should be expressed in relative rather than fixed terms. In an ideal world the target would be drawn from the external environment: beating the market, the performance of our competitors or some other valid benchmark. A relative goal promotes the action required to ensure the survival of the organization in its economic ecosystem. If external reference points are hard to come by, the performance target could be drawn from the performance of peers from within the organization or from the unit's own past performance – so promoting 'continuous improvement'. As a result of adopting a different approach to target setting, managers do not try to *meet* a negotiated number – meeting a quota – they aim to *beat* a performance standard.

2. Rewards system: 'from meet to beat'

Typically incentives are linked, in a mechanistic way, to the achievement of targets based on a belief that 'people need to be incentivized to meet targets'. From this perspective, incentives – where the link between performance and pay is defined in advance – are taken to be 'necessary to motivate people' and promote 'fairness'.

Too often however, incentives succeed in motivating people – but in the wrong way. Fortunately Enron, WorldCom and the rest are rare extreme cases. Usually the dishonesty induced by mechanistic reward systems 'only' manifests itself in negotiating a less stretching target or 'managing performance', or the numbers that measure it, around period ends. Such behavior, while not fraudulent, is dysfunctional and unhealthy.

In order to eliminate the dysfunctional and damaging behavior often associated with the setting up or achievement of targets, incentives need to be decoupled from fixed negotiated targets.

There is no one 'right' way of achieving this but examples drawn from Beyond Budgeting cases involve managers exercising judgment 'after the event'. This makes sense since it is only after the event that we know what actually happened in the business environment – rather than what we assumed would happen – and how performance compares to our competitors or peers.

3. Planning and forecasting: 'from predict and control to project and act'

For many businesses, the annual planning process is an elaborate exercise of target and (by implication) pay negotiation. The original purpose – the requirement to anticipate the future and put in place appropriate plans – has often been forgotten. Planning arteries become clogged with accounting cholesterol because of the need to produce detailed arguments to support the case for targets (or budgets) to be lower or higher, depending which side of the negotiating table you sit. Forecasts become distorted by the political process.

Once agreed, the plan becomes a 'contract'. Changing the plan involves breaking this 'contract'. Deviation from plan signals a potential failure to deliver.

However, once the critical step of decoupling targets and reward has been made, the forecasting and planning processes are free to do the job that they need to do – to anticipate what the future might look like and so help ensure that plans are in place to steer the performance of the business, exploit opportunities and mitigate risks.

4. Measurement and control: 'from comply to plan to signals from noise'

The constricting nature of conventional planning processes is made worse by over-reliance on one measurement tool: variance analysis. Variance analysis reduces the complexity of the real world to a single number – usually the result of a comparison between an actual and a plan. This exercise is unlikely to provide useful insight because most budget-based plans at best represent an informed guess made many months previously. In addition, modern information systems produce enormous quantities of data all of which is infected by 'noise' (random variation) which conventional variance-based analytical approaches are incapable of distinguishing from important signals.

The world is a complex and dynamic place. In order to understand it properly we need a range of measures that help us detect those trends and patterns that are important for the health of the business. Visual displays of these measures provide insight into performance dynamics; variance analysis against forecast is used to help learn and adapt rather than as an instrument of control. Beyond Budgeting approaches also use filtering techniques to separate 'signals' from 'noise'.

5. Investment management: 'from entitlement to earn'

In a conventional system, the process of building annual plans and negotiating targets usually involves allocating resources to projects or areas of the business. Because they then form part of a fixed performance contract it is difficult to change budgets dispensed in this way. In addition budgets are often regarded as an entitlement which the system encourages managers to spend. Since spare resources cannot be carried forward managers are encouraged to spend regardless of need on the basis of 'use it or lose it'.

Because our knowledge of the future is incomplete, the wisdom of allocating spend so far in advance is questionable. Do we know what the money will be spent on? Do we know how effective the spend is likely to be? Are we aware of the alternative uses for these resources? Do we even know whether we can afford to spend at this level? If the answer to any of these questions is no, it is likely that money will be wasted and opportunities missed.

We need a dynamic allocation process where resources are committed as and when needed (and not before) based on a full understanding of the merits of any particular investment and those of the available alternatives.

6. Coordination: 'from push to pull'

Except in very small businesses, annual plans come together to form an interlocking network of fixed financial contracts. In the name of 'organizational alignment' this network of interdependent plans can severely limit the ability of an individual business to respond to the demands of the marketplace.

If we have created a set of adaptive processes, along the lines advocated by Beyond Budgeting, how do we ensure that in exercising this new found freedom it doesn't result in chaos? How do we coordinate the activities of semi autonomous responsive business units without imposing order from the top down in the form of fixed plans?

The answer is to build processes which continuously coordinate the activities of multiple business units so that collectively they continue to work in a synergistic way. Rather than order being imposed from above it should be created 'bottom up' by the continuous synchronization of activities around demand (actual and forecast) or by some form of lightly regulated internal pricing mechanism. In this scheme, alignment of resources and plans is achieved by the action of the market which *pulls* resources through the business, not *pushing* fixed plans.

THERE ARE SIX ORGANIZATIONAL PRINCIPLES IN THE BEYOND BUDGETING MODEL

1. Performance climate: 'from fulfilling to winning'

In a traditional system, 'good performance' is defined as meeting a target, by fulfilling the 'annual contract'. If success is defined in this way it colors the collective psychology of the business. It influences what is deemed a 'good year', how people are rated by their peers and so on. It has an impact that extends far beyond the mechanical operation of the budgeting process.

Businesses operating successfully without budgets put competitive success – beating as opposed to meeting goals – squarely at the heart of their entire approach to business. Success is defined in terms of performance relative to competition, peers or their own past record in the struggle to win customers and satisfy shareholders. This approach to performance influences all aspects of business life, including the way people talk, behave and interact.

2. Governance: 'from compliance to freedom within boundaries'

Policies, rules and procedures are one form of governance. It is an approach that seeks to regulate behavior in detail, by defining *what should be done*. There are circumstances where this 'command and control' may work – at least for a time. For instance, in emergencies or in circumstances where there is a big gulf between the knowledge and expertise of managers and workers.

The Beyond Budgeting model argues that this form of management is inappropriate for twenty-first century businesses which need more than dumb compliance from their employees. Instead of rules and regulations governance should rely more on principles and values. Taken together, principles and values provide boundaries and a compass – a framework which gives freedom for employees to exercise their initiative and to contribute more fully consistent with the common good. The focus on setting boundaries, being extremely clear about what can *not be done*, is analogous to that of liberal market economies where citizens enjoy freedom but within the rule of law.

3. Empowerment: 'decentralization to devolution'

The conventional model was created to enable centralized control to be exercised over decentralized business units in an era without modern communications and information systems. Without the ability to monitor what was going on 'from a distance' in real time, the activities of business units had to be tightly constrained by the need to seek permission from the center – permission which often took the form of agreement to budgets or budget adjustments.

The Beyond Budgeting model espouses a philosophy of empowerment – the devolution of decision-making authority. Typically this is granted to small cross-functional groups since they have the necessary qualities to respond quickly and effectively to the needs of the situation: an intimacy with the issues and sufficient expertise to determine how best to respond (consistent with the principles and values of the enterprise). Control is exercised by holding managers accountable for relative performance and adherence to governing principles. 'Head Office functions' only exist because activities *can't* be devolved or they *need* to be performed centrally in order to support efficient devolution.

4. Capability: 'from command and control to lead and coach' or 'from instruct to inspire'

Accountability for relative performance and the devolution of decision-making authority will succeed only if employees are motivated and have the capability to use their freedom wisely.

The Beyond Budgeting model places stress on leadership rather than on management. Rather than being given instructions and having their 'faults' corrected, business teams need to be helped to operate in a way which is consistent with the collective success of the organization as whole. In practical terms, this means enrolling them in the ideals and goals of the business and so inspiring them to perform. This also needs to be backed up by a commitment to the development, training, and the provision of practical support when and where needed.

5. Focus: 'from predict and sell to sense and respond'

The ethos of the classical management model is expressed in the conventional organization chart. This gives us an image of a large number of people 'at the bottom' of a pyramid, responsible to progressively 'higher' levels in the organization. In this model ultimate authority rests with the Chairman who is accountable to the owners of the business: the shareholders. Like the conventional military organization that was its inspiration, it is designed to create and exploit economies of scale. The purpose of this system is taken to be creating wealth for shareholders, and the role of customers is to 'feed' the economic machine. This requires that customers have needs that can be organized in a way that can be met on a large scale.

The Beyond Budgeting model takes a contrary position, effectively inverting the pyramid. Finding, creating, and satisfying customers are the focus of the organization, not shareholders. Shareholder wealth is a *consequence* of success in meeting customer needs rather than customers being a requirement to satisfy shareholders. In practice, this means that the organization is structured and operated as an externally focused network rather than an internally focused hierarchy. Power – the capacity to influence – is placed in the hands of those best placed to understand

and respond to customers rather than exclusively in the hands of those at the apex of the pyramid. By building the organization from the outside in – by adopting a sense and respond strategy – the organization is better able to adapt to its environment.

6. Information: 'from need to know to share and learn'

In a conventional model most information flows vertically – up and down 'the line' – in the form of 'reports' with a fixed format and frequency. It serves to help coordinate the activities of the enterprise and manage conformance to plan, thereby making performance more predictable. Senior people are assumed to be more knowledgeable and trustworthy than their juniors, and therefore better placed to make use of information. Therefore, in this model, information only need be disseminated to the extent that is necessary to help employees fulfill their designated role.

The Beyond Budgeting model is founded on a commitment to openness and integrity of information; it is a critical resource to everyone to help them do their job better – not a privilege of rank. To a business unit manager the information he or she needs might take the form of the profitability of individual customers and the efficiency and effectiveness of transactional processes. Leaders might use the same data sources to look at trends pertinent to the well being of the organization as a whole. Everyone in the business might use peer performance information to help them to spot opportunities for improvement, help identify risk or better anticipate the needs of business units that they support. Open access to high quality consistent information supports the external focus of the business and its responsiveness and alignment. The goal of information management is therefore to promote transparency. This requires high levels of data integrity but openness itself helps promote honesty and information quality and in so doing helps build the trust necessary to operate in the way advocated by Beyond Budgeting. Transparency of information is a prerequisite for freedom.

SUMMARY

Budgeting is at the heart of the classical management model which has underpinned business practice for the best part of the century. There is a strong case for scrapping this approach since most of the assumptions it makes about the world, the way a business needs to be organized and how people behave are no longer valid for the first decade of the twenty-first century. In essence it is based on a mechanistic view of organizations. A replacement model needs to be 'organic' and promote flexibility and an external focus. It should also avoid creating relationships within the business that lead to 'bad behavior' such as 'biasing' forecasts, gaming target setting, suboptimizing total business performance and so on. The 'Beyond Budgeting' model is a candidate for being part of the 'new management model'. The forecasting practice advocated within this book could be one of the foundational stones on which a 'Beyond Budgeting' implementation is built.

KEY LEARNING POINTS

The 20 questionable assumptions of traditional management practice

1. The world is predictable.
2. The actions of other organizations can be predicted.
3. It is possible to set realistic fixed targets and objectives 'in advance'.
4. We know enough to be able to specify the optimal set of interventions for our business.
5. Only senior people in the business can make good judgments about plans and targets.
6. Senior people are motivated purely by the welfare of shareholders.
7. It is possible to construct a set of fixed plans delivery of which ensures success.
8. The external world shares our definition of success.
9. Deviations from a fixed plan should be eliminated.
10. Correcting deviations will not require a significant change in resources.
11. Holding managers accountable for different parts of the plan will improve the chances of collective success.
12. The greater the precision and level of detail the greater the chances of success.
13. Managers only require information relating to their part of the plan.
14. Without fixed plans the organizations will quickly descend into chaos.
15. Financial incentives are necessary to motivate.
16. Financial incentives will not encourage the manipulation of the system.
17. Twelve months is the most appropriate unit of time.
18. Any changes required within a year will be relatively minor.
19. Strategy will not change within the timescale of a year.
20. Operational activity has no impact on fixed plans.

Beyond Budgeting Process Principles

1. Target Setting: 'from ceiling to threshold'
2. Rewards System: 'from meet to beat'

3. Planning and Forecasting: 'from predict and control to project and act'
4. Measurement and Control: 'from comply to plan to signals from noise'
5. Investment Management: 'from entitlement to earn'
6. Coordination: 'from push to pull'.

Beyond Budgeting Organizational Principles
1. Performance Climate: 'from fulfilling to winning'
2. Governance: 'from compliance to freedom within boundaries'
3. Empowerment: 'decentralization to devolution'
4. Capability: 'from command and control to lead and coach' or 'from instruct to inspire'
5. Focus: 'from predict and sell to sense and respond'
6. Information: 'from need to know to share and learn'.

NOTE
1 Skinner was an influential psychologist who, as a 'behavioralist', believed that human behavior was programmed through reward and punishment. He is famous for experiments involving pigeons. Behavioralism is now largely discredited.

Chapter 11

CONCLUSION:
reconnection

Throughout history, probably as long as we have existed as a species, human beings have tried to divine the future. We have used sticks, spiders, stones, turtles, tea leaves, livers, stars and intestines, none of which have succeeded in opening the window into the future. And yet, despite over 3000 years of recorded history of failure, and the fiercely held belief in our own free will – our capacity to choose, to make our own lives – many business people still seem to be held in thrall to the idea that the future can be predicted.

Science can now explain what experience has taught us, that we cannot predict the future. To believe otherwise is naïve and damaging to our enterprise in life, whatever it is. And yet, ironically, once we humbly abandon the idea that we can predict, and accept that our destiny does not exist 'out there' waiting to be discovered, we find that the future is not unknowable. Constrained only by the laws of nature, the actions of our fellow human beings and our shared recent history, we do have the capacity to shape the future, and so predict *a* future – one of our choosing.

This is the 'big idea' in this book, and we have described what you need to do to exploit this insight.

We have explored the six principles of forecast mastery:

Mastery of Purpose, based on recognition of the difference between a forecast and a target.
Mastery of Time, based on an appreciation of lags associated with the life cycle of decision-making.

Mastery of Models, involving an appreciation of the limitations of any specific approach, in particular those involving judgment.

Mastery of Measurement and how to differentiate between unavoidable and avoidable errors.

Mastery of Risk and how an understanding of it sharpens organizational reflexes.

Mastery of Process, based on an appreciation of where and how to align actions and behaviors.

We have also discussed how you might set about introducing change and tackle some of the road blocks you will encounter along the way. In particular we have discussed the pernicious effect of traditional budgeting practices and behaviors.

The purpose of this book has been to provide readers with a practical guide to understanding and improving a business process, one that is essential to the long term health and survival of any organization. We have gone beyond merely asserting the validity of our ideas; we have endeavored to demonstrate it by logical argument, reference to real life examples and also by demonstrating how they are consistent with our scientific understanding of the way that nature works – as engineered by billions of years of evolutionary trial and error. The subliminal message of this book is that what we do as managers, as social animals, is not set apart from nature, it is part of it. To manage well – effectively, efficiently and with due care to our obligations to our employees, society and to the environment that we share – we should learn from nature and seek to structure and run our organizations accordingly.

We conclude by telling the subliminal story.

As human beings we swim in a deep ocean of data, most of which is irrelevant to our purpose. If we are to survive we need to discard most of it to isolate that tiny proportion that we can use. Since our purpose is to create the future, we need to be clear what kind of future we want and what tools are available to help us bring it about. Anything which is not pertinent to those actions needs to be eliminated – and one of the most important things to jettison is the idea that perfect accuracy is either possible or necessary.

Any attempt to make sense of the world involves information and working, like a sculptor, to eliminate that which is irrelevant and so expose the meaningful form. But information about the future is of a completely different nature to most of the information we handle in business; it is not collected – it is created. Moreover, like it or not, it is created in large measure by the collective intellect of the individuals working in the organization. 'Scientific models' can certainly help, but like turtles and tea leaves, they are not truth machines. Forecasting techniques can do no more than tell us what the future will be if it is like the past, which is helpful, but only up to a point. Our reliance on the honest, balanced judgment of human beings, particularly when we are faced with environmental turbulence and novelty, means that we have to take care to create a healthy environment that promotes the growth of rationality, integrity but also skepticism. We have to recognize our own intellectual limitations which we share with our coworkers. Our brains are not computing machines; they are a pattern-recognizing jelly, bathed in powerful chemicals. They are immensely powerful and efficient, engineered by millions of years of Research and Development; but they can fail. Reward and punishment are powerful substances which can create collective hallucination or, like testosterone, an unjustified confidence in our own abilities. Our organizational brain can also become delusional, selectively eliminating not just irrelevant information, but also that information that does not fit our beliefs about the way the world works and the way we think it is or would like it to be. The only thing that separates forecast from fantasy is a firm anchor in the facts, and differentiating between them requires an ability to separate reality from the randomness that our pattern hungry brains often mistake for meaning.

Nonetheless, however good we are at rigorously testing our model of the world against reality, nature is so organized that the only thing we can be sure of is that the predictions of our models will be wrong. Our error may be minor; a blurring of the edges of our image of the future, but it could be that we have misread the signals and created a completely false picture. Furthermore, once we have created our model, it becomes one of the tools we use to decide what information is relevant and what is not, what to discard. So, if we have no concept that something is possible, we literally will not see it; at least not until it is so close to us that we cannot fail to recognize it – by which time it may be too late. Nature knows this. The visual field of our eyes is only five degrees. The picture we have of the world is built up by our eyes continuously scanning the environment to build up a composite picture, supplemented by our peripheral vision which covers the 'left field'. And our brains are continuously at work, wondering 'what if, what if'. As Andy Groves says 'only the paranoid survive' (Grove 1997). But thought without action leads to neurosis; we also need to prepare ourselves – to create a repertoire of responses to match the range of possible futures so that we can anticipate not merely react and so – just a little – cheat time.

None of this will happen by itself; it needs to be organized. But the organizational models which we have bequeathed, particularly the budgeting model, are not a good fit for the way of working we advocate. They are too mechanistic, based on a too simplistic model of the world and an impoverished view of human nature, making no allowance for free will and mankind's need for meaning and purpose. We need to rethink the way that we structure and run information-based processes in business, exploiting what the natural world teaches us about the best way to deal with the complexity and uncertainty of life, working with the grain of human nature. We hope that, in our own modest way, we have helped point the way forward and provided some practical guidance about how to get started.

Thank you for accompanying us on the journey.

GLOSSARY

Behavioral bias   Bias associated with **judgmental forecasting**.

Bias   Systematic error: the mark of a poor forecast process. Manifest as a sequence of errors with the same sign (positive or negative). See **variation** and **behavioral bias**.

Buckets   The units of time used to build up a forecast.

Budget   A sum of money allocated to an activity or action to which an organization has committed itself.

Budgeting   The process of setting **targets** and allocating resources to groups of activities or processes.

Business forecasting   Forecasting used to help steer the activities of an organization given a set of **targets**. Business forecasts are longer term than **operational forecasts** but shorter term than **strategic planning**.

Central forecast   A 'single point' forecast. See **range forecast**.

Chaos Theory   The study of systems which, because of the complex, nonlinear nature of their relationships, behave in ways that cannot be predicted. See **Systems Science**.

Cognitive bias	Systematic error caused by defects in reasoning. A form of **behavioral bias**.
Concertina horizon	A forecast where the period of time being forecast (horizon) varies depending when the forecast is made. Traditional financial 'year-end' forecasting is an extreme form of concertina horizon. See also **rolling horizon**.
Contingency plans	A complex set of plans designed to cope with (**mitigate** or **exploit**) a possible set of circumstances.
Continuous risk	'Smooth' **risk** which can assume any value along a scale.
Coupling	A word used to describe the nature of the relationship between two or more parts of an organization. If changes in one part have a direct and immediate impact on another, they are said to be 'closely coupled'. Otherwise they may be 'loosely coupled', or even 'uncoupled'.
Cybernetics	The science of control and communication (in man and machine). See **Systems Science**.
Cycle	The elapsed time between forecasts (i.e. the frequency of forecast).
Cycle time	The length of time required to produce a forecast.
Decision-making lead time	The time between taking a decision to do something (an **intervention**) and its impact being manifest.
Dependent risks	**Risks** which tend to vary in proportion to each other (strongly correlated). Dependent risks can be added arithmetically.
Discrete risk	'Lumpy' **risk** that tends to assume one of two (or a very limited number of) values – often one value may be 'zero'). See also **continuous risk**.
Domain knowledge	Knowledge about/experience of the situation being forecast.

Driver-based forecasting	A forecast generated from inputs that are assumed to have a significant impact on outcomes. A form of **mathematical model**.
Event risk	**Risk** attached to an **intervention**.
Exploitative actions	Actions taken to exploit a positive situation. See **mitigating actions**.
Feedback	Information about the state of a system which is returned (fed back) into the system in order to change its state.
Feedforward	Information about the potential future state of a system, generated by a forecast **model**, which is used to influence its future state.
Forecast	A description/estimate of likely future outcomes ('where we think we will be') based on assumptions about the environment and organization's plans. A form of **feedforward** information. See **target** and **prediction**.
Forecast decay	The phenomenon of forecasts becoming increasingly unreliable towards the end of the horizon as a consequence of a decline of knowledge about the detail of **plans**.
Forecast error	The difference between actual and forecast outcomes for a **bucket** of time.
Forecast lead time	The time between the completion of a forecast to the start of forecast horizon.
Horizon	The length of time covered by a forecast. See **rolling horizon** and **concertina horizon**.
Independent risks	Unrelated **risks** that do not vary in proportion to each other (not highly correlated): these need to be combined statistically (or estimated judgmentally).
Intervention	Any activity designed to change a forecast outcome to which (for the purposes of forecasting) an incremental impact can be ascribed. See **event risk** and **momentum**.

Judgmental forecast   A (subjective) estimate of future outcomes based on the judgment of individuals (using a tacit mental **model**), unlike forecasts produced using numerically based **mathematical** or **statistical models**.

MAPE (Mean Absolute Percentage Error)   The average of a set of errors, ignoring sign. A measure of **variation**.

Mathematical model   An explicit arithmetical representation of a situation used to generate a forecast. See **driver-based model**.

Mitigating actions   Actions taken to offset negative consequences of a situation. See **exploitative actions**.

Model   A simplified representation of (part of) reality, used to generate a forecast. See **judgmental forecasting, mathematical model, statistical model**.

Momentum forecast   A forecast of underlying trends; not significantly affected by the impacts of **interventions** in the short term.

Motivational bias   Systematic (**judgmental**) forecast error attributable to the perception of reward or punishment for certain types of forecast outcome. A form of **behavioral bias**.

MPE (Mean Percentage Error)   The average of a set of errors, taking account of the sign. A measure of **bias**.

Operational forecasting   Short term forecasts used to determine the scale and nature of response to a future outcome that an organization cannot influence.

Option   A potential **intervention**.

Plan   A set of future actions (**interventions**) designed to reach an objective.

Planning   The process of defining a set of future actions (**interventions**) with the aim of achieving an objective.

Prediction   A statement about the future based on (scientific or supernatural) insight into the workings of the world. See **forecast**.

Process A set of related actions whereby a set of inputs is transformed into a set of outputs.

Range forecast An estimated spread of possible outcomes (**risk**) around **the central forecast** with a defined level of probability. The result of **sensitivity** and 'what if' analyses.

Reliable A quality of a good forecast: accurate enough for the purposes of the decisions being made. Reliable forecasts are without **bias** and exhibit acceptable **variation**.

Risk A possible deviation from a **central forecast** (positive or negative) where a probability of occurrence can be estimated with a degree of confidence. See also **uncertainty**.

Rolling horizon (forecast) A forecast where the period of time being forecast remains constant. In principle the length of the **forecast horizon** should be determined by the longest **decision lead time**. See **concertina forecast**.

Run chart A graph showing values of a variable over time. Forecast error should be plotted on a run chart to help identify **bias**.

Sales and Operations Planning An approach to coordinating the activities of different parts of an enterprise in order to efficiently and effectively fulfill customer demand, usually centered on a forecast of demand.

Scenario Planning An approach to assessing **uncertainty**. It usually involves the production of (radically differing) alternative scenarios by making completely different *sets of assumptions* about political, economic, social, technological or environmental factors. Scenario Plans can be used to help create **contingency plans**.

Sensitivity analysis	An approach to estimating **risk** (often expressed in the form of a range forecast) by varying the assumptions made about **continuous risk**. See also **'what if' analysis**.
Skewed	A skewed probability distribution is one where risk is not uniformly distributed around the **central forecast**.
Social bias	Systematic **error** attributable to a tendency to conform to group norms (which distorts/overwhelms fact-based analysis). A form of **behavioral bias**.
Statistical model	An approach whereby historic trends are extrapolated, using a statistical model, to create a forecast. See **model**.
Strategic planning	A process whereby choices are made about the scope, goals and structure of the business, usually based on some form of long-range forecast of the environment. See also **business forecasts** and **operational forecasts**.
Systems science	The study of interconnected entities, in particular the phenomenon of organizations and the complex nature of causality of systems. See **cybernetics** and **Chaos Theory**.
Target	A desired future outcome (where we would like to be). See **forecast**.
Uncertainty	Possible future outcomes (with positive or negative implications) where the probability of occurrence cannot be estimated with a degree of confidence. See also **risk**, **scenario planning** and **contingency planning**.
Underlying risk	Risk around a momentum forecast. The level of risk may be estimated based on historic patterns of variation around a trend. See **event risk**.
Variation	Unsystematic error manifest as errors which do not exhibit extended sequences of the same sign. See **bias and error**.
'What if' analysis	Estimating alternative possible forecast outcomes by making different assumptions about **discrete risks**. See also **sensitivity analysis**.

Appendix I

DESIGN PRINCIPLES: A SUMMARY

Use this questionnaire to test your understanding of the five principles of forecast mastery. Alternatively, use it to audit your existing forecast processes or to test the robustness of the design of a new process.

1. **What is the purpose of your business forecasting process?**
   - Clarity of purpose is essential in order to design an effective process and align the organization around it.
   - The purpose will most likely include a phrase like 'to support the steering of the business by …'.
   - It is also important to be clear about what the purpose is not:
     i. It is not about trying to prophesy the future. When you respond to a forecast, you change the future.
     ii. It is not about making a commitment. This is the purpose of a target which is not the same as the purpose of forecasts.
     iii. It is not to support the fulfillment of customer demand. This is the province of operational forecasting.
     iv. It is not to speculate on longer term trends. This is the role of strategy.

2. **Specifically, what are the kinds of changes that you might wish to make in response to your forecast?**
   - In order to design an effective process you need to be clear about the kind of decisions that you will be making, based on a forecast.

- This will involve making interventions which can be thought of as projects that you might want to:
    i. Stop
    ii. Start
    iii. Bring forward
    iv. Push back
    v. Change.
- A change can include a change in external communication (perhaps to shareholders), but it is unlikely to be the sole purpose of a forecast process.

3. **What kind of changes lie outside the scope of your forecast process?**
    - It is not sensible to design a process which will accommodate every kind of decision which might be made to steer the business.
    - Identify minor decisions that are not material for steering the business at the level of the organization in focus. Then either build a subsidiary (aligned) process to support decision-making at this level or, if this cannot be justified, exclude them altogether from the formal process architecture.

4. **Is everyone involved in the process clear what your purpose is, and is not?**
    - It is not enough to be clear about the purpose yourself. It needs to be effectively communicated to everyone involved in the process, which may be a large group of people.

5. **What information do you need in order to make the kind of decisions you need to make?**
    - The information you need for decision-making is likely to be very different from that you might normally produce as part of a budgeting exercise for example.
    - In particular, because decision-making involves making changes to 'projects', you will need to be clear about the incremental impact of each of them. Such information may be spread about a normal chart of accounts or not routinely available at all.

6. **What information is irrelevant for the decisions that you need to make?**
    - If information is not needed for decision-making, and does not contribute to improving the reliability of the forecast, then it should not be collected at all.

- In particular, increased level of detail, especially if it is produced using judgmental techniques, often degrades the quality of forecasts.

7. **How far in advance will you need the information that drives your decisions?**
    - The process should be designed around decision-making (what decisions need to be made and when) not the other way round.
    - It may be preferable to have a less 'accurate' forecast quickly rather than a 'perfect' one too late.

8. **Is everyone involved in the process aware that reliability is the aim rather than accuracy?**
    - The objective is to produce 'good enough' information for decision-making.
    - Improved 'accuracy' which does not lead to improving the quality of decisions is likely to reduce, not enhance, the value of the process.
    - Since it is often misunderstood, it is important that you communicate the aim widely and effectively.

9. **Is everyone involved in the process familiar with the importance of eliminating bias?**
    - The most important characteristic of a reliable process is that it be unbiased. This means that the number of positive forecast errors should be approximately the same as the number of negative forecast errors.
    - This is often poorly understood. Indeed, often people think that some form of bias is good or 'part of the game'.
    - Most forecast processes involve input from a large number of people. For the overall outcome of the process to be reliable it is important that the need to eliminate bias is communicated effectively.
    - In particular it is important to regulate 'adjustments' made to forecasts outside of the formal system since they often introduce bias rather than help eliminate it.

10. **How precise does the forecast information have to be in order to support the kind of decisions that you need to make?**
    - The second characteristic of a reliable process is that it is 'accurate enough'. In other words, the average size of errors is not large enough to prejudice the quality of decision-making.
    - It is important that you roughly quantify the level of 'acceptable variation' and you make all the contributors to the process aware of these tolerances.

11. **What other processes exist in your business that have similar or related purposes to your own?**

    ● It is likely that there will be other forecasting processes in your organization, for example sales forecasting processes. If they are seeking to influence the same sort of decisions as your process, it is imperative to align the two processes. Not to do so is to invite chaos.

    ● If there are processes that are related to yours, for example an innovation project management process, then it is necessary to align them to make sure that the right projects (i.e. related to purpose and affordable) are being worked on and that the forecast represents the reality of what is being planned in the business.

    ● It is possible that there will be other forecasting processes in your organization that have different purposes and are not related in any other way. In these circumstances, it is important to recognize explicitly that they serve different purposes and that it is acceptable for them not to be aligned, formally.

12. **What benefit do you want to derive from your forecast process and what level of commitment of time and money is consistent with this?**

    ● One way to ensure that your forecast process is cost effective is to define the amount of resource (time, money and manpower) you can justify allocating to it and design your process round this.

13. **Which kinds of decisions have the longest lead times?**

    ● The need to forecast is a result of the fact that all decisions in business take time to enact, sometimes a very long period.

    ● Therefore, in principle, the lead time of the decision with the longest time lag should determine the length of the overall forecast horizon.

14. **Are there other decisions that have significantly shorter lead times?**

    ● Most probably, there will be other kinds of decisions with significantly shorter lead times.

    ● If these decisions require a different kind of information it may be necessary to create sub horizons with different information structures (perhaps more detail, updated more frequently).

15. **How do you divide time?**

    ● The forecast horizon needs to be subdivided into 'buckets' of time.

    ● This subdivision will need to take account of factors such as the best way of producing the information, and the most effective way of communicating the results.

- If in doubt, it is easier and less risky to produce data forecasts using consistent bucket sizes and to aggregate data produced in small buckets (e.g. a month) rather than disaggregate data produced in large buckets (e.g. a quarter).

16. **How quickly do those things become important for decision-making change?**
    - The frequency of forecast updates should be related to the rate of change of variables which could cause plans to change.
    - This means that different forecast elements, and different parts of the forecast horizon, will be updated at different frequencies.

17. **Is your resource allocation process operating on the same frequency?**
    - Changes in commitments arising from a forecast need to be put into effect in a timely fashion. This requires that the resource allocation process operate at the same frequency as the forecast process.

18. **How are resource allocation decisions linked to the forecasting process?**
    - In order to properly align the resource allocation process and the forecast process there should be a clear protocol governing when and how projects are incorporated into the forecast.
    - For instance, it may be that only when a project moves from the feasibility stage into capability is it included in the forecast.

19. **How do you deal with your lack of knowledge about your intentions at the distant end of the forecast process?**
    - The further out you look the less knowledge you have about the project portfolio. This degradation in knowledge is called 'forecast decay' and it is possible that it may be misinterpreted as a degradation in performance.
    - It is important that forecast decay is recognized and dealt with, either by acknowledging its existence and allowing for it or by compensating for it in some way.

20. **What types of models do you use to populate your forecast and why?**
    - Models (a set of assumptions about the future) are used to produce forecasts.
    - There are three basic types: judgmental, statistical and mathematical.
    - A forecast process is likely to use all three types in combination.
    - Each type of model has its strengths and its weaknesses that make it more or less suitable for different purposes.

- It is important that you make the choice of the technique to use in a deliberate fashion, mindful of these strengths and weaknesses.

21. **What measures are in place to mitigate the weaknesses of the modeling approach you have chosen?**
    - In particular, it is important to recognize and to take steps to mitigate the weaknesses of the different approaches.
    - The major weakness of judgmental forecasting is that it is particularly prone to bias.
    - The major weakness of mathematical and statistical modeling is that they cannot easily accommodate novelty, which means that forecasting is always likely to rely on judgmental methods to a certain degree.

22. **How do you ensure that your models use consistent assumptions?**
    - All the key assumptions underpinning a forecast should be clearly documented.
    - A business is a form of system, made up of elements interconnected in time and through time.
    - It is important that the impact of changes in one element of the forecast is properly reflected in other elements in the same and in subsequent time periods.

23. **How is measurement made part of your routine forecast process?**
    - No forecasting methodology will ever be perfect at any one point of time, and the world is in a constant state of flux.
    - There is a need to constantly measure the performance of our forecasting process in order to calibrate and improve and to ensure that it continues to present a reliable picture when the world, or your organization, changes.
    - One can only draw meaningful conclusions about forecast quality by observing the patterns of errors over time.
    - In addition, the measures need to be acted upon in order to ensure that the reliability of the forecast can be maintained and improved.
    - Measurement needs to be embedded in the design of the forecast process.

24. **How do you measure forecast quality?**
    - In order to interpret patterns, measurement of errors needs to be made in a consistent fashion.
    - This means using the same time buckets, with the same lag. The process should only be measured within decision-making lead times, to ensure that you exclude from the measure the effect of decisions made in response to forecasts.

25. **Are your intervention criteria sound, and are they clearly communicated?**
    - Interventions in the forecast process should be made with the aim of eliminating bias and reducing variation to the extent that it compromises good decision-making.
    - We cannot make a definitive conclusion about the existence of bias, only a probabilistic assessment. Therefore, base the criteria on an understanding of probabilities and apply them consistently throughout the organization.

26. **Is the assessment of risk part of your routine forecast process?**
    - No forecast can anticipate everything; even in a relatively stable business environment the further ahead you look the greater the chances of error. Therefore, it is important routinely to assess the risk attached to the forecast.
    - Risk assessment should therefore be built into the design of the forecast process.
    - A risk assessment is also a useful way of surfacing and acknowledging dissenting views while maintaining a collaborative spirit.

27. **How do you assess risk?**
    - It is important to understand the scale of the risk, but assessing the scale of risk is fraught with traps for the unwary.
    - There needs to be a well defined approach to assessment which covers, among other things, what nature and scale of risks are to be included and how to treat discrete risk and dependent and independent events. This should include the impact of changes to key assumptions.

28. **What measures are in place to mitigate or exploit outcomes uncovered by your risk assessment?**
    - The purpose of assessing risk is to put in place measures to mitigate the impact of negative events and exploit the opportunities provided by positive outcomes.
    - Therefore, there needs to be a formal procedure to capture options and do whatever work is necessary to ensure that these can be deployed quickly when needed.

29. **What procedures are in place to assess uncertainty?**
    - Uncertain events have a low probability of occurrence but may be very large. In extremis they could threaten the continued independent existence of the organization.

- By their nature, they are difficult to anticipate since they represent discontinuities: radical departures from an established trend. As a result a different process is needed to assess uncertainty, possibly including the generation of alternative future scenarios.

30. **How do you plan to respond to uncertain events?**
   - Due to the nature and scale of uncertainties it may be difficult to deal with them by adjusting plans.
   - It is necessary therefore to establish what might be done to avoid negative outcomes altogether.

 More

Other sources of information on forecasting best practice
Do not despair if you fail to answer the majority of these questions satisfactorily. We have already referred you to the 'Forecasting Principles' website hosted by Wharton University (Various, 2009), as a source of excellent advice on forecast models. There you will find 139 forecasting principles detailed: the result of extensive consultation among experts. It is interesting to note that on average only 19% of these principles are cited in text books on the subject! (Armstrong, 2003).

Appendix 2

IMPORTANT CONCEPTS IN SYSTEMS AND CYBERNETICS

> In this appendix you will be introduced to a number of key concepts in cybernetics and systems, particularly those that underpin the analysis presented in the main body of this book. In addition there are recommendations for further reading for those whose interest has been awakened.

Many of the ideas in this book are practical applications of elements of systems theory. When we use the word 'system' in this context we are not referring to ICT systems, although they are one kind of system. The words 'system' and 'systemic' are in common use (as in 'the systemic failure of the banking system' for instance) but for most people the words do not have a precise meaning. Nor is there a widespread appreciation that systems are something that can be studied scientifically and used to understand and intervene in the real world. If we claim to be using 'systems science', how does this differ from the kind of science we might have learned at school?

Conventional science is based on the study of parts – reductionism – based on the assumptions that the whole can be explained by its parts

Conventional science, such as that practiced by Newton and his successors for the last 400 years, has proved to be a spectacularly successful piece of social technology. One of the characteristics of this kind of science is that it acquires knowledge through a process of 'reductionism'. This involves isolating a small number of variables (usually two) and seeking to establish a causal relationship between them, often through experimentation. The aim is to understand how changes in one thing affect the others and express this, mathematically, as a law or theory, such as Newton's Law of Gravity or Einstein's Theory of Relativity. The implicit assumption behind this approach (put very simplistically) is that if all natural laws were known then, simply by combining these laws, the world could be completely understood; it would be completely predictable.[1] Systems science rejects this assumption.

Systems science is based on the study of 'wholes' subject to the principle of emergence: 'the whole is greater than the parts'

A system is a set of elements which interact with each other. Unlike conventional science which focused on simple unidirectional causality (A influences B), systems science explicitly studies circular causality (A influences B which influences A). The justification for studying phenomena in this way is that systems, beyond a certain level of complexity, behave in ways that conventional science, using simple cause and effect logic, cannot easily explain. Indeed complex systems often exhibit novel properties; properties that do not exist in any of the component parts. Thus common salt is made up of sodium and chlorine, neither of which exhibits the property of 'saltiness'. The property whereby 'new' things are observed at higher levels of connectedness or complexity is called 'emergence'.

So systems science is not a study of 'things'; it is about how things are connected. Systems scientists set out to study the properties associated with such 'connectedness'. One consequence of this is that, if elements are connected in the same way, they will behave in the same way, irrespective of their material form. So knowledge gleaned from the study of physical systems (e.g. molecules, organisms) can be applied to social (e.g. economics) and even logical systems.[2] Whereas conventional science seeks to understand by breaking things up to isolate the qualities of simple 'parts', systems science studies the properties and behavior of complex 'wholes'. Systems scientists argue that this makes it more appropriate to the study of complex wholes like biological organisms and social organizations.

Systems science as a formal discipline is a relatively recent phenomenon

The originator of idea of the study of systems as a science was an Austrian biologist, Ludwig von Bertalanffy, who in the 1930s proposed and subsequently promoted the concept of 'General Systems Theory' (GST). GST is an attempt to formulate scientific laws that can be applied to systems of all types, in the same way that gravity applies to bodies of all types. In 1948, the mathematician Norbert Weiner coined the word Cybernetics to describe another new endeavor: the 'science of control and communication in man and machine' (Weiner, 1948). While Weiner's Cybernetics was developed independently of GST, it soon became clear that the two approaches had the same object of study: the behavior of connected wholes. Cybernetics differed from GST in that it was exclusively focused on goal directed behavior. As an intellectual movement, Cybernetics influenced early thinking in computing and life sciences, but did not take hold as an independent discipline and fell out of fashion in the 1970s.[3] In the last 15 years systems science has enjoyed a revival in the form of 'Complexity Science' most notably associated with figures such as Stuart Kauffman, Duncan Watts, Chris Langdon, Brian Arthur and others associated with the Santé Fe Institute (Waldrop, 1992).

Cybernetics is the strand of systems science most suited to the study of the management of organizational performance

In this book, we tackle the question 'how do we design systems that help us effectively achieve an objective?' – the domain of cybernetics. Our daily life is populated by simple 'goal seeking systems' of all sorts such as thermostats, cruise control on cars and so on. The way we manage businesses employing tools such as 'targets', 'reporting' and 'planning' is, without most managers being aware of it, based on a very crude set of cybernetic concepts; or more accurately a set of cybernetic concepts employed in a very crude fashion.

Progress in management thinking depends on acquiring a better grasp of cybernetic concepts and thought

We believe that we will accelerate progress in management thinking and be more consistently successful in practice by better understanding the science behind management and learning how to use this knowledge to design better systems and processes. In this appendix, we set out some of the basic systems and cybernetic ideas we have exploited in this book, which we hope will help readers gain a deeper appreciation of the ideas and perhaps inspire some to explore further. We have used examples from engineering or from nature to help illustrate these ideas. The same basic 'rules' govern the behavior of all systems but social systems are considerably more complex than most other sorts, so we should be wary of making simplistic comparisons.

The concept of 'a goal'

A good place to start is with the concept of 'a goal'. A goal is a set of system states[4] that are selected in preference to other states. This might be the result of evolutionary pressure – e.g. other states induce death (e.g. hypothermia) – or because they have been consciously selected by a human being as being desirable, as is usually the case in business. A goal could take a wide variety of forms. It may take the form of a small range of values (point regulation); it could be a specific cycle of states (path regulation) or a particular spatial, temporal or functional relationship (self-organization). In complex social organizations there will be many sorts of goals many of which will not be part of a formal control process.

What all these forms have in common is that the system acts in order to seek these states out – a process called regulation. How does regulation work? In cybernetic theory, information is central to regulation (the maintenance of control). Regulation may be applied from outside the system, but cyberneticians have a particular interest in self-regulation – from within the system.

The role of information in control: four archetypes

Goal orientated systems are in a state of dynamic equilibrium. Unlike a ball in the bottom of a bowl – which is in static equilibrium – goal orientated systems are always being 'knocked off balance'. They are 'disturbed' by perturbations; sometimes from outside itself (its environment), often from other parts of the system. What makes the system goal seeking is that whenever it is disturbed – when it moves away from its desired state(s) – it returns to it, by acting upon information which the system receives about its own state. In this context 'information' need not take the form of numbers on a page or computer screen. Changes in price, for instance, are a form of information, as is behavior (e.g. the expression on the face of your boss). In fact any 'difference which makes a difference' (data capable of being acted upon) is information.

Figure A.1 shows four different ways in which these information flows can be arranged.

The first type of system is termed 'information less' (or open loop) since, while a goal exists, no information about the performance of the system with respect to the goal is made available to the system. An example of this form of goal orientated system might be a central heating system activated by timer alone (i.e. without a thermostat). For obvious reasons a system designed in this way is not very effective – the heater might be turned off on a cold spring day for example. In practice a human being often 'closes the loop' – i.e. introduces information into the system – for instance by turning the boiler on when it gets too cold.

What this example illustrates is that effective achievement of a goal (let's call it 'control' from now on) can only be reliably achieved if information about the state

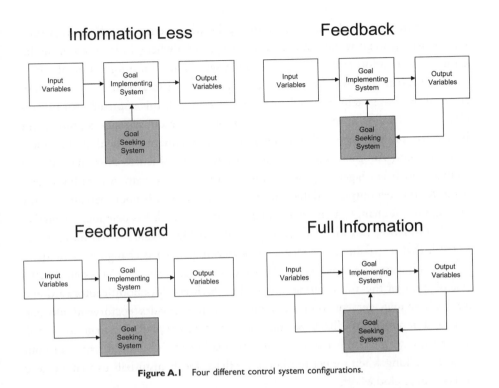

Figure A.1 Four different control system configurations.

of the system (specifically the variables which we are trying to control) is 'fed back' to the goal seeking system (by the thermostat for instance). The goal seeking system then takes appropriate action based on the difference between the output variables and the goal. This is the 'feedback' based system often referred to as an 'error controlled system'. The majority of electromechanical control systems designed by engineers are of this sort. Control engineering is exclusively devoted to the study of such control arrangements but most of the processes in our body are controlled by feedback systems of some sort. Indeed, the term often used to describe dynamic equilibrium in organisms – 'homeostasis' – was coined by Walter Cannon in 1932 (Cannon, 1932) to describe the mechanism whereby the body is able to maintain a constant temperature through such mechanisms. We can say with confidence, even though we may not be able to identify the mechanism at work, that **any system which exhibits stable patterns of behavior over time is dominated by feedback control**. The fact that trends exist (which we are able to forecast) is evidence of this. If a system was not feedback controlled the system would be chaotic and so unforecastable.

An error controlled system is controlled by what went on in the past. A third type of arrangement is the 'feedforward' based system where, instead of waiting for error (output) information, the goal seeking system acts on information about its potential future state with the aim of anticipating (and so avoiding) errors. Where the goal seeking system has a reliable predictive model, this approach can provide effective control. An example of this is an automatic cut out system – a power surge is detected and the system closed down before any damage can be done to a piece of equipment. Another example of feedforward control is the shivering reflex in animals which is triggered by skin temperature, not by a drop in core body temperature (the key output variable). If, however, the model is poor, perhaps because of a significant change in environmental conditions which has degraded its predictive performance, this kind of controller is unreliable. Because it has no feedback to tell it that it is failing, it is incapable of learning – that is changing its 'model'.

For this reason, complex systems (including biological and social systems) make extensive use of the 'full information' model which employs both feedforward and feedback. In management control systems forecasting provides feedforward information, and 'reporting' feedback. So, for example, if we are preparing to go for a walk in the snow we put on extra clothes in anticipation of the cold, but after an hour or so of walking when we get too hot, a feedback mechanism tells us that we need to take some clothes off.

Complex social and biological systems may have many thousands of information loops at work simultaneously, helping regulate the behavior of the system. **Formal systems of regulation, such as those described in this book, modify and supplement the feedback/feedforward channels which already exist in every viable system,[5] in order to help the organization more effectively achieve its goals.**

The importance of time to regulation

In goal orientated systems time – specifically the speed of response – is a critical factor determining the behavior pattern of the system (see Figure A.2 below). In order for feedback to be effective in maintaining control it needs to have a rate of response (i.e. have a 'relaxation time') that is faster than the rate of the environmental disturbances operating on the system. Depending on the relationship between the rate of disturbance and the speed of response, the system will gradually come back under control, oscillate, behave chaotically or even 'explode'. This fact was demonstrated by Maxwell as long ago as 1868 (Maxwell, 1868) when he explained the behavior of steam engines regulated by Watt's 'governor'. Why so many of them

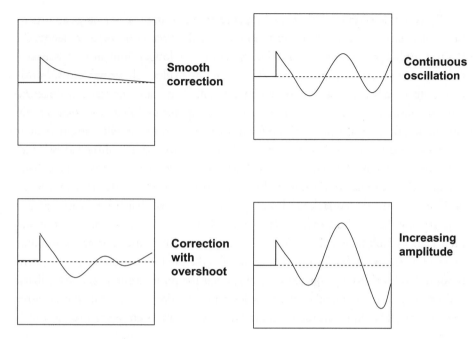

Figure A.2 The role of time in regulation of a system.
Examples of different forms of system behavior resulting from differences in the timing of corrective action.

literally exploded had been, up until then, a mystery. We can see the effect of long lead times in economic cycles, for instance. Economic boom and bust is often associated with the long lead times of the construction industry. So, for example, had banks received more immediate feedback about the performance of sub-prime mortgages our current travails might have been avoided.

In complex systems, lead times can often be significantly longer than the rate of external disturbance and organisms and organizations use a range of strategies to bridge this gap. One of the stratagems involves using feedforward (forecasting) information[6] to compensate for the lags in the feedback circuit.

The important destabilizing role of positive feedback (and feedforward)

Thus far we have focused exclusively on the 'negative' form of feedback (or feedforward); the sort of feedback which results in the value of a variable, such as the deviation from the goal, being reduced. There is a second type that results in deviations being amplified: it is called positive feedback (or feedforward). This is the mechanism behind the so-called 'vicious circle' (or 'virtuous circle').

Every viable system – that is one capable of sustaining itself, such as an organism, organization, ecosystem or an economy – is dominated by negative feedback. Positive feedback is fatal to any kind of system in the longer term since it is associated with the system 'running away' (i.e. becoming explosively unstable). But positive feedback does have a role to play in control, in at least one respect, since the ultimate in stability is death. If any system was incapable of doing more than simply eliminating deviations from goal, no form of change, such as growth, improvement or learning would be possible. Sometimes deviations from an established stable state can generate system characteristics which are more desirable, and positive feedback is required to amplify deviations rather than correcting them. But this cannot go on forever. Positive feedback (and the existence of 'errors' that it can work on) is a critical component of adaptive goal orientated systems (ones capable of changing their goal variables) of the sort that are ubiquitous in nature, but at some point however negative feedback must reassert itself as the predominant force if the system is not to 'explode'. Most complex natural systems use positive and negative feedback and on occasions the positive feedback loop may be dominant – but the negative feedback modality must ultimately prevail for any system to survive as a recognizably independent entity.

Natural systems, such as economies and ecologies, tend not to completely disintegrate through runaway positive feedback, but if they are not properly regulated (by the application of judicious negative feedback) such that their growth is maintained in line with the carrying capacity of the environment, they can overshoot and collapse, as shown in the diagram below (Figure A.3). In economies this phenomenon is often described as a 'bubble', and ours has just burst.

The existence of positive feedback loops is probably one of the reasons why we see 'fat tails' in the probability distributions described in Chapter 6 and the switch between negative and positive polarity is a source of discontinuities in systems (as shown in Figure A.3). Because of the nature of complex systems, particularly social systems characterized by the interplay of actors with free will, the nature and timing of discontinuities are impossible to predict with any confidence. Even when we know a system is in an unsustainable unstable condition (for instance a bubble will *always* lead to a collapse[7]) we cannot reliably forecast when the adjustment will take place and how large the correction will be. Understanding the nature of the phenomenon will, however, give you a head start in forecasting. In addition, managers might wish to exploit this characteristic of systems, deliberately trying to destabilize a system by introducing positive feedback, as in the case of innovation and change.

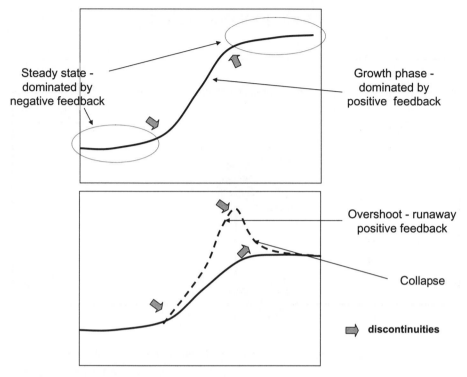

Figure A.3 A systems diagnosis of patterns of change.
The typical shape of a change process is associated with changes in the relative strength of positive and negative feedback processes. Excessive dominance of positive feedback ultimately leads to collapse.

System order: the architecture of complex control systems

Large, complex systems, such as economies, can and (as recent experience has taught us) should be regulated in order to maintain a healthy balance between stagnation (too much negative feedback) and explosion (an excess of positive). But complex systems require a more complex set of control arrangements than the ones we have so far discussed. The goal orientated arrangements shown in Figure A.1 are all examples of 'first order systems', so called because there is only one set of 'closed loops' and the goal is imposed from outside the system. Simple engineering systems work like this, as does budgetary control. More complex systems have additional control 'layers'.

For example, so called 'second order' control systems are sometimes termed 'adaptive' since the goal is not imposed from outside the system but provided by a second control level – a goal generating system (see Figure A.4).

Multi goal orientated

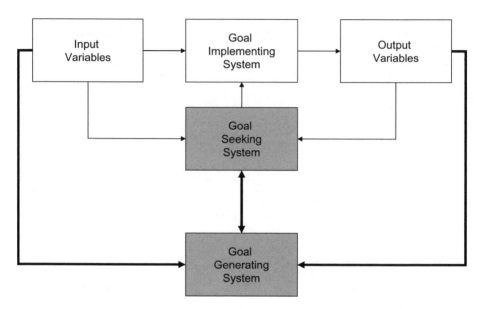

Figure A.4 A second order feedback system.

In this case, because the goal generating system has a 'memory' it is able to choose from a range of control repertoires, changing the goal, and consequently the behavior (output), of the system. In this case a feedback signal doesn't merely generate regulatory action, it also triggers a change in the model used to regulate behavior – it can 'learn from experience'. This is the concept of 'double loop' learning we encountered in Chapter 5.

It is possible to conceive of further control layers, including ones which respond to the state of the system itself in addition to perturbation from the environment. Such systems display a reflective capacity, a form of 'self-awareness' or consciousness. William Powers (Powers, 1974) hypothesizes that human systems, which of course do exhibit consciousness, have nine control layers. Systems with multiple control layers are self-regulating, and can exhibit the ability to change their own structure and behavior patterns. Most biological and social systems operate at this level. Ackoff (Ackoff and Gharajedaghi, 1996) categorizes goal seeking systems based on whether the whole or its parts is able to 'choose' its goals (higher order or, in his terms, 'Purposeful') or simply reacts to phenomena over which it has no control (lower order or 'Deterministic').

		WHOLE	
		DETERMINISTIC	PURPOSEFUL
PARTS	PURPOSEFUL	Ecologies	Social Systems e.g. organizations
	DETERMINISTIC	Machines	Animalistic Systems e.g. human beings

The practical application of the science of control: cybernetic technology

Like any other science, an understanding of cybernetics begets technologies – the use of knowledge to develop tools that can be used help achieve an objective. In our case the objective is to design systems capable of helping complex organizations effectively regulate themselves.

Simple 'first order systems' only require the following to be able to exercise effective control:

1. The goal and performance function (that is: a definition of when a systems performance can be deemed to satisfy the goal).
2. A suitable goal seeking variable.
3. A knowledge of how changes in the goal seeking variable can be generated.

In first order systems such as those designed by engineers, the goal is externally determined, and the designer will also be aware of how to bring about changes in the goal seeking variable. Usually the goal seeking variable will be one that is easily quantified.[8]

In higher order systems, it is usually not possible to satisfy all these conditions. Arguably, one of the reasons why the classical model of management (and budgeting in particular) is ineffective is that it treats organizations *as if* they were simple first order machines. Social organizations are many orders of magnitude more complex; so complex that they are incapable of being understood in detail. In addition, unlike simple first order machines, they are probabilistic rather than deterministic systems. It is not possible to ever precisely 'know' the state of the system or what will happen to one variable when another is changed.

Despite this complexity and uncertainty, control by cybernetic means is still possible. Indeed the creator of Management Cybernetics, Stafford Beer, argues that cybernetics *is* the science of communication and control in 'exceedingly complex probabilistic systems' (Beer, 1959). His analysis of different sorts of systems and what type of control system is required to regulate them is shown below in Figure A.5.

	COMPLEXITY		
	Simple	Complex	Exceedingly Complex
Deterministic	Pulley Billiards Typewriter	Computer Planetary System	Empty Set
Type of Control	Control input	Control input	Control input
Probabilistic	Quality Control Machine Breakdowns Games of Chance	Inventory Levels All conditioned behavior Sales	Firm Humans Economy
Type of Control	Statistical	Operations Research	Cybernetic

(Left side vertical label: PREDICTABILITY)

Figure A.5 Control technologies.
Different types of control arrangements are required for different kinds of systems.
(Cybernetics and Management (Stafford, 1959)). (Reproduced by permission of Cwarel Isaf Institute.)

If we accept this analysis, this means that the relatively simple control concepts used by control engineers cannot be applied to more complex and probabilistic systems of the kind found in biology and the realm of social affairs. In his book *The Brain of the Firm* (Beer, 1981), Beer proposes a model of control (the 'Viable Systems Model' or VSM) based on an analysis of the mechanisms used by the brain to control the body (and using certain key cybernetic concepts such as Ashby's Law of Requisite Variety). He claims that the VSM exhibits all the capabilities required for the control of any exceedingly complex probabilistic system.

There are a number of interesting parallels between Beer's VSM and the Beyond Budgeting Model but this is outside the scope of this chapter, which has done no more than scratch the surface of systems science. For those wanting to learn more about this fascinating and increasingly important subject, we recommend some further reading:

Further reading

The works of Stafford Beer arguably represent the most sophisticated and profound pieces of thinking about social organization, but his own writings (listed in the References) are daunting and often difficult. For an easy introduction to his thinking we recommend recent books written by Patrick Hoverstadt (Hoverstadt, 2008) or William Christopher (Christopher, 2007).

In recent years there has been a renaissance of scientific research in systems, which has unfortunately not yet been reconciled with the earlier work of cyberneticians like Beer. Complexity science has provided insight into such topics as the emergence of order but has, as yet, made little contribution to the understanding of regulation and control of organizations. Eric Beinhocker's book (Beinhocker, 2006) provides an excellent overview of this recent work and usefully employs it to analyze the failings of classical economics.

We also recommend two books from different traditions in systems science. Russell Ackoff, like Stafford Beer, has worked extensively with business organizations. His writing is accessible and entertaining; we recommend *Ackoff's Best* (Ackoff, 1999). Many scientists have come to systems from the biological sciences, perhaps because they have come to appreciate how important an understanding of interconnectedness is to making sense of the natural world and to the responsible stewardship of it. Frederik Vester was a German biochemist and his book (*The Art of Interconnected Thinking*) is accessible and also an important counterpoint to Anglophone bias (Vester, 2007).

For wide ranging and more general enquiry into the implications of systems science for the leadership of organizations Margaret Wheatley's book is recommended (Wheatley, 1999).

NOTES

1 This sentiment was famously expressed by Laplace, the 'French Newton' in 1814: '[W]e may regard the present state of the universe as the effect of its past and the cause of its future. An intellect which at a certain moment would know all forces that set nature in motion, and all positions of all items of which nature is composed, if this intellect were also vast enough to submit these data to analysis, it would embrace in a single formula the movements of the greatest bodies of the universe and those of the tiniest atom; for such an intellect nothing would be uncertain and the future just like the past would be present before its eyes' (Laplace, 1951).

2 We have used analogies extensively in this book, for example the analogy of sailing. Systems scientists claim that this is more than a linguistic device to enrich communication (i.e. a metaphor). Used with care, an analogy is a form of *scientific model* that can be used to analyze and explain the behavior of other phenomena (in this case forecasting and decision-making in business).

3 For example, James Lovelock originally described his Gaia hypothesis – where the whole earth is conceived of as a giant self-regulating whole – as a 'cybernetic system' (Lovelock, 1975).

4 Formally, a system is described as a set of related variables and its state the value of these variables at a moment of time.

5 A viable system is one capable of maintaining an independent existence.

6 So-called 'leading indicators' are a form of feedforward information.

7 Classical economic theory has difficulty explaining such phenomena since it assumes that, as a result of actors having perfect rationality and perfect knowledge, the system is perfectly self-regulating, never departing far from equilibrium. This is what Alan Greenspan was referring to when he admitted to there being a 'flaw' in the model he had used as head of the US Federal Reserve. Economics is one area where systems science is currently gaining ground, since the discipline historically relied on techniques better suited to 'simple' systems (such as those studied by physics). See Beinhocker (2006) for more.

8 This is no longer necessary. In recent years even common household electrical devices (e.g. digital cameras) use control systems based on so called 'fuzzy' measurement concepts such as 'more', 'less', 'good', 'better', 'worse', and there is evidence that the human brain works in this way.

REFERENCES

ABRAHAMS, P. (2001) Cisco pays high price for low revenue growth: Quarterly losses show inventory levels were a gamble. *Financial Times*, May 10, p. 32.

ACKOFF, R. L. (1999) *Ackoff's Best*, New York, John Wiley & Sons, Inc.

—— and GHARAJEDAGHI, J. (1996) Reflections on Systems and Their Models. *Systems Research*, 13–23.

AIKEN, C. and KELLER, S. (2009) The Irrational Side of Change Management. *McKinsey Quarterly*, April, 101–109.

ALLAN, D., KINGDON, M., MURRIN, K., and RUDKIN, D. (1999) *How to Start a Creative Revolution at Work*, Oxford, Capstone.

ANON (1902) Lord Kelvin's Assurance. *New York Times*, August 3.

ANTHONY, R. and GOVINDARAJAM, V. (1995) *Management Control Systems*, Chicago, Irwin.

ARGYRIS, C. and SCHON, D. (1978) *Organisational Learning: A Theory of Action Perspective*, Reading, MA, Addison-Wesley.

ARIELY, D. (2008) *Predictably Irrational: The Hidden Forces that Shape our Decisions*, London, Harper Collins.

ARMSTRONG, J. S. (1985) *Long Range Forecasting: From Crystal Ball to Computer*, New York, Wiley Interscience.

—— (ed.) (2003) *Principles of Forecasting*, Norwell, MA, Kluwer.

ASCH, S. E. (1955) Opinions and Social Pressure. *Scientific American* 193, 31–35.

AXSON, D. (2003) *Best Practices in Planning and Management Reporting: From Data to Decisions*, Hoboken NJ, John Wiley & Sons, Inc.

BAZERMAN, M. H. (2006) *Judgment in Managerial Decision Making*, Hoboken, NJ, John Wiley and Sons, Inc.

BECKHARD, R. and HARRIS, R. T. (1987) *Organizational Transitions*, Reading, MA, Addison-Wesley.

BEER, S. (1959) *Cybernetics and Management*, New York, John Wiley & Sons, Inc.

—— (1979) *The Heart of the Enterprise*, Chichester, John Wiley & Sons, Ltd.

—— (1981) *The Brain of the Firm*, Chichester, John Wiley & Sons, Ltd.

BEINHOCKER, E. D. (2006) *The Origin of Wealth: How Evolution Creates Novelty, Knowledge, and Growth in the Economy*, Boston, MA, Harvard Business School Press.

BLOOM, A., WOLLASTON, A., and MCGREGOR, K. (2009) *Analysis of profit warnings*, London, Ernst and Young July 2009.

BOGLER, D. and MICHAELS, A. (2000) Attempting to shift the stretch-goal posts: To his cost P&G's Jager took risks and failed. *Financial Times*, June 9, p. 32.

BOGSNES, B. (2009) *Implementing Beyond Budgeting*, Hoboken NJ, John Wiley & Sons, Inc.

BRIDGES, W. (1991) *Managing Transitions: Making the Most of Change*, New York, Perseus.

BRYAN, L. and FARRELL, D. (2008) Leading through uncertainty. *McKinsey Quarterly*, December 2, 2008, http://www.mckinseyquarterly.com/article_print.aspx?L2=21&L3=37&ar=2263.

CANNON, W. (1932) *The Wisdom of the Body*, New York, Norton.

CHAPPUIS, B., AIMEE, K., and ROCHE, P. (2008) Starting Up as CFO. *McKinsey Quarterly*, March.

CHRISTOPHER, W. F. (2007) *Holistic Management*, Hoboken, NJ, John Wiley & Sons, Inc.

COHEN, N. (2009) Financial meltdown blamed on risk models. *Financial Times*, February 14, p. 15.

CORAM, R. (2002) *Boyd: The Fighter Pilot who Changed the Art of War*, New York, Little, Brown and Company.

CROAKE, J. (2008) American Express Planning Transformation. *BBRT Membership Interviews*. Dallas, Beyond Budgeting Round Table.

DANIEL, C. (2001) Marconi starts assault on doomsayers: As the telecoms group reorganizes around 'solutions' rather than products, critics see a lack of focus. *Financial Times*, April 11, p. 26.

——, GUTHRIE, J., and PRETZLIK, C. (2001) Marconi staff warned management over trade: Executives remained upbeat before profits warning despite workers concerns. *Financial Times*, August 2, p. 1.

DANIEL, C. and PRETZLIK, C. (2001) How the men from Marconi got their wires crossed on reality. *Financial Times*, August 2, p. 29.

DENNETT, D. (1991) *Consciousness Explained*, London, Penguin.

DURFEE, D. (2004) It's Better (and Worse) Than You Think. *CFO Magazine*, May 3.

EIU (2007) Forecasting with Confidence: Insights from Leading Finance Functions. *KPMG*.

FRITH, C. (2007) *Making Up the Mind*, Malden, MA, Blackwell.

GEUS, A. D. (1997) *The Living Company*, Boston, MA, Harvard Business School Press.

GIGERENZER, G. (2002) *Reckoning with Risk*, London, Penguin.

—— (2008) *Gut Feelings*, London, Penguin.

GILES, C. (2008) The Vision Thing. *Financial Times*, November 25.

GLADWELL, M. (2002) *The Tipping Point*, New York, Back Bay Books.

GLEICK, J. (1998) *Chaos: Making a New Science*, London, Heinemann.

GOEDHART, M. H., RUSSELL, B., and WILLIAMS, Z. D. (2001) Prophet and Profits. *McKinsey Quarterly*, 2, 11–15.

GROVE, A. (1997) *Only the Paranoid Survive*, London, HarperCollins.

HACKETT (2008) Aligning Forecasting Practice with Market Dynamics. *The Hackett Group*, Vol. 12 No. 1.

HOPE, J. (2005) Tomkins Plc. Beyond Budgeting Round Table.

—— (2006) *Reinventing the CFO*, Boston, MA, Harvard Business School Press.

—— and FRASER, R. (2003) *Beyond Budgeting: How Managers Can Break Free from the Performance Trap*, Boston, MA, Harvard Business School Press.

HORNGREN, C. T., FOSTER, G., DATAR, R. M., and ITTNER, C. (2008) *Cost Accounting: A Managerial Emphasis*, Upper Saddle River, NJ, Pearson Education.

HOVERSTADT, P. (2008) *The Fractal Organisation*, Chichester, John Wiley & Sons, Ltd.

HUNT, B. and ROBERTS, D. (2002) Weinstock, 'Britain's best manager', dies. *Financial Times*, July 24, p. 1.

JARVIS, M. (2008) Interview with author.

JOHNSON, T. and BROMS, A. (2000) *Profit Beyond Measure*, London, Brealy.

—— and KAPLAN, R. (1987) *Relevance Lost. The Rise and Fall of Management Accounting*, Boston, MA, Harvard Business School Press.

KARAIAN, J. (2009) By the numbers: top ten concerns of CFO's. *CFO Europe*, September 2009 11–12.

KNIGHT, F. (1921) *Risk Uncertainty and Profit*, Boston, MA, Houghton Mifflin Co.

KOTTER, J. P. (1996) *Leading Change*, Boston, MA, Harvard Business School Press.

LAPLACE, P. S. (1951) *A Philosophical Essay on Probabilities*, New York, Dover Publications.

LOVELOCK, J. (1979) *Gaia*, Oxford, Oxford University Press.

—— and MARGULIS, L. (1975) The atmosphere as circulatory system of the biosphere – the Gaia Hypothesis. *Coevolution Quarterly*, 31–40.

MANYIKA, J. (2008) Google's View of the Future of Business. An Interview with CEO Eric Schmidt. *The McKinsey Quarterly*, September 2008.

MAXWELL, J. C. (1868) On Governors. *Proceedings of the Royal Society*, 100.

MCCARTHY, K. (2001) Marconi shares 'worthless'. http://www.theregister.co.uk/2001/09/27/marconi_shares_worthless.

MCKINSEY, J. O. (1922) *Budgetary Control*, New York, The Ronald Press Company.

MEADOWS, D. H., MEADOWS, D. L., RANDERS, J., and BEHRENS, W. W. (1972) *The Limits to Growth*, New York, Universe Books.

MENTZER, J. T. and COX, J. E. (1984) Familiarity, application, and performance of sales forecasting techniques. *Journal of Forecasting* 3, 27–36.

MERGENTHALER, R., SHIVA, R., and SURAJ, S. (2008) CEO and CFO Consequences to Missing Quarterly earnings benchmarks. Harvard Business School, Working Paper 09-014.

MODIS, T. (1992) *Predictions: Society's telltale signature reveals the past and forecasts the future*, New York, Simon and Schuster.

MOORE, G. A. (2002) *Crossing the Chasm: Marketing and Selling Disruptive Products to Mainstream Customers*, New York, HarperCollins.

MORLIDGE, S. (2005) Just 15 Minutes: Unilever Foods Poland DPM Case Study. Unilever.

NEAVE, H. R. (1990) *The Deming Dimension*, Knoxville, The SPC Press.

PLENDER, J. (2002) Mayo's handy guide to Marconi's road to ruin: No accounting for lost shirts. *Financial Times*, January 19, p. 13.

POWERS, W. (1974) *Behaviour: The Control of Perception*, London, Wildwood House.

PWC (2007) Budgeting and Forecasting Study. Prague, PwC Advisory.

RANDALL, J. (2001) Analysis: where did Marconi go wrong? http://news.bbc.co.uk/1/hi/business/1423642.stm.

ROBERTS, D. (2001) Many customers were warning of slowdown several months ago. *Financial Times*, July 6, p. 18.

ROEMER, F. (2008) Interview with author. London.

RYAN, V. (2008) Future Tense. *CFO Magazine*, December 10, 2008. http://www.cfo.com/printable/article.cfm/12668080.

SANWAL, A. (2007) *Optimizing: Corporate Portfolio Management*, Hoboken, NJ, John Wiley & Sons, Inc.

SAWERS, A. (2008) Future Shock: Creating the 'No Surprises' Organization, Hoboken NJ, John Wiley & Sons, Inc.

SCHWARTZ, P. (1998) *The Art of the Long View*, Chichester, John Wiley & Sons, Ltd.

SEDDON, J. (2008) *Systems Thinking in the Public Sector*, Axminster, Triarchy Press.

SENGE, P. (1990) *The Fifth Discipline*, London, Random House.

SHEWHART, W. A. (1931) *The Economic Control of Manufactured Product*, London, MacMillan and Co.

SIMON, H. (1957) *Models of Man*, New York, John Wiley & Sons, Inc.

SLOAN, A. P. (1967) *My Years with General Motors*, London, Pan.

SOLOMANS, M. (2001) Think Marconi and what do you see? *Financial Times*, April 10, p. 18.

STERMAN, J. D. (2000) *Business Dynamics: Systems Thinking for a Complex World*, Boston, MA, McGraw Hill.

STERN, S. and MARSH, P. (2008) The Chaos Theory of Leadership. *Financial Times*, December 2.

SUGHRUE, L. (2007) Greenspan Defends Low Interest Rates: Former Federal Reserve Chairman Talks to Lesley Stahl about Subprime Mortgage Meltdown. *60 Minutes*.

SUROWIECKI, J. (2004) *The Wisdom of Crowds*, London, Abacus.

TALEB, N. N. (2001) *Fooled by Randomness*, New York, Texere.

—— (2008) *The Black Swan*, London, Penguin.

TURNER, G. (2008) Special Report. *New Scientist*, 2678.

UNKNOWN (1997) Planning. 04/09/2007, http://www.au.af.mil/au/awc/awcgate/mcdp5/fore.htm.

VARIOUS (2008) Aligning Forecasting practices with Market Dynamics. *The Hackett Group*.

VARIOUS (2009) Principles of Forecasting Website. http://www.forecastingprinciples.com/index.php?option=com_frontpage&Itemid=1.

VESTER, F. (2007) *The Art of Interconnected Thinking*, Munich, MCB Verlag.

WALDROP, M. M. (1992) *Complexity: The Emerging Science at the Edge of Order and Chaos*, New York, Simon & Schuster.

WEINER, N. (1948) *Cybernetics*, Cambridge, MA, MIT Press.

WELCH, J. and BYRNE, J. A. (2001) *Jack: Straight from the Gut*, New York, Warner Books.

WHEATLEY, M. J. (1999) *Leadership and the New Science: Discovering Order in a Chaotic World*, San Francisco, Berrett-Koehler Publishers.

ZHU, J. (2009) Cashing In. *CFO Magazine*, December 2008–January 2009.

INDEX

rewards 192
  decoupling from targets 238, 249
  linked to targets 104, 234
risk 151, 265
  aggregating 167–8
  assessing 159–69
  and contingency planning 172–3
  continuous and discrete 165–6
  definitions 153–4
  and diversification 155
  improving judgmental estimates of 166
  overstatement of 168
  own actions changing 168–9
  perception of 155–8
  range estimates 158–9
  range vs. single outcome 152–3
  skewed distribution of 162–4
  timing issues 162
  versus uncertainty 153–8
  see also uncertainty
Roemer, Fritz 12, 42, 49, 95, 97, 190
roles and responsibilities 209–15
rolling horizons 64–6, 265
'rule of four' errors 135–8
run charts 106, 133–42, 265

'S' curve 222–3
sales and operations planning (S&OP) 216, 265
Sanwal, Anand 75
scenario planning 169–75, 265
Schon, Douglas 128–9
'scientific' approach, adopting 26
Sciver, Richard 52, 74, 174
second order control systems 283–4
semantic schizophrenia 17–18
Senge, Peter 129
sensitivity analysis 166, 266
Shewhart, Walter 148–9
shower example 59–61
Simon, Herbert 98
Simpson, George, Marconi CEO 4, 6, 7, 9
single loop learning 128–9
skewed distribution, risk profiles 162–4, 266
Sloan, Alfred 13, 14, 15, 70, 85, 123–4

social bias 101–4, 266
social conformity 101–3
socio-pathological behavioral patterns 22
software therapy 24–5
Southwest Airlines 71
speed of forecasting 45–7
Stalin, Joseph 13–14
standardization 188–9
statistical models 94, 110–11, 266
  advantages of 111
  drawbacks 111–12
  for momentum forecasting 114–15
statistical therapy 23–4
StatoilHydro 50, 63, 64, 235
'strategic horizon' 66, 67
strategic planning 66–7, 266
'stretch goal forecasting' 201
'structural breaks' 94–5
substitution effects 119, 120
success, redefining 26–7, 251–2
Suroweiki, Joseph 103
Svenska Handelsbanken 204–5
Symbios, systems dynamic models 109
symptoms of forecasting illness 17–22
systematic error 50
  cognitive bias 89, 98–101
  eliminating 143–4, 145, 269
  and judgmental forecasting 97–8
  motivational bias 104–5
  social bias 101–4
systems dynamics 62, 109
systems science 266, 276–7
  systems dynamics 62, 109
  see also cybernetics

Taleb, Nassim Nicholas 137, 156
'tampering' by managers 135
TARAC mnemonic 45, 54–5, 91, 198
targets 42–3, 266
  decoupling from rewards 238, 249, 250
  forecasts converted into 201
  negotiation, weakening of 237–8
  relative versus fixed 236–7, 248–9
technical expertise 211–12
technological therapy 23–5
Telecoms New Zealand 73–4
thinking systems 98

Index compiled by Sophia Clapham